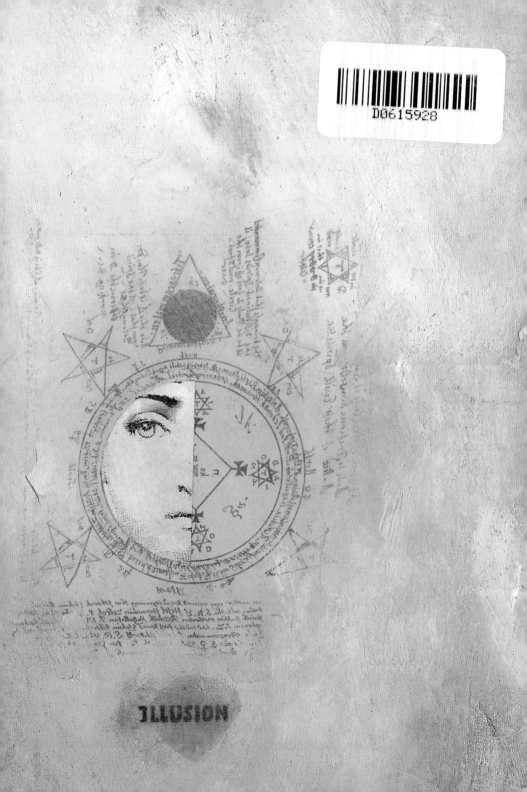

ILLUSION

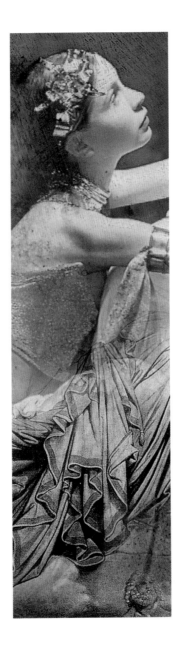

AUGUST 2001

—how fortunate are you and i, whose home
is timelessness: we who have wandered down
from fragrant mountains of eternal now
to frolic in such mysteries as birth
and death a day (or maybe even less)

e.e. cummings

ⅼive

oot

rth

COHEN — because

ety + because

is Canadian, + because

is when we were ALL,

So very young!

ations by

S AND IAN JACKSON

Stoddart

Published in 2000 by Stoddart Publishing Co. Limited
34 Lesmill Road, Toronto, Canada M3B 2T6
180 Varick Street, 9th Floor, New York, NY 10014

First published in the UK by Galileo Multimedia Ltd
Text copyright © 1966 by Leonard Cohen
Art and concept copyright © 2000 by Galileo Multimedia Ltd
Text from *Beautiful Losers* used with permission of McClelland & Stewart Ltd,
Canada & Random House Inc (USA)

Distributed in Canada by:
General Distribution Services Ltd.
325 Humber College Blvd., Toronto, Ontario M9W 7C3
Tel. (416) 213-1919 Fax (416) 213-1917
Email cservice@genpub.com

Distributed in the United States by:
General Distribution Services Inc.
PMB 128, 4500 Witmer Industrial Estates, Niagara Falls, NY 14305-1386
Toll-free Tel. 1-800-805-1083 Toll-free Fax 1-800-481-6207
Email gdsinc@genpub.com

Canadian Cataloguing in Publication Data
Cohen, Leonard, 1934-
    God is alive, magic is afoot
    Poems.
    ISBN 0-7737-6180-2
    I. Title.
    PS8505.O22G62 2000   C811'.54   C00-932437-2
    PR9199.3.C65G62 2000

U.S Cataloging-in-Publication Data
Available from the Library of Congress

Printed in Spain by Artes Gráficas, Toledo

for Steve Smith
1943-1964

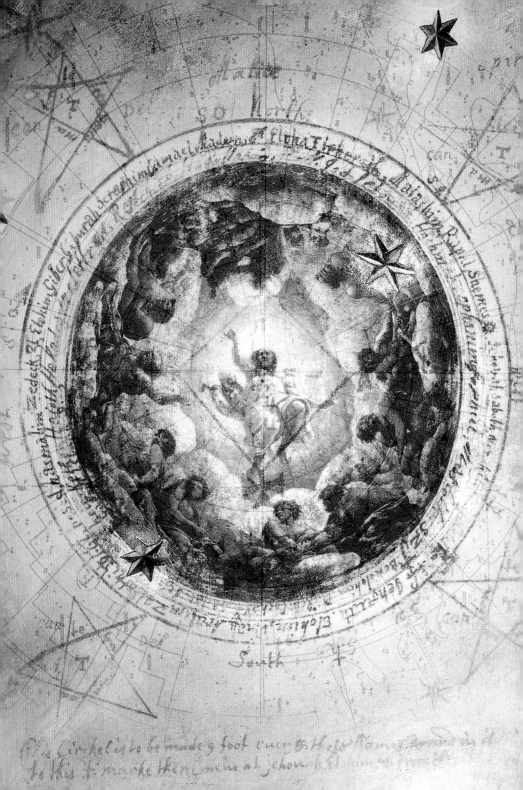

god is alive

magic is afoot

GOD IS ALIVE

magic is afoot

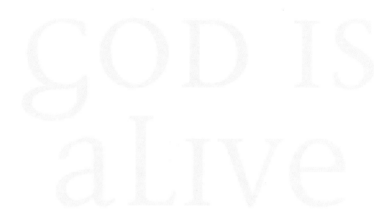

GOD IS afoot

magic is alive

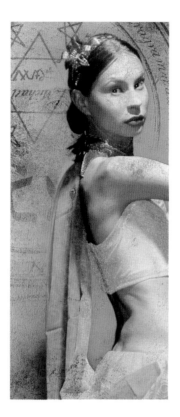

aLive is afoot

magic never died

GOD NEVER SICKENED

MANY POOR MEN LIED
MANY SICK MEN LIED

magic never weakened

magic never hid

magic always ruled

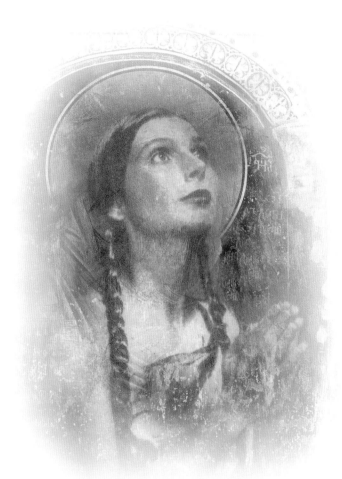

god is afoot

god never died

god was ruler

though his funeral
lengthened
though his mourners thickened

magic never fled

THOUGH HIS

SHROUDS WERE HOISTED

THE NAKED

GOD DID LIVE

THOUGH HIS WORDS

WERE TWISTED

THE NAKED MAGIC THRIVED

GOD
IS aLive
magIC
IS
afoot

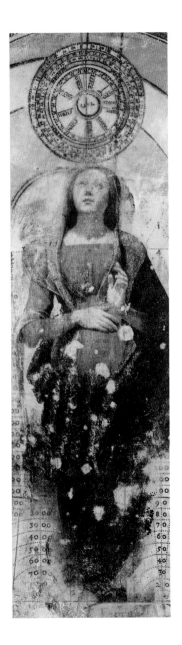

THOUGH HIS DEATH WAS

PUBLISHED ROUND AND

ROUND THE WORLD

THE HEART DID NOT

BELIEVE

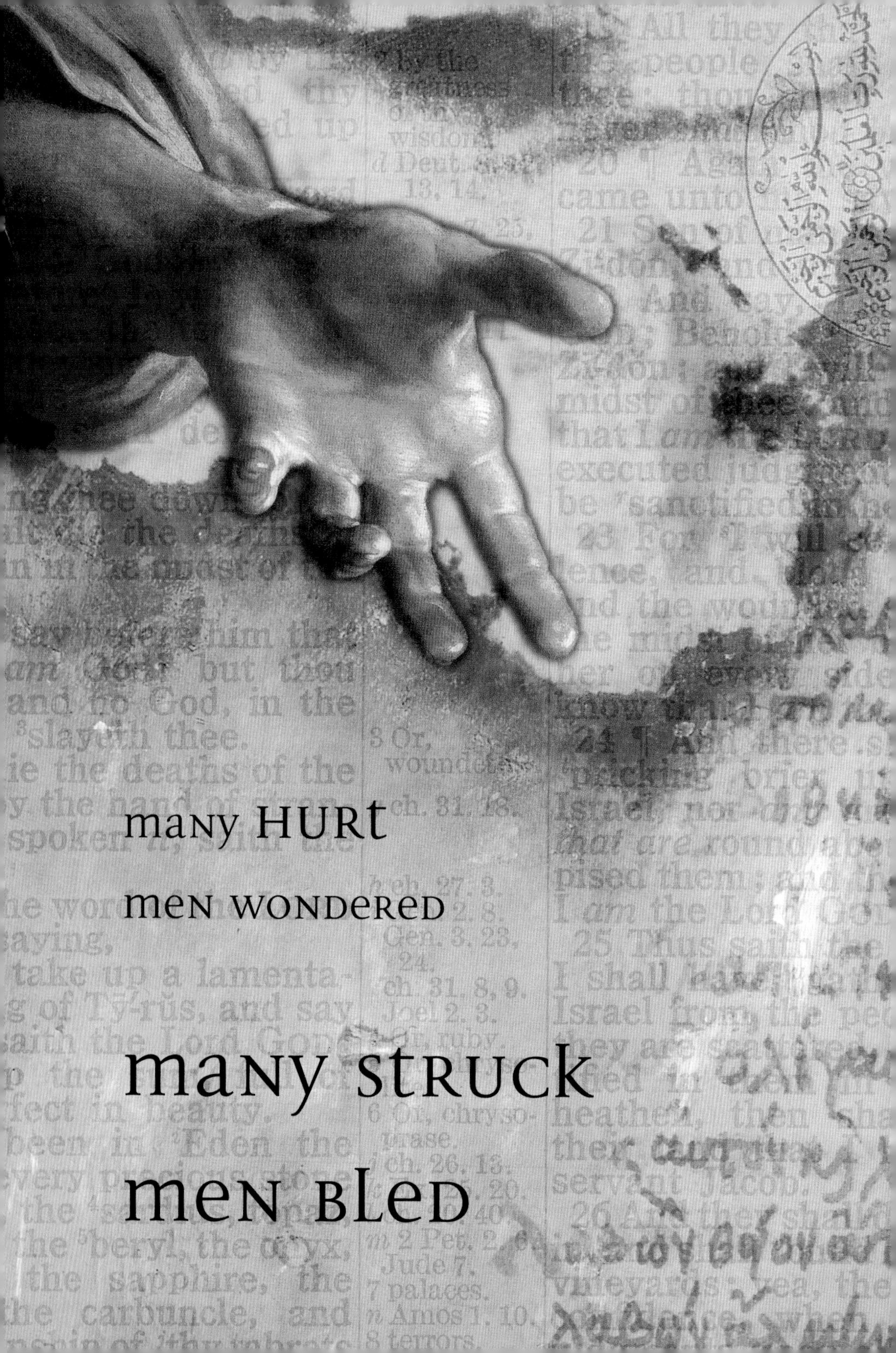
many HURT
men WONDERED
many STRUCK
men BLED

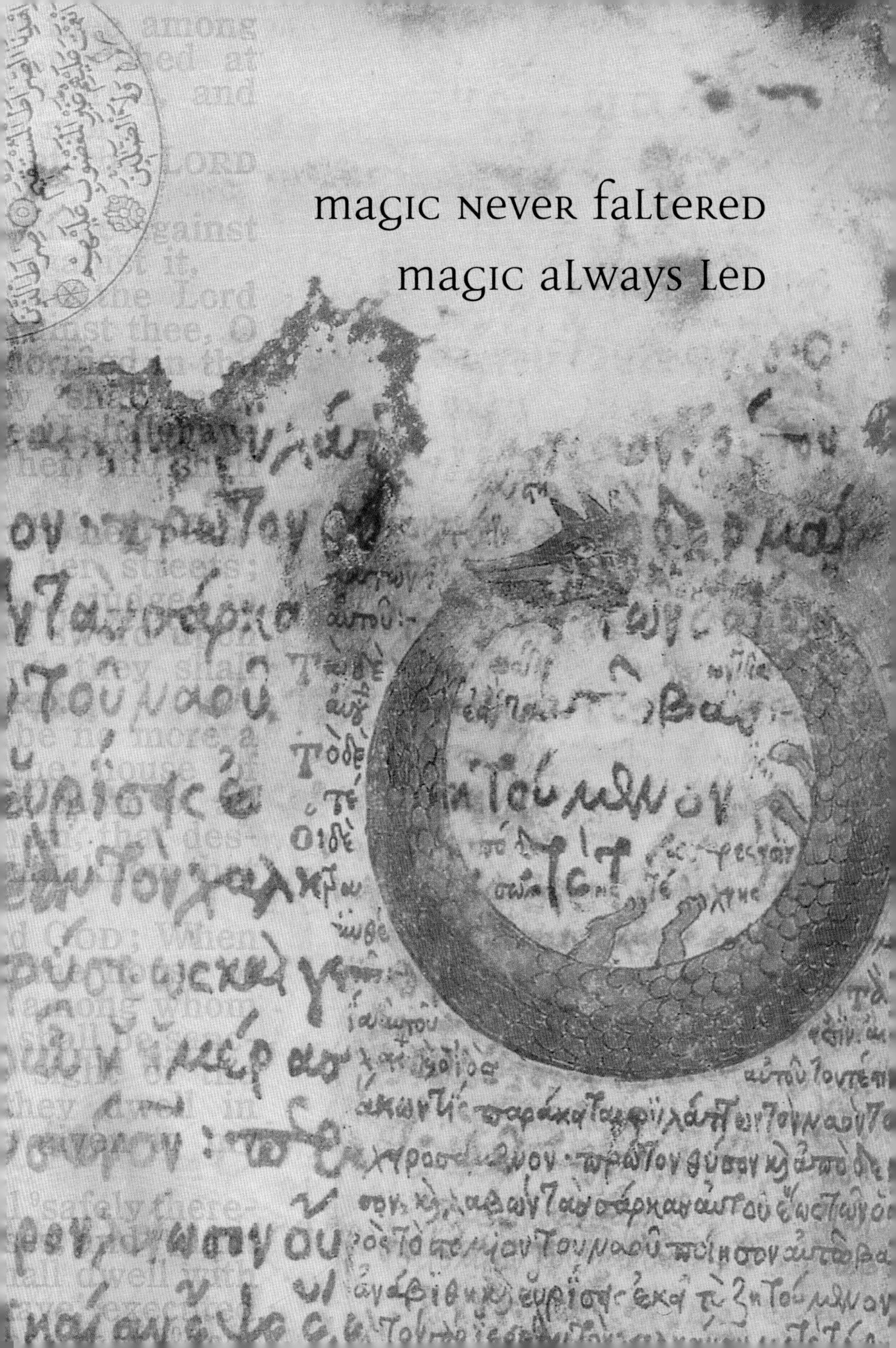

magic never faltered
magic always led

many stones were rolled but
god would not lie down

many wild men lied

many fat men listened
though they offered stones

magic still was fed

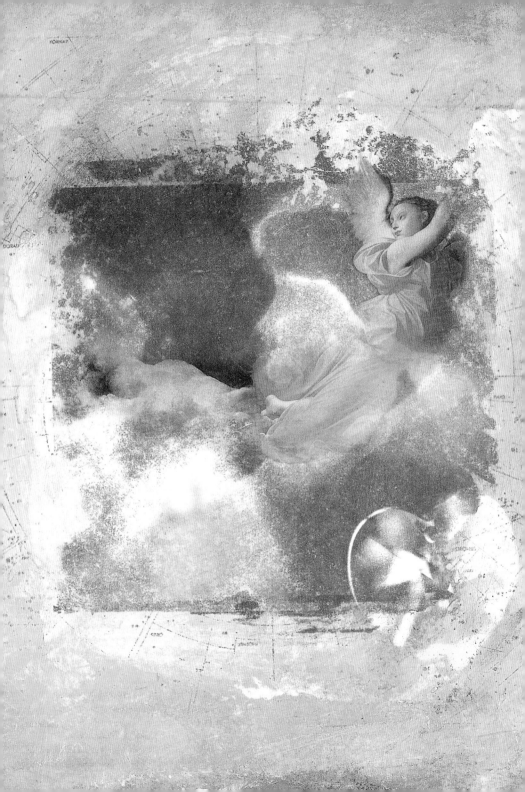

though they locked
their coffers

god was always served

magic is afoot

god rules, alive is afoot
alive is in command

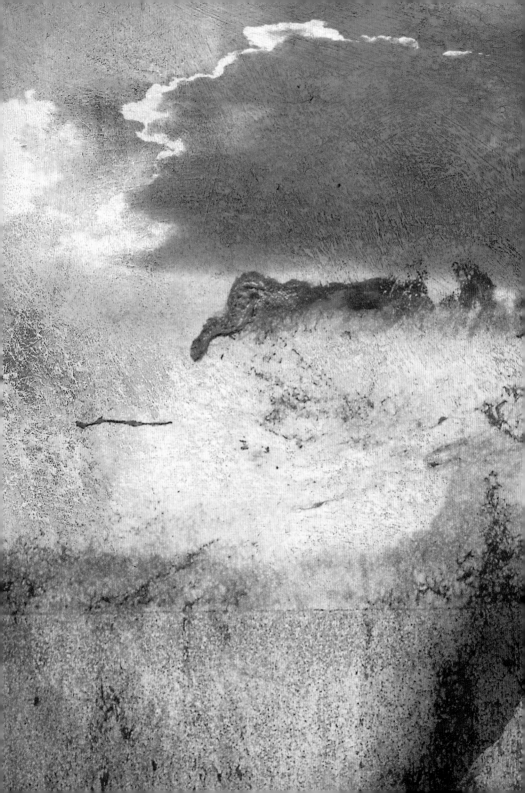

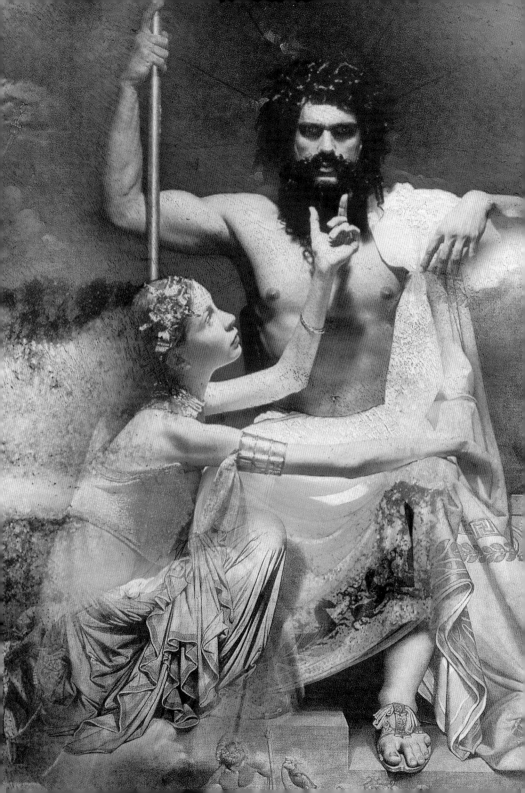

many weak men hungered
many strong men thrived

though they boasted solitude

god

was at their side

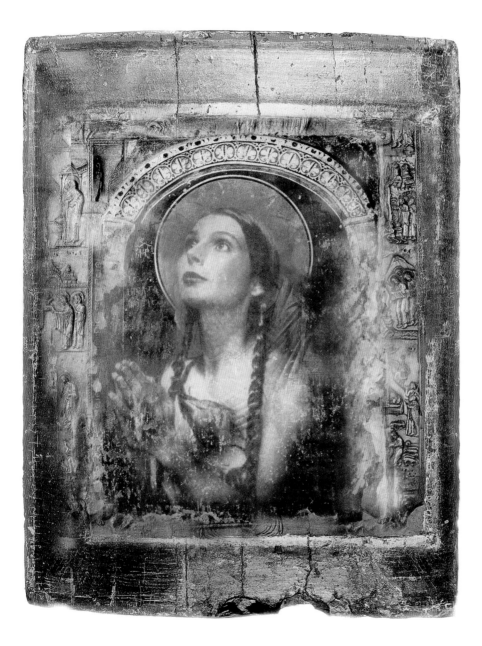

NOR the DREAMER IN HIS CELL
NOR the CAPTAIN ON the HILL
magic is alive

THOUGH HIS DEATH

was PARDONED

ROUND AND ROUND THE WORLD

THE HEART WOULD

NOT BELIEVE

though laws
were carved in
marble they
could not
shelter men

though altars built in
parliaments they could
not order men

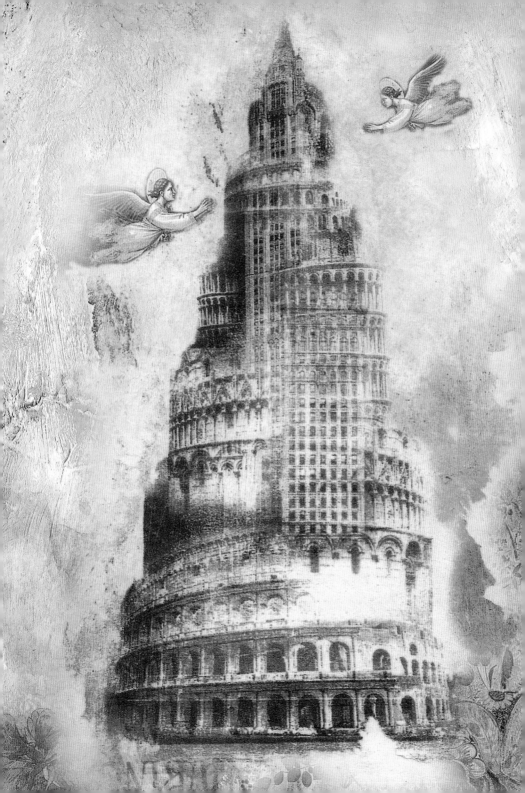

POLICE ARRESTED MAGIC
AND MAGIC WENT WITH THEM

for magic Loves
the HUNGRY

but magic would not tarry
it moves from arm to arm

it would not stay with them

magic is afoot

★

it cannot come to harm

it rests in an empty palm

it spawns in an

empty mind

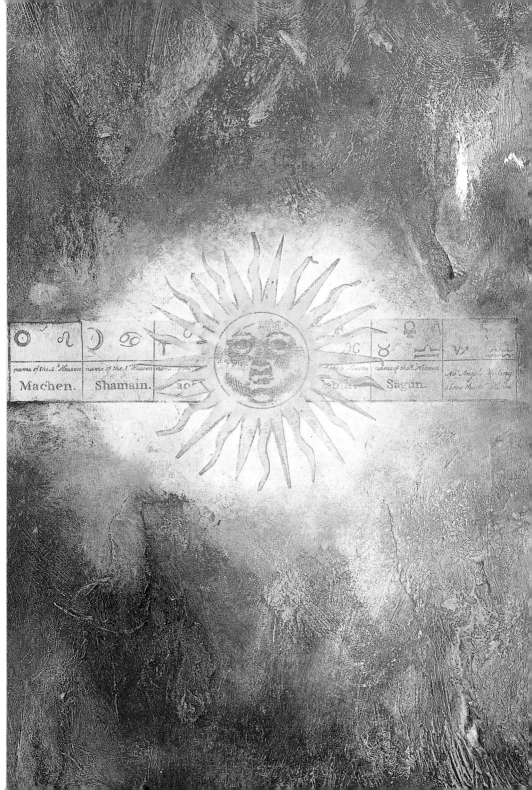

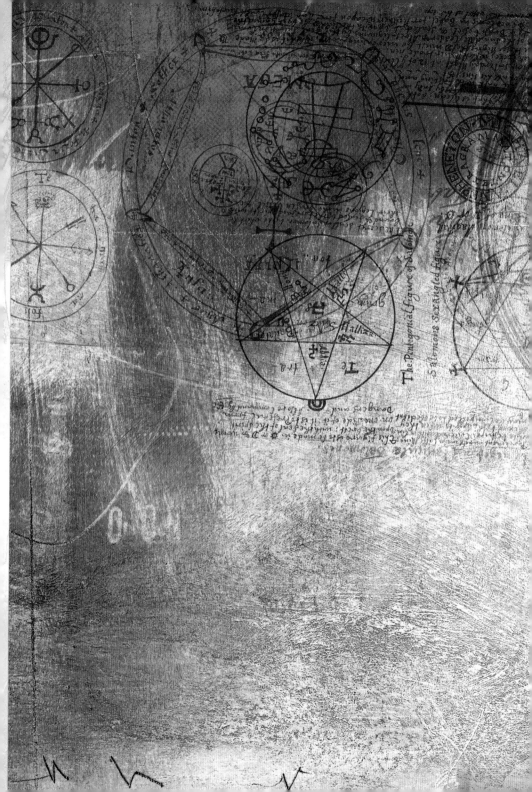

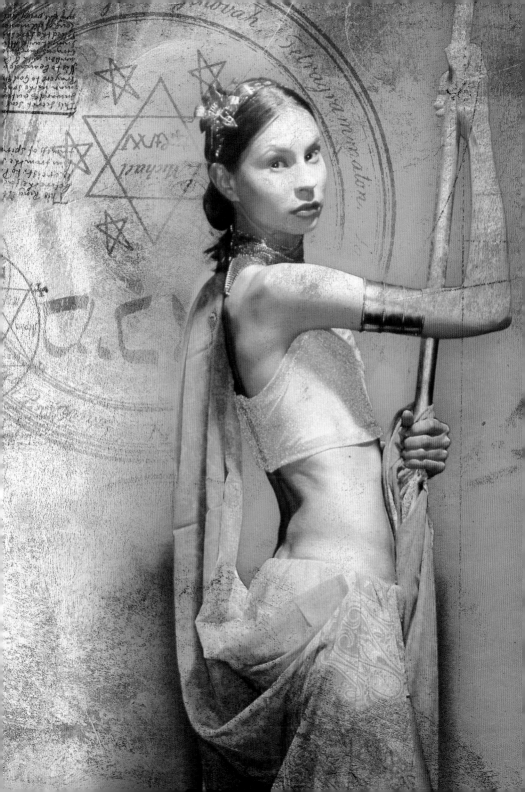

many strong men lied

they only passed

through magic

and out the other side

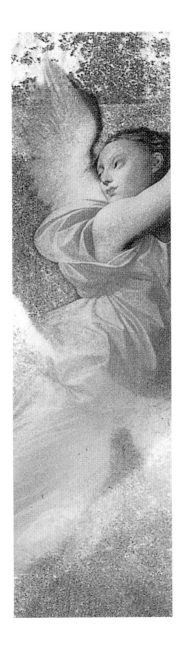

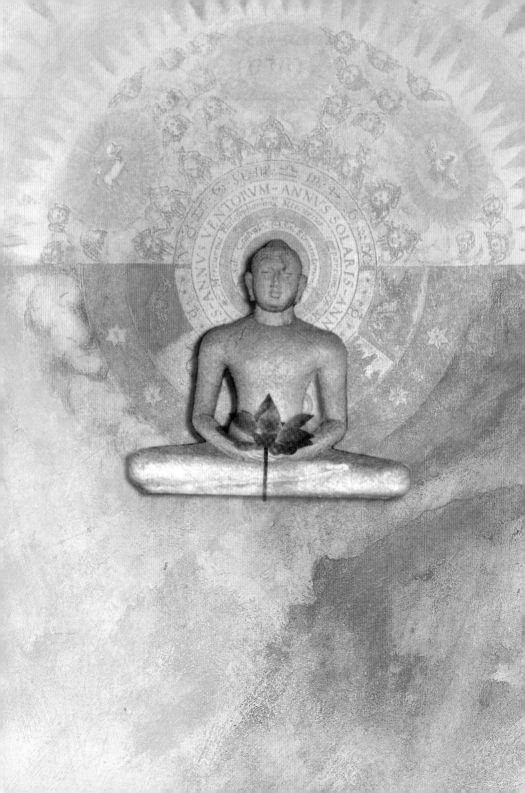

many weak men Lied

they came to god in secret
.and though they Left him nourished

they would not

tell who healed

though mountains danced
before them

they said that
god was dead

though his shrouds were hoisted

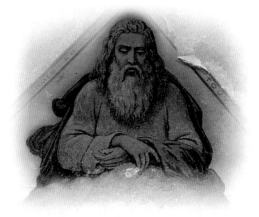

the naked god did live

THIS I MEAN TO WHISPER
to my mind

THIS I MEAN TO LAUGH
WITH IN MY MIND

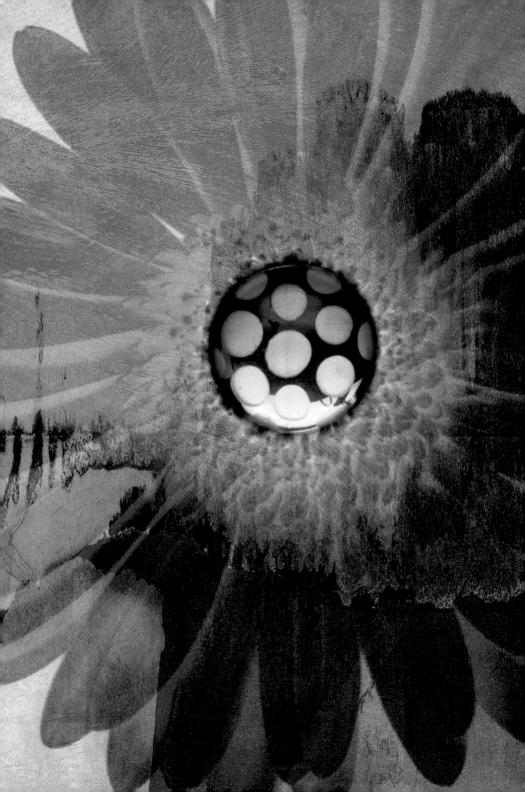

this i mean
my mind to serve
till service is
but magic

moving through
the world

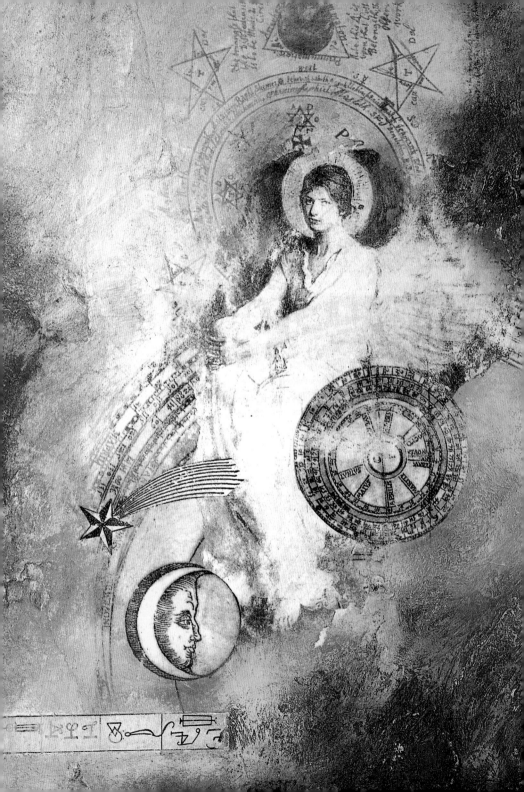

and mind itself is magic
coursing through the flesh

and flesh itself is magic

god is
afoot

dancing on
a clock

and time itself

the

magic length
of god

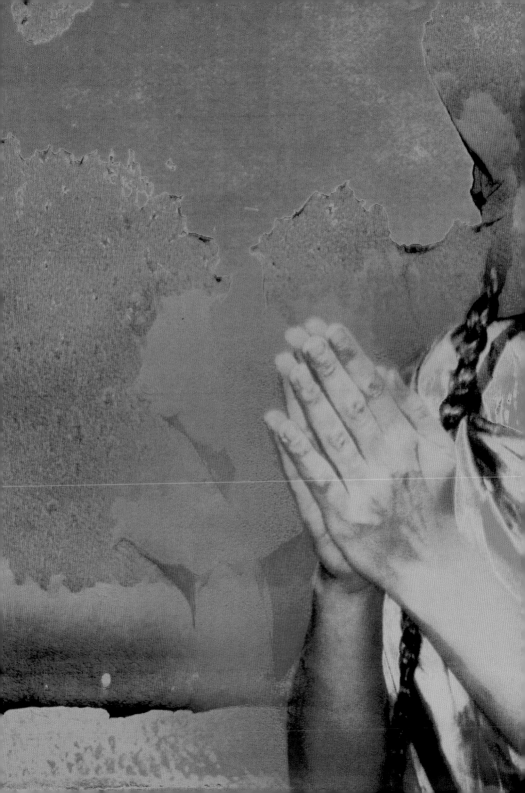

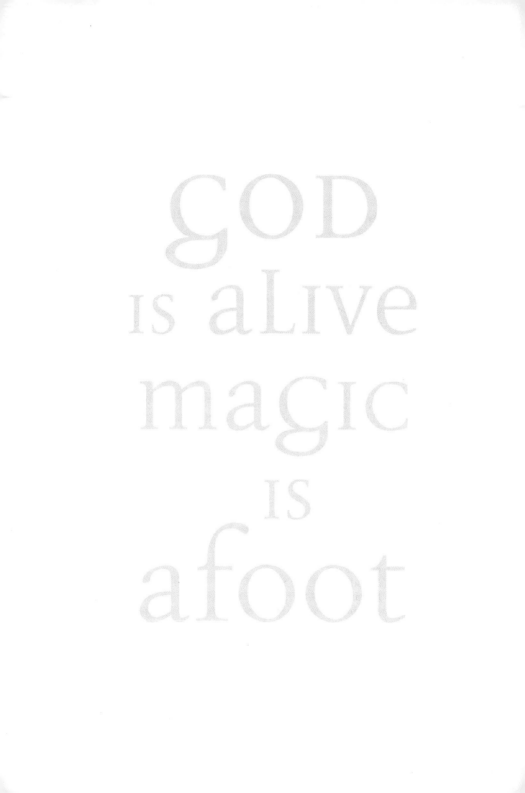

çod is aLive, maçic is afoot

God is alive. Magic is afoot. God is alive. Magic is afoot. God is afoot. Magic is alive. Alive is afoot. Magic never died. God never sickened. Many poor men lied. Many sick men lied. Magic never weakened. Magic never hid. Magic always ruled. God is afoot. God never died. God was ruler though his funeral lengthened. Though his mourners thickened Magic never fled. Though his shrouds were hoisted the naked God did live. Though his words were twisted the naked Magic thrived. Though his death was published round and round the world the heart did not believe. Many hurt men wondered. Many struck men bled. Magic never faltered. Magic always led. Many stones were rolled but God would not lie down. Many wild men lied. Many fat men listened. Though they offered stones Magic still was fed. Though they locked their coffers God was always served. Magic is afoot. God rules. Alive is afoot. Alive is in command. Many weak men hungered. Many strong men thrived. Though they boasted solitude God was at their side. Nor the dreamer in his cell, nor the captain on the hill. Magic is alive. Though his death was pardoned round and round the world the heart would not believe. Though laws were carved in marble they could not shelter men. Though altars built in parliaments they could not order men. Police arrested Magic and Magic went with them for Magic loves the hungry. But Magic would not tarry. It moves from arm to arm. It would not stay with them. Magic is afoot. It cannot come to harm. It rests in an empty palm. It spawns in an empty mind. But Magic is no instrument. Magic is the end. Many men drove Magic but Magic stayed behind. Many strong men lied. They only passed through Magic and out the other side. Many weak men lied. They came to God in secret and though they left him nourished they would not tell who healed. Though mountains danced before them they said that God was dead. Though his shrouds were hoisted the naked God did live. This I mean to whisper to my mind. This I mean to laugh with in my mind. This I mean my mind to serve till service is but Magic moving through the world, and mind itself is Magic coursing through the flesh, and flesh itself is Magic dancing on a clock, and time itself the Magic Length of God.

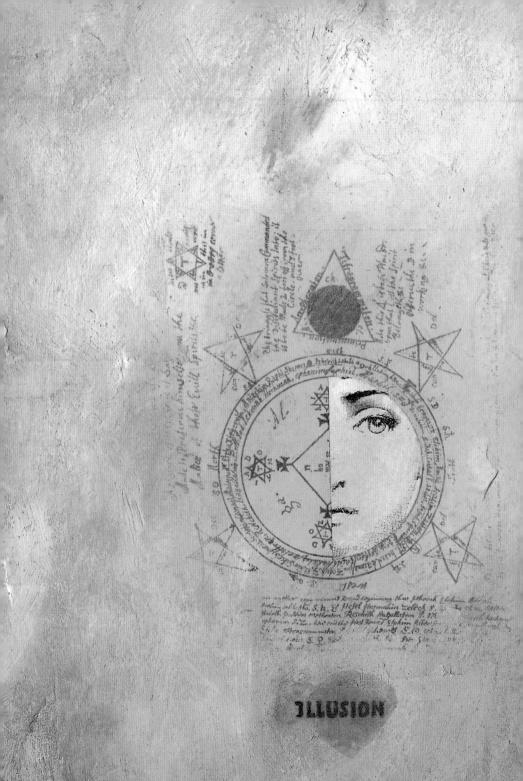

ILLUSION

Kelly Elliott

USA Today Bestselling Author

BROKEN

Visit my website at http://www.authorkellyelliott.blogspot.com

ISBN-13: 978-0-9887074-8-1

CONTENTS

Dedication

This book is dedicated to my husband, Darrin, and my daughter, Lauren.

It is also dedicated to anyone who has ever felt lost and broken at some point in life.

"STRENGTH OF CHARACTER
ISN'T ALWAYS ABOUT HOW MUCH YOU
CAN HANDLE BEFORE YOU BREAK.
IT'S ALSO ABOUT HOW MUCH
YOU CAN HANDLE AFTER YOU'VE
BEEN BROKEN."

–ROBERT TEW

PROLOGUE

-》》》》》》》》》》》《《《《《《《《《《《《-

Whitley

Graduation Night

"Oh, sweetheart, you look beautiful! Roger is going to go nuts when he sees you in this dress."

I turned and looked at my mother and then back in the mirror. I smiled at my reflection.

I'm so blessed. I was blessed with wonderful parents, with the greatest best friend in the world—who had picked out this dress for Roger's graduation party—and with the handsomest and sweetest boyfriend ever. Roger was the love of my life.

"Mom, you know Roger is leaving right after graduation to work for his dad's company in New York City. He wants me to go, and I really want to."

My mother sighed. "College, Whitley."

"Mom, I want to learn all about the party-planning business. I want to have my own company someday. New York City is the best place for me to get started." I rotated and faced my mother. "Don't be mad."

"Ah hell, Whit. That usually means I'm going to be mad."

I let out a small laugh. "Mom, I talked to Michelle Durkin. She said I could start working under her as soon as possible. She'll teach me everything she knows about parties, weddings, birthdays, and reunions. Everything. Mom, this is something I really want to do. And who better to learn it from than your best friend from college?"

"Whit, you're so smart. You can get into any college you want. Your father and I are both doctors. Why don't you want to go to med school?"

"Ugh, Mom! I don't want to be a doctor. I can't even stand to see a paper cut. Please, Mommy, I really want this. Plus, I can be with Roger. I love him more than life, Mom."

My mother smiled and glanced over my shoulder. I turned to see my dad standing there, smiling.

"Do we let her?" my mother asked my father.

When he looked at me, his smile grew. I'd already talked to him about New York. I hated to say it, but I had my daddy wrapped around my finger.

He would do anything if he thought it would make me happy. I tried not to take advantage of that, but this time, I used it for my benefit.

"I guess we let her. You know, Whit, if things don't work out, all it takes is one phone call. One call, and I'll personally come take you away from that hellhole of a city."

My father hated New York City. We lived in Rhinebeck, New York, and my parents loved the country and small-town life. I, on the other hand, couldn't wait to leave Rhinebeck and move to New York City. I loved the country life, but right now, I needed to be a city girl for a bit.

I jumped up and down and clapped my hands. "Don't worry, Daddy! Nothing would ever make me want to come back here! Roger is going to make me so happy." I ran into my father's arms.

"He better, baby girl. He's promised me that his only goals in this life are to make you happy and keep you safe."

I smiled as I thought of Roger talking about New York City and how wonderful it was going to be. His dad was starting him out with his own condo in Manhattan and a more than generous pay to learn the family business. It would be nothing but parties, shopping, and more parties.

I can't wait to start my new life with Roger!

Life couldn't get any better.

➤➤➤➤➤➤➤➤➤➤➤➤✖◀◀◀◀◀◀◀◀◀◀◀◀◀

Present Day

The moment his fist hit my face, I felt extreme pain in my jaw.

Tonight might be the night he finally kills me.

The force of the blow had been so strong that I was literally seeing stars. I stumbled backward, and I started to fall down the cold steel stairs that I hated more than anything.

I saw the look on Roger's face. *Is he smiling?*

Then, all I could see were the metal beams across the ceiling as my body began falling back. My head slammed against one of the stairs.

Holy shit! My head...oh God, it hurts.

After I hit the bottom landing of the staircase, I slowly stood, and the room started spinning. I saw Roger walking up to me.

He grabbed my arm. "This is your fault, goddamn it! If you had just listened to me, Squeak, none of this would have ever happened!"

It's always my fault. Always. "I didn't do anything wrong."

I felt his grip tighten around my arm. My head was killing me, and my jaw felt like it was broken. He'd never hit me this hard before.

"You didn't do anything wrong? You were flirting with him, Squeak. I saw the way you were touching him and dancing with him. Did you flirt with him just to piss me off?"

When I looked into his eyes, the anger caused a chill to run up and down my spine. I tried to pull away from him. I knew I shouldn't have talked to Nick, let alone danced with him. He was Roger's biggest competition, and they were both up for the same job promotion at work.

Roger had been dancing and hanging all over Lucy Waters, and he hadn't so much as said two words to me all night. At one point, I'd seen him grab her ass and whisper something into her ear. I got pissed, so I'd sought out Nick and started to talk to him. We'd danced only one time, and as I was thanking him for the dance, I'd placed my hand on his upper arm. The moment I did it, I knew I'd made a drastic mistake.

"It was just an innocent dance, and I was thanking him for his kindness since you seemed to be making plans with Lucy for later." I attempted to jerk my arm out of his grip.

He pulled my arm so hard that I heard something pop. I dropped to my knees and let out a scream. When I looked up, I saw the expression on his face turn from anger to hate.

Oh my God, he's going to kill me.

He pulled me up, and tears started rolling down my cheeks from the pain in my jaw, head, and now, my shoulder. As he put his face right up to mine, I could smell the alcohol on his breath. It turned my stomach, and I tried to turn away. He grabbed my jaw and turned my face back to him, causing me to yell out again.

"Look at me when I'm talking to you, you fucking bitch! You. Don't. Touch. Other. Men. *Ever!* You are mine, Whitley. You've always been mine, and you always will be. You need to be taught a lesson, so you don't whore around like you were tonight. You showed up at that dinner party, looking the part. I told you, no strapless dresses ever!"

He yanked the top of my dress so hard that the fabric tore and fell off my body. I watched as he looked me up and down and licked his lips.

No. Please, God, no! "I wasn't flirting, Roger! He asked me to dance, and I didn't want to be rude." My jaw hurt more with every word I spoke.

Roger threw his head back and laughed. When he finally peered at me, he shook his head. "Did you want him, Squeak? Did you want to fuck him?"

What in the hell is he saying? How could he even think that?

"Answer me, Whitley!" Roger yelled, causing me to jump.

"No!"

"You're lying to me. That beautiful dress you had on tonight—the only reason you can afford to dress like that is because of me. These nails..." He pulled my hand up to his face and then bent my hand back, causing me to

drop to the floor in pain. "These nails are possible because of me, Squeak. Your hair, your sweet-smelling soft hair—this belongs to me. It's all because of me. This beautiful condo in Manhattan—this is all me, baby."

He pulled my hair, but I couldn't even call out in pain anymore. All I wanted was for the pain to go away.

I need to get away from him. "You're hurting me, Roger."

Usually, if I said he was hurting me, he would know I was at my breaking point, and he would stop. Then, he would leave and go drink until he couldn't walk, and he'd stay at the Ritz for the night. The next day, he'd come back, beg for forgiveness, and tell me how much he loved me and how afraid he was of losing me.

Yanking me closer to him, he reached down, tore off my panties, and then began touching me.

"Did. You. Want. To. Fuck. Him?" he slowly whispered in my ear. "If you want to, Whit, I can arrange it. Maybe I could even watch the two of you together and then join in."

I sucked in a breath of air and looked into his eyes. *He's gone crazy!*

"I heard Nick likes threesomes. We could have a little fun, Squeak. You would like that, wouldn't you? You're such a dirty little whore. You'd like to be fucked by that asshole, wouldn't you?"

I shook my head, the pain growing twenty times worse. I tried to open my mouth to say no, but Roger started to penetrate me with his fingers.

"Hmm...you're not very turned-on, baby. Let's get you good and wet. Do I need to call Nick to help out with that?"

I pushed him away from me and found the strength the talk. "Don't ever touch me again, you sick bastard! I don't want Nick, and I don't want you!" My skin started to crawl with the disgust I felt from being near him.

The look in his eyes changed. I didn't even see it coming until it was too late. He slapped me across the face, and then he grabbed my hair. When I saw Roger's fist coming straight toward my face again, I closed my eyes and waited for the blow.

I'm going to die tonight.

LAYTON

High School

"Is he ever coming back, Mike?" I asked my older brother as I watched him gut a deer.

"No, Layton. I don't think he's ever going to come back."

"He might." I started the fire and zipped up my jacket.

It was such a cold night out, and all I wanted was a warm bed. It wasn't uncommon for it to be cold in Texas in October.

Shit, I'm just so sick of being cold.

And hungry.

Mike stopped gutting the deer, took a deep breath, and turned around to look at me. "Layton, he's been gone for almost two years. He only sends us the tax money, so we can keep the ranch—the only damn thing he ever cared about. We couldn't even afford to keep the cattle on this place. I've just about used up all the money we got from selling them off. He left us. He left us in a house that wasn't finished. We have no heat and no air conditioning and no fucking running water! He doesn't care about you or me. He never has. All we are is a reminder of Mom."

I thought about my mother. She had passed away from cancer about two and a half years ago. My dad had started to build her dream home on top of one of the hills on our ranch, but then they found out she had cancer, and we'd had to move to Austin to be closer to the doctors.

She'd lived six months to the day after they'd sat Mike and me down on the sofa and told us she had breast cancer. I thought my world had ended there. I was wrong. It had ended two more times after—with her death and then our father leaving us.

I glanced over toward Mike and watched him work on the deer.

We had pretty much learned to survive on our own. Our dad had moved us back to Llano to our ranch after our mom passed away. He'd raised cattle, and he had also been big into racehorses. He'd made good money at both, so it made no sense to anyone why he would just up and walk away.

He'd said he was going to New York to look at a racehorse, and that was the last we'd heard from him. The only thing he'd done for us since then was provide the tax money on the ranch, so it would stay in the family, and that was sent through his lawyer.

We never had anyone come to the house. It looked finished from the outside, but if anyone knew that we lived in a shell with no running water or heat and air conditioning, they would put us both in foster homes. There was no way we would let that happen. We had a hot plate, a microwave,

and a small refrigerator. We hunted for all our meat, and we had a small garden, using seeds that we'd found in our mother's box of stuff that our dad had packed up and stored.

We were doing okay though—Mike and me. All we needed was each other.

"You know, Layton, with a little bit of hard work and both of us working like we are, we can buy a few racehorses and get some more cattle. We can make a name for ourselves and build the kind of ranch our old man dreamed of," Mike said.

I nodded. "Yeah, I know, Mike."

It was more Mike's dream to have the ranch, especially with racehorses. He was just like our father when it came to that. He had a gift, too. He had a few older friends who placed bets for him, and we were doing pretty well with the amount of money we were saving.

He turned and smiled. "You should go hose off, Layton. Isn't that party at the high school tonight?"

I smiled and nodded.

"You still like that girl?"

"Who? Olivia?"

Mike laughed. "Yeah, Olivia, the barrel racer. You've only had the hots for her since…what? Fifth grade?"

I grinned and kicked the ground. "Fourth."

"Go get ready, Layton. I've got this. There's some chili. Heat it up, and we'll have some before heading into town."

I turned and started to walk toward the house. I glanced back and looked at my brother. He was almost eighteen, and I was sixteen. I smiled and shook my head.

Yeah, we are going to make kick-ass cattle ranchers and raise some of the best fucking racehorses around. Then, when the old man comes back, we will rub it in his goddamn face. I'll make Mike proud of me.

As I walked into the house, I thought about tonight.

Maybe tonight, I'll finally get lucky with Olivia. Damn girl is stringing me along.

We'd almost had sex last night in her barn, but her damn brother had come in and caught us.

Fucker. My jaw was still killing me.

Tonight though, tonight my dreams would come true, and I would finally be with the girl I knew I was meant to spend the rest of my life with—my blonde-haired, blue-eyed beauty, Olivia.

That was all I needed in this life—Mike and Olivia.

I could keep working for Olivia's daddy on his ranch and put the money away to have the biggest and best damn cattle ranch in Texas—with a little bit of Thoroughbred horses thrown into the mix.

Present Day

I sat in the bar and downed another Bud Light. I was well on my way to getting drunk—again. I felt someone slap my back.

"What the hell, Layton? Again?"

I turned and saw my best friend, Reed, sitting next to me. He ordered a beer and flirted a bit with Misty, the bartender, who worked nights during the week. Misty wanted nothing to do with Reed, and all Reed wanted was a chance to get into her pants. All Misty wanted was a chance for me to get into her pants. She had practically begged me yesterday, and I'd almost given in. I'd do anything to forget about Olivia.

If only sex would make me forget everything…and everyone…

"Fuck off, Reed," I said.

Reed took a deep breath in and slowly let it out. "Dude, I know the last few months have been hell for you, but you have to snap out of it. Have you been to Lucky's to check on the horses? He's got…what? Three there that he's training? Mike believed in those horses, Layton."

Just the mention of my brother's name caused me to feel sick. "I know what my fucking brother believed in. You don't have to keep reminding me, Reed. I'm going to do him proud. I promised him."

"I know you did, Layton. I know you did." Reed took a sip of his beer.

"It's just…I keep expecting him to walk through that door with a big ole smile on his face from winning a race. I keep waiting…but he never comes."

I could tell Reed was staring at me, so I turned and looked at him. I smiled, winked, and finished off my beer. I looked up and saw Misty giving me that pathetic sympathy smile that everyone had been giving to me for months since Mike had died. I was sick of it.

"Misty, what are you doing after work?" I winked at her.

She slowly smiled and bit down on her lower lip. My dick instantly got hard as I thought about fucking her in the backseat of my truck.

"Going home with you?" she asked.

I casually gave her my dimple smile that I knew drove the girls crazy. "Fuck yeah, you are."

Reed slammed his beer down on the counter and turned to face me. "You know, Layton, sometimes, you can be a real prick." He grabbed his cowboy hat and headed out the door.

I watched him leave and then nonchalantly looked back at Misty. It was just us in the bar now.

"Can you close up early?" I asked.

She smiled and walked toward the front door. She pulled the cord, and the Open sign turned off. She locked the front door and shut off all the lights, except for the ones over the pool tables.

As she walked toward me, she started to take off her clothes. By the time she reached me, she was only in her bra and thong. She had a smokin' hot body and looked hot as hell standing there in her red lace bra and G-string. I stood, picked her up, and made my way over to a pool table.

Maybe she can make me forget for a few minutes.

ONE

-->>>>>>>>>>>><<<<<<<<<<<<--

Whitley

I could hear Courtney talking to someone, and I strained to hear what she was saying.

"She won't tell us what happened, Ms. Will, but we know she was assaulted by someone. I can't help her if she won't tell me who did this."

"I can tell you who did it. It was that motherfucking, good-for-nothing boyfriend of hers. Can't you just go arrest him? I mean, he put her in the damn hospital, for Christ's sake."

"Not unless she tells me who did it. I've called the police, and she refuses to talk to them. She said she *fell*. They questioned the boyfriend, and he said he was at his office late that night. He said that Whitley left the party without him, and he had to stay for an emergency. He has witnesses saying he was there. He told the police that when he got home, she was lying at the bottom of the stairs."

Court let out a small laugh. "Of course. He has it all neatly wrapped up, like always. She must have done something to really piss him off. He's pretty good about hiding it. I only just found out a few months ago that he has hit her before."

I coughed to let them know I was awake, but the pain that shot through my head and jaw about had me yell out.

"Whit, don't move, honey. You're in the hospital." Court leaned down and whispered in my ear, "I'm going to kill that asshole for doing this to you."

I slowly smiled. I looked over her shoulder at the tall, dark-haired woman standing there. I remembered her talking to me earlier.

"Can I only have certain people come into my room?" I asked.

She slightly grinned. "Yes, but your fiancé would like information on how you're doing. He was in here earlier and left you those roses." She gestured toward the window.

I turned and saw two-dozen pink roses. "Please throw them out," I said as I felt tears building in my eyes.

"Gladly! Fucker couldn't even get red." Courtney walked over and picked up the roses. "I think I'll leave them in the sweet lady's room next door."

I watched as she walked out of the room with the roses in hand. I glanced back at the woman standing there. "I know what you think of me."

She shook her head. "No, Whitley, you don't. You see, I've been exactly where you are right now—feeling so broken, like there is no way out. But there is. There are people who can help you if you would just let them."

"I'm sorry. What's your name again?" I asked.

"Monica."

"Monica, I just want to leave New York City and forget I ever met him. Please just let me do this my way."

She took a deep breath and looked me in the eyes. "Whitley, please, please press charges against him. Let him know he can't do this to you or any other girl for that matter."

Courtney walked back in, stopped, and glanced between Monica and me. "Should I leave?"

I smiled at Monica and shook my head. "I was just telling Monica about my plans to move and leave New York as soon as possible."

Monica's smile faded just a bit, but she nodded. "I hope you know what you're doing, honey. Please do it. Please leave him as soon as possible."

I smiled. "I promise, I will."

Courtney watched Monica step out, and then she turned to face me. "Why, Squeak? Why won't you put his ass in jail?"

"Court...please don't ever call me Squeak again. *Please.*"

Since middle school, I'd been called Squeak because I had such a high-pitched voice. Court had started it, but Roger loved the nickname, and he'd called me that since we began dating.

I thought back to the night before when he had touched me and whispered it in my ear. I felt sick to my stomach.

Never again.

Court looked at me funny and made a face. "Whit, what did he do to you? How long has this been going on? I want the truth please."

I closed my eyes and felt tears building. When I opened my eyes, the tears began rolling down my face. "About six months after we moved to New York, while we were getting ready to go to a dinner party, we got into a fight about what I was wearing. He told me I looked like a whore, and I called him an asshole. He slapped me so hard that I had to put makeup on to cover the mark on my face. The whole way to the party, he begged me to forgive him, and he even cried."

Courtney shut her eyes, and when she opened them, I saw her tears. I smiled weakly at her.

"The next time?"

"It was months later. Things were great until I talked to a neighbor outside our apartment building. He was a runner, like me, and he was telling me about a marathon. Roger saw us chatting when he walked up. The moment we stepped into our apartment, he grabbed my arm and started yelling at me. When I told him to stop, he pushed me, and I fell. I hit my head on the coffee table and started crying. He begged me to forgive him...and I did.

"I just accepted the fact that he was jealous, so I never talked to guys—any guys, even old friends from home. But it got worse. It continued with the clothes I wore or how I walked in front of other men. Once, I embarrassed him in front of his coworkers at a Christmas party, and when we got home, he yelled at me. We were at the top of the stairs, and when I tried to push past him, he grabbed me and shook me so hard that the room started spinning. I told him he was hurting me, and when he let me go, he pushed me, and I fell down the stairs. That was how I really broke my wrist."

Courtney let out a gasp. "Oh my God, Whitley! You told everyone you tripped while you were running! Is that why you've pulled away from me so much? You didn't want me to find out?"

I closed my eyes and nodded. "I'm sorry, Court. I really thought he would change. At first, I thought it was me, that I was doing something wrong. He always found ways to tell me how he'd given me everything, how I wouldn't have anything if it weren't for him."

I opened my eyes and stared down at my hands. "I'd met a girl who wanted to open up a party-planning company with me, and I was so excited, but he told me I couldn't do it. He said I didn't even have a college degree. When I reminded him I didn't have a degree because I'd followed him to New York, he just slapped me and called me ungrateful. It has been a never-ending cycle."

"Fuck him, Whit. You can do anything you want."

I smiled and looked directly into her eyes. "I need your help."

Her smile faded. "Okay. I know people."

"Huh?"

"If you want to take him out, I know people who know people. It can look like an accident. Easy."

I just stared at her. "Oh. My. God. Are you being serious?"

"Shit yeah, I am."

I shook my head to clear my thoughts. "As much as that sounds like a solid plan, honey, I think I'll pass. Do you remember in high school when my parents and I met that guy from Texas, and he talked about his hometown?"

"Yeah, it was like an animal name, Llama or something like that."

I started laughing.

God, I love this girl, like she's my sister.

I'd loved her since the moment we met on the playground in kindergarten. She'd pushed me and told me I had a squeaky voice, and I'd pushed her back and told her to choke on her lollipop. We'd been best friends ever since.

There wasn't a damn thing I wouldn't do for Court, and I knew she felt the same way.

"It was Llano, Courtney, but you were close, hon."

"Potato, patatoe. What about it?"

I smiled at her and tilted my head. "I called my dad this morning and told him I was leaving Roger because he was cheating on me. I said that I wanted a fresh new start, and Llano, Texas is where I wanted to go."

The smile that spread across Court's face lit up the room. "No fucking way! We're going to Texas?"

I let out a laugh. My head was already feeling better from knowing that my very best friend was ready to just up and leave everything behind to go to Texas with me.

"Depends on if you want to help me run a party-planning business there."

"Ah, yeah, I do! When do we leave? After we go pick up your stuff at the apartment?"

I took a deep breath. This was going to be the tricky part. "Um…I actually need to leave, like, right now. Roger is in New Jersey for the next two days at some summer retreat with his dad. He left me a text, saying he's been trying to call the hospital, and they won't give him any information even though he's my fiancé."

I looked down at my finger at the diamond he'd given me two years ago. We'd never even talked about a wedding after he put the ring on my finger. It was all for show for his job. I knew that now.

Courtney smiled and turned to walk out the door before looking back over her shoulder. "I'm on it. I already have the doctor's phone number. I bet I can get those discharge papers ready for you in an hour."

"That's all you need?" I asked with a laugh and a wink.

"Get dressed, bitch. We're busting you out of New York City and heading to Texas!"

TWO

-»»»»»»»»«««««««««-

LAYToN

I stood on my front porch, looking out at the cattle. I smiled as I thought about how Mike would be happy to see that our cattle herd was so big. I heard Blake Shelton blaring from the white F-350 truck coming down the driveway.

I smiled as I watched Reed pull in, jump out, and then walk up to the porch.

"My God, I can't believe you've been fucking Misty for the last two weeks, you motherfucker. You *knew* how much I liked that girl."

I took a sip of coffee and smiled.

Liked her? He only wanted to sleep with her. "Twice, bro. It's only been twice."

Reed twisted his baseball cap around and grabbed a chair. He sat down as he faced me. "Really? 'Cause, according to my baby sister, Wes said she heard you've been screwing Misty in the bar for the last two weeks. Misty has been telling everyone y'all are a couple. She even said you were packin' some heat there, cowboy. I'm never going to be able to play pool in that bar again, you asshole."

I threw my head back and laughed. "Dude, don't worry. I have absolutely no interest in Misty whatsoever. She was something that got my mind off of Olivia and Mike for a few minutes, that's all."

Reed let out a deep breath and shook his head. "Layton, Mike's death was over six months ago. I know y'all were each other's world, dude, but you've got to move on."

I turned toward the pasture. "I not only lost my brother, but I also lost the love of my life."

I closed my eyes and pictured making love to Olivia for the first time in the deer cabin…and the last time in the barn. Watching her get up and walk away from me that morning while telling me she was leaving me for another man had about killed me.

"Layton, she left you the day after your brother died. She's a bitch. If she ever loved you, she would have never walked away from you when you needed her the most. She's not worth the heartache."

I rotated around and faced Reed with a smile. "You're right. That's why I'll never trust another woman again. I'll never let another person into my heart ever."

Reed let out a laugh and slapped my back. "Sure, dude. You keep telling yourself that. You headed out to check the fence line?"

"Yeah. You want to ride along?"

Reed smiled that smile of his. "Nah, I'm going on a picnic with Jennifer." He lifted his eyebrows up and down.

I shook my head and laughed as I walked away. "Have fun with that."

◄ۣۣۣۣۣۣۣۣۣۜۜۜۜۜۜۜۜ ►

I rode along the fence line, just trying to clear my head. This was where I did my best thinking. I loved it out here. I could get lost, just being in the quiet of it all.

"Motherfucker! Son of a bitch! Stupid-ass car! Oh my God, I hate you!"

What in the hell?

I came up over a small hill and saw a silver Lexus RX pulled off on the side of the road. The girl standing next to the car, kicking the wheel, was obviously from the city. She was dressed in light gray slacks and a sheer white blouse. Her brown hair was pulled up and piled loosely on top of her head. The way she was screaming at the tire and yelling at the car made me smile instantly.

Too fucking cute. Damn city girls.

"Piece-of-shit car!"

I let out a small laugh. "Excuse me, ma'am. You've got a problem with your car?"

She spun around and threw her hands on her hips as she tilted her head. When she crinkled up her nose, I guessed it was something she did when she got mad.

"No, cowboy. I like standing on the side of the road in Texas in the middle of July, yelling at my piece-of-shit car. I get a kick out of it."

Wow. What a bitch. Yep, city girl. Bet she's from New York or somewhere like that. "Wow. Full of spit and fire, and here I was, trying to be a Southern gentleman and help you out. If you prefer that I keep moving along, I'll be more than happy to—"

"No! Wait! Oh God, please don't go. I've been here for almost an hour, and not one car has gone by. Not one! My cell phone doesn't have a signal, and you're the first person I've seen. I'm sorry. I didn't mean to be such a bitch. I'm late for my first big job interview, and I really wanted this to go so differently."

When she tried to hold back a sob, my heart sank.

Ah, shit.

I guided Cricket up against the fence, and then I pulled my leg over and jumped.

"Oh shit! Aren't you afraid your horse is going to run away?"

I smiled at her and turned to look at Cricket, who seemed just as amused by her comment as I was. "You know, I think Cricket might actually like you. She's not one for taking to people, but look at how she's staring at you."

I turned to see the city girl peeking over at the horse with a serious face. She slowly turned back to me and smirked.

"Are all Texas cowboys so...*friendly?*" She used air quotes as she said *friendly.*

I gave her my oh-so-famous smirk with a dimple. She didn't want to, but her lips cracked with the slightest grin. My heart dropped, but I quickly pushed away the feeling.

"Nah, I'm one of a kind," I said with a wink. "What's going on with the overpriced piece of junk?"

She looked back at the car and then at me. "I didn't call it that."

"No, ma'am, you didn't. I did."

She took a deep breath and shook her head. "I'm not sure. It just died. It won't turn over or even make a sound. Nothing. Can I use your phone to call a tow truck? I just moved to town, so if you could recommend, maybe, where to have it towed, that would be awesome. Oh, also, do you know a Mrs. Pierceson?"

"Yes, she's my neighbor."

She jumped up and down and started clapping her hands together. "Oh my God, is there any way you can take me to a phone or to her house? I'll pay you! I mean, with cash."

Holy shit. I felt slightly offended. "Um...ma'am, you're in the country in Texas. We help our neighbors out. I don't want your money. I'd be happy to bring you up to my house to make your call, and then I can take you on over to Mrs. Pierceson's."

She smiled the biggest, most beautiful smile I'd ever seen. I couldn't help but smile back.

"Great! Let me grab some shi—I mean, some stuff out of my car."

When she took off her sunglasses to look at me, I was taken aback by her green eyes. They were the most beautiful shade of green I'd ever seen. They were just as breathtaking as Olivia's blue eyes.

I stood there and watched her as she searched in her car. She took a box out of the backseat and placed it on the ground. Then, she grabbed a laptop carrier and slung it over her shoulder. When she shut the door, she reached for the box and just looked at me. I just stared at her and the box she was holding.

"Oh, um…I thought you were going to get your truck or something."

I looked all around me, then at Cricket, and then back at her as I let out a laugh. "You're joking right?" I asked.

Her smile faded slightly.

"Sweetheart, if you want me to give you a ride, you're climbing onto the back of Cricket here."

Her mouth dropped open, and I couldn't help but smile at her expression.

"You want me to get on your horse? With all my stuff? How?"

I sighed and prayed that someone would just put up a sign outside of Llano that read, _No more city folk allowed._

"Ma'am, how in the world—"

Balancing the box in one hand, she held up the other and shook her head. "Okay, first off, I'm pretty sure you're older than me, so please stop calling me ma'am. My name is Whitley. And your name, cowboy?"

What a bitch!

I turned and started to walk back over to Cricket. I stopped and spun around. "Well, Whitley, I'm twenty-five years old, and it's a Southern thing to address a lady as ma'am. If you want a ride up to my house, you'll have to get off your damn high-society horse and realize you're out in the middle of the goddamn country. I own five-thousand acres. My neighbor is a good way away, but my house isn't too far on horseback. If you want a lift, you'll get your ass over here, and then I can help you up and over this fence, so you don't rip your pretty little outfit. If you'd like to wait for a car to come by, good luck. And my name is Layton, not cowboy." I stood there with my arms folded over my chest, trying to contain my anger.

She managed to open her car door, and then she tossed the box back inside. Still clinging to her laptop carrier, she grabbed her purse and then started to make her way over toward me.

"You so much as touch me wrong, and I'll knock the shit out of you, cowboy."

I reached for her and picked her up. When I lifted her over the fence, she let out a little gasp. After I set her down on the other side, she tried to adjust her balance.

"The name's Layton, not cowboy."

She glared at me as she put her hand on Cricket.

"Let me help you up," I said.

She slammed her purse and laptop carrier into my chest. "Just hold these, will you? I know how to get on a damn horse."

I smiled as she climbed up onto my girl. She certainly did know what she was doing. She moved behind the saddle and reached down for her things. I smiled as I handed them to her.

"What? No tip of your hat? No, 'Well done, city girl'?" She arched her eyebrow.

"Do you need me to tell you that you did a good job?"

She turned her head and sighed.

I climbed onto Cricket and said, "Hold on."

We rode along in silence for a bit before she finally started to talk.

"So, you've always lived here?"

"Yes, ma'am, my whole life."

She let out a sigh, and I smiled, knowing I was agitating the shit out of her by calling her ma'am.

"Family? Are you married?"

"Nope."

"Nope to not married? Or nope to no family?"

I turned around to look at her. Her eyes caused me to catch my breath. I'd never seen such beautiful green eyes. I'd always been one for blue eyes, but this girl's eyes just did something to me.

"Both."

I felt her tense up and grab on to me tighter.

"Oh. Do you mind if I ask where your family is?"

"Are you going to see Mrs. Pierceson regarding business? Or is it personal?"

She let out a gruff small laugh. "I'll take that as, it's none of my business. I'm meeting her for business. I'm starting an event-planning company here. She's my first client."

"Really?"

"Really. She's throwing a sixtieth birthday party for her husband. I met her in the coffee shop in town, and we got to talking. She's very nice, and once she found out I was new to town, she couldn't wait to help me out by being my first client."

"Well, she's pretty well-known in Llano, so if you do a good job, you'll most likely get more work out of it. One thing we like to do in the country is throw a damn good party."

"Oh shit. That just makes me more nervous. Damn it. Why'd you have to tell me that?"

I rolled my eyes and shook my head. "Just be yourself, CG, and you'll do fine."

"CG? What in the hell does that stand for?"

I let out a laugh. "City girl!"

"Oh my God. No. You did not just give me a nickname, and to top it off, a lame nickname at that!"

"Lame? That is not a lame nickname. Are you not from the city? I mean, come on. New York City, I bet, right? You can't get any more city than that."

"Whitley, that's my name. Please call me Whitley."

"Fine. Whitley, it is."

"Fine."

"I already said fine."

"Jesus Christ, no wonder you're not married."

I started to laugh. This girl was full of spit and fire. "What about you?"

"What about me?"

"Married? Boyfriend? Family here? What brought you to Llano? How old are you?"

I felt her tense up.

"I'm single and plan on staying that way. My family lives in New York, and my best friend, Courtney, moved here with me. I needed a fresh start, and Texas was it. I'd heard about Llano years ago, and I decided this was what I wanted—small-town, country living. And I'm twenty-four."

"You running from someone?"

"What? Why would you ask me that?"

Jesus, she was instantly on guard. *Yep, she's running from something...or someone.*

"It was just a question, CG."

"No, I'm not running. Shit, I thought you were supposed to be a Southern gentleman, not an asshole."

"Ouch. Now, I see why *you're* single."

"Can we just not talk anymore? Please."

"Fine by me," I said.

"Good."

When she placed her head on my back, I instantly felt like a dick. Just by the way she was holding on to me, I could tell she was upset. I should have just dropped it. My heart actually hurt, knowing I might have caused her pain.

We rode the rest of the way to the house in silence.

THREE

→»»»»»»»»»»«««««««««««←

Whitley

I couldn't believe I was trying to get to my first appointment with my first client on the back of a horse with a damn cowboy—and a smart-ass cowboy to top it off.

Wait until I tell Court about this. She would be pissed. My first official contact with a cowboy, and she wasn't with me.

I smiled, just thinking about telling her.

Shit. Why did my car have to break down?

Damn it! Why does he have to smell so good?

Breathe out of your mouth, Whitley. Don't breathe in his heavenly scent.

I closed my eyes and thought back to fifteen minutes ago when I saw him for the first time and felt like I'd died and gone to heaven. He was about five-eleven and built like a god. He had the bluest of blue eyes. I'd never in my life seen eyes that looked like they were piercing into my soul.

His smile…good God, his smile. I swore my panties had combusted the moment he'd flashed that smile. *Fucker had to have a dimple, too. Ugh.*

I opened my eyes and looked at the back of his head. He had on a black cowboy hat, but his brown hair was peeking out. My eyes moved down to the tattoos covering his arm. I saw the name Mike and a date, but I couldn't make out the numbers.

That would be another reason Courtney was going to be pissed. She loved guys with tats. I could take it or leave it.

He turned his head and said something, pulling me out of my thoughts.

"I'm sorry. What was that?"

"My house is right up the way a bit. It's just another couple of minutes."

"Perfect! I can still make my appointment and not be too terribly late."

When we came up over a hill, the house in front of me literally took my breath away.

"Holy shit. Is that your house?" I stared at the most amazing house I'd ever seen.

"Yes, ma'am, it is. My brother and I built it."

"It's…it's breathtaking." I shook my head.

This house looked almost exactly like the dream home I had planned in my head. It was a two-story house made of stone and wood. Most of it was a sandstone rock, and the chimneys on the ends made it look like a log cabin. It even had a silver tin roof. The porch pretty much wrapped around the whole house. On the second floor, I noticed a huge balcony that had to belong to the master bedroom. There was a three-car garage, and behind the house was an even bigger barn.

As Layton headed to the barn, I saw a young man running toward us.

"Mr. Layton! My dad said you might need some help this summer. I couldn't wait to ask you. I'll do anything, sir, anything you want. You want me to take Cricket and get her cooled off and fed, sir? I'll take care of her for you."

I had to let out a laugh. Whoever this little boy was, he certainly looked up to Layton. After bringing Cricket to a stop, Layton leaned back and asked for me to sit tight. He jumped down, took my purse and laptop bag, and then handed them to the little boy. Then, Layton turned and reached for me. As much as I wanted to tell him that I was very capable of getting off a horse by myself, I also longed for his touch, which really surprised me. So, I let him help me down. The moment he touched me, I felt a surge go through my whole body.

What in the hell was that?

He slowly slid my body down while looking in my eyes the whole time. I couldn't catch my breath. The way he was staring at me gave me goose bumps.

"Um…thank you, um…Layton." I looked everywhere but at him.

When I did look back at him, he smiled that drop-dead gorgeous smile of his.

Good Lord. I could have dropped to my knees on the spot.

Then, he smirked.

Fucker. He knows he's having an effect on me. That bastard! He's doing it on purpose.

"Ryan, why don't you take Cricket to the barn and get her settled? I'll talk to your dad about you helping Mitch and me out this summer. I'm going to take Miss…"

I looked at the little boy, who was smiling from ear to ear, and I let out a giggle. "Reynolds."

"Reynolds. I'm going to take Miss Reynolds up to the house, so she can call a tow truck. Then, I'll be driving her to Mrs. Pierceson's place." Layton took my purse and laptop bag from Ryan and handed it back to me.

"Okay, Mr. Layton. I'll take real good care of her. The horse, I mean."

Layton snapped his head over and looked at Ryan. He threw his head back and laughed. "Ryan, you're gonna be a heartbreaker."

Ryan took the reins and headed down to the barn. Layton gestured toward the house. We walked side by side as we approached the back door. The closer we got, the bigger the house got.

"Jesus...this house is huge. It's just you living here?"

He let out a laugh and walked up onto the back porch. As we walked into the house, we came right into an eating area. It was nothing but windows, looking out onto the beautiful Texas hill country. Then, we moved into the kitchen, and I almost let out a whimper. I thought my parents had a beautiful kitchen. This one was straight out of a magazine.

"Holy shit. I could have an orgasm from just standing in this kitchen."

I walked around and ran my hand along the granite-top kitchen island as I took everything in. When I looked up at Layton, he had removed his cowboy hat, and all I saw was a pile of messy brown hair.

Holy shit.

He had that just-fucked hair that Court was always talking about.

Be cool, Whitley. Be. Cool.

Layton grinned. "Well, I've never heard anyone say that about my kitchen before."

"You have to have a party here! I mean, if this is just the kitchen, I can't imagine what the rest of the house looks like."

His smile faded, and he walked away.

Shit. What did I say?

I followed him past a butler's pantry, then past a huge formal dining room, and into a breathtaking living room. I'd never seen a living room so big in my entire life. It was nothing but floor-to-ceiling windows, again looking out to the country hills.

Then, I saw them. I slowly turned around and saw nothing but dead animals on the walls. A huge elk was hanging above the fireplace, just staring at me.

Deer...turkey...

Oh. My. God. Is that a fox?

"You have a fox. You have a dead fox on your wall!"

Layton chuckled. "Yes, ma'am, I do. I like to hunt."

I spun around and glared at him. "Please tell me you at least eat the meat, and you're not one of those men who just likes to hunt to kill."

"I make some of the best elk beef stew around. Want some?"

"Eww, gross! No, thank you."

Just then, two labs came running up to us. One was black, and the other was brown.

Oh, I love labs! I bent down and was attacked with nothing but wet kisses from both.

"All right, y'all, leave her be. Kennels."

And with that, they both ran into another room.

I looked up at him with a questioning look. "Kennels?"

"Yep. I just have to say it, and they go lie down in their kennels."

Damn. The thought of him training his dogs to listen so well was a total turn-on.

I pulled out my cell phone. *Shit! Still no signal.* "Um…I still don't have a signal. Do you have a landline I could use?"

Layton walked over and picked up a telephone. He also pulled out a book and flipped through a few pages before he started dialing a number.

"Jack? Hey, it's Layton Morris."

Morris. Something about his name was so damn sexy.

Oh my God…what in the hell is wrong with me? Stop it, Whitley. You're done with men—forever. They are nothing but evil bastards who only want to take everything from you and then leave you empty and alone.

"Yep…it's on the south side of my property on Old Mills Road. Yeah, sure. It's Whitley, and it's…" He looked over at me and raised his eyebrow.

Really? He forgot my last name already?

"Reynolds," I said with a sarcastic tone as I rolled my eyes.

"Your cell or home number, so he can reach you?" he asked with a smirk.

"Oh…" I rattled off my cell phone number and my home number.

While Layton was talking with Jack on the phone, I took advantage and looked around his house. I walked to another room and peeked in to find a huge den and office. Again, the room was covered in dead animals. If I didn't know any better, I would swear that the deer was turning its head and following me.

Yuck! I'd have nightmares from living here.

I saw a desk and noticed a few pictures on it. I made my way over and picked up a picture of Layton and another guy who looked to be a few years older than him.

Brother maybe? Damn, these two boys are drop-dead gorgeous.

"Jack is on his way to get your car."

I jumped and damn near dropped the picture. "Shit! You scared the hell out of me."

"You enjoy walking around, snooping in people's homes?"

I felt my cheeks instantly turn hot. I placed the picture back down on the desk and quickly walked out of the room.

As I passed him, I whispered, "I'm so sorry."

I made my way back into the living room, through the kitchen, and out the door onto the back porch where I stood and took in a few deep breaths. The breeze was just enough to help me cool off from the instant hot flash that had swept through my body. I didn't know if I was pissed at how he had just treated me or embarrassed that I had been caught snooping in his office.

I heard the door open and close, followed by his footsteps on the wooden porch. Then, he came and stood next to me.

"I'm sorry. That was rude of me. I'm just not used to people walking around in my office."

I slowly turned and looked him in the eyes. There was such sadness there. I wanted to ask him who was in the picture with him, but just by his reaction, I had a feeling I already knew who it was.

"No, I shouldn't have walked into your study like that. I'm terribly sorry. So, um…you'll let me know who's coming to get my car?"

"Oh yeah…here. I wrote it down for you. Jack is probably the best mechanic in town. You're in good hands."

As he handed me the paper, our fingers touched. He jerked his hand back and then ran it through that messy hair before putting his hat back on. I shoved the paper into my purse and then looked back out toward the hills.

"I bet the sunsets are amazing from this porch," I said as I glanced over at him.

He smiled, but then it faded. "Yeah, they're pretty amazing."

"Surely, there's someone special you share all this with?" I asked with a smile.

He glanced at me, and the hurt in his eyes was more than I could stand.

"No, Whitley, there's no one. I'll take you to Mrs. Pierceson's place now."

He turned and started to walk toward the garage as I followed. A silver Ford F-350 was parked right outside the garage. He went up to the passenger side and opened the door for me.

"Christ almighty, is everything in Texas big?" I said with a slight smile.

He smiled and winked. "Yes, yes, it is."

He held his hand out for me and helped me up and into the truck. He shut the door and strolled around the front.

I didn't want to admit that I was glad I'd made him smile. The idea of him being sad bothered me for some reason.

"You've got your purse and laptop?" He looked me in the eyes.

"Yep, got 'em."

"Good. I wouldn't want you needing an excuse to come back and take another peek around my house."

And there was the asshole I'd met a bit ago.

I rolled my eyes and turned away from him. "Don't worry. I won't be gracing you with my presence ever again, Mr. Morris."

He laughed as he took off down his driveway. "It's a small town, Miss Reynolds. I wouldn't make promises you can't keep."

I glanced over at him and saw that smile again.

Ugh. Bastard.

I just needed to get away from him and get to my first client. The start of my new life was waiting for me, and now, I was going to have Layton Morris breathing down my throat as I tried to sell myself as the best party planner Mrs. Pierceson would ever hire.

"How will I get home? I forgot to call Courtney."

He didn't even waste a second. "I'll drive you back into town. I have some business I need to take care of anyway."

"Fine. But don't utter a word. I'm doing business, and the last thing I need is you making some crack about me being from the city."

He laughed as he looked over at me. "Oh, don't you worry your pretty little self now. I promise not to let Mrs. P in on my nickname for you, CG."

"Ugh…just don't talk. Better yet, just wait in your truck."

As he laughed and shook his head, I had a strange feeling that Layton Morris was going to be nothing but a pain in my ass.

FOUR

>>>>>>>>>>><<<<<<<<<<<<

LAYTON

Whitley did nothing but fiddle with her damn hands the whole way to Mrs. P.'s. She seemed nervous as hell.

"Just relax, CG. Be yourself, and you'll do fine."

I saw her head snap over toward me as she let out a sigh. I knew calling her CG was getting on her nerves, which only made me do it even more. I quickly glanced at her, only to see her shooting me a dirty look.

"Why do you insist on calling me that?"

I shrugged my shoulders as I turned into the driveway. I rolled down the window and hit the call button.

"Hello?"

"Mrs. P, how are you today? It's Layton."

"Layton! My Lord, boy, where in the hell have you been? I've missed you. We're neighbors, for God's sake!"

I laughed and shook my head. "I'm delivering a Miss Reynolds. She has an appointment with you, and her car broke down. Jack is coming to pick it up."

The giant iron gate started to open.

"Come on up, sweetness."

"My God, everything in Texas really is bigger. I think her entrance is bigger than yours," Whitley said as we headed down the driveway.

Mrs. P lived damn near toward the back of her property, so we had a bit of a drive just to get to her house.

"Where in the hell is the house?" Whitley looked at me with a smile. "Does she have just as much land as you do?"

"Just about. Her husband was big into cattle. I pretty much bought all his cattle, so he could retire. They only have one son, who wants nothing to do with the cattle business."

Whitley turned slightly in her seat. "So, you raise cattle?"

"Yep. That's one of the things I do."

I glanced over, and she tilted her head somewhat.

"What else do you do, cowboy?"

I smiled. "I also raise Thoroughbreds."

She smiled bigger. "No shit? For racing?"

Ah...so my CG likes horse racing, does she? "Yes, ma'am, for racing."

"I used to love going to the racetrack with my parents. My father made some good money on a few horses he owned."

I nearly slammed on the brakes. "You mean to tell me that you grew up around horses?"

She gave me that damn cute little smile of hers and then turned back and looked straight ahead.

"Yes, sir, I did. I was on my first horse when I was three years old."

Well, damn.

"You must be good at what you do, considering you have so much land, and your house is..."

"My house is, what?"

"Nothing. I'm being rude by just even talking about your income. I'm so sorry." She looked out the window and started messing with her hands.

"I've learned not to put all my eggs in one basket, Whitley. I've made investments in real estate, horses, and stocks. You know, those sorts of things. The property is owned outright, so—"

"Please, Mr. Morris, you don't owe me any explanations at all."

"Now, we're back to Mr. Morris. Okay, Miss Reynolds, we're almost to the house."

She shifted in her seat, and I wanted to ask her why she'd done a one-eighty and gone all formal on me.

We rounded the corner, and my heart dropped to my stomach.

Fuck! What's she doing here?

I wanted nothing more than to turn around and leave, but I didn't want to be rude to Whitley. I pulled up and parked next to the white BMW convertible.

"Wow! Mrs. Pierceson drives a nice car."

I jumped out of the truck and walked around to help Whitley out. She had her purse and laptop carrier in one hand as she allowed me to help her down, much to my surprise.

"That's not her car."

Whitley turned and looked at me. I was sure she had heard the fear in my voice.

"Whose car is it then?" She raised her eyebrow.

"Her niece's. Let's go. Mrs. P is waiting for you, and you're already late."

I gently took her by the arm to lead her in, but then she jerked away from me. I looked at her, and her face was white as a ghost.

"Please don't touch me like that—ever again."

She smoothed out her pants and shirt and walked past me up to the porch. She stopped for a brief second and took a deep breath before walking up the steps and ringing the doorbell.

I stepped up to her and leaned down. "I'm sorry, CG. I don't have some weird kind of country disease or anything. I'll make sure I never touch you again."

She snapped her head up and was about to say something when the front door opened.

"Well, looky here, if it ain't my handsome Layton! Son, you have to come over more often! Mr. Pierceson is down at the barn, doing God knows what, if you want to say hello."

Mrs. Pierceson turned and started to walk into the house, and I gestured for Whitley to go in first. When we walked into the foyer, Mrs. P turned around and smiled at Whitley.

Whitley grinned back and put out her hand.

She's in for a surprise.

"Oh, pishposh, girl. Come in for a hug!" Mrs. P grabbed Whitley and pulled her into an embrace.

Whitley let out a gasp and then giggled. "I'm so very sorry I'm late, Mrs. Pierceson. My car broke down, and...well, Mr. Morris here came to my rescue, sort of."

I smiled and winked before I started heading toward the kitchen to go out to the barn. "Your knight in shining armor, I believe you said I was, CG."

I turned to see her mouth hanging open while Mrs. P was smiling from ear to ear.

"CG? What does that stand for, my dear? Is that what you prefer to be called?"

Right as I opened the back door, I heard Whitley say, "No! God, no. Please just call me Whitley."

As I made my way down to the barn, I could hear Mr. P singing away to some old George Jones's song. I smiled to myself, thinking about how Mike used to come and talk to Mr. P for hours. I never knew what all they had talked about, but I was pretty sure Mr. and Mrs. Pierceson had known how we had lived. They had always left food at the gate but never bothered to come down to the house. My guess was they'd paid a visit when we weren't home one day, and they probably never really knew how to talk to us about it.

Just as I was about to walk into the barn, I heard someone call out my name.

"Layton?"

The sound of her voice rang through my whole body. I hadn't talked to Olivia since the night she'd told me she was leaving me.

I just stopped. I didn't move. I was frozen.

After I took a deep breath, I started to walk into the barn.

"Layton, wait, please. Talk to me for just a second."

I felt her hand on my arm, and I fought against wanting to take her into my arms. I slowly turned around and looked into those beautiful blue eyes. My heart began pounding.

I cleared my throat. "Hey, Olivia. I'm just heading to say hi to your uncle. If you'll excuse me…"

"*Please.* I just want to know how you're doing. I've heard, um…I've heard things have been tough for you, baby."

I looked her up and down. *Fuck, she looks good.*

She was wearing tight-ass riding pants and a white T-shirt. I could see her nipples through the shirt, and I was starting to get a hard-on from just looking at her.

"I'm doing fine, Olivia. Things have been great. No worries on my end. Just one big party."

I went to walk away, but she held on to my arm.

"Layton, I'm sorry I hurt you. I didn't mean to."

I just looked at her. "Really, Liv? 'Cause you leaving me right after my brother died was a pretty big thing. Not sure how you didn't think that one would hurt."

She took a deep breath and threw her head back. "Layton, I'll always love you, baby, but—"

"Please, Liv, I can't deal with this right now, okay?"

Just when I feel like I'm moving on and finally forgetting her, I have to fucking see her. Fuck!

"Baby, I just want to be friends, and when I hear about you whoring around with the town slut, I get a little worried. I don't want you to sell yourself short. You deserve so much more, Layton. Baby, would you like to have dinner tonight?"

I just stared at her. I was tempted to say yes. I wanted nothing more than to spend time with her. She took a step closer and ran her hand up and down my chest as she leaned into me. My knees felt weak, and I longed for her to touch me more.

"Layton, I've missed you, baby," she whispered against my neck.

Olivia…I've missed you.

I tried to talk, but all that came out was a low moan.

"Hmm, I've missed hearing those sounds you make, Layton. Have you missed me? Touch me, and tell me you've missed me."

I closed my eyes and placed my hand on her hip. I pulled her even closer to me, so she could feel my hard-on.

She let out a small giggle and then moved her lips up to my ear. "Who's the girl, Layton? Are you seeing someone new?"

My eyes flew open. *What? What girl? Who's she talking about?*

I pulled back and looked at her. "What?"

She licked her lips and grabbed my dick. "Is this for me? Or for the brunette you pulled up with?"

Just then, I heard Justin's voice calling out for Olivia. She moved her lips to my mouth and bit on my lower lip before stepping away from me.

I couldn't even think straight. I watched as Justin walked over with a smile as he saw Olivia. She strolled right into his arms and kissed him. I felt sick to my stomach.

What in the fuck just happened?

Justin pulled back, and that was when he noticed me.

"Shit, I'm sorry. I didn't know you were here, Morris. Um, Liv, is everything okay?"

Did he just call her Liv? That's my nickname for her, not his. Fucking prick.

Olivia turned back and looked at me. "Oh yeah, baby. Layton was just going to visit my uncle, and we ran into each other. You never did tell me why you're here, Layton." Her voice was now cold toward me.

I glanced between her and Justin. Out of the corner of my eye, I saw Mrs. P and Whitley coming toward us.

Fuck.

I turned and started to head inside the barn toward Mr. P's singing voice. I needed room to breathe.

What in the hell did she just do to me? Who is she talking about? What brunette—

Just as I reached Mr. P, it hit me. She must have seen me helping Whitley out of the truck.

She thinks we're together.

"Hey, Layton! What a great surprise!" Mr. P yelled out.

I smiled and held my hand up in a wave. "Hey, Mr. P. Um…I'll be right back."

I turned and stormed out of the barn. As I walked up, I could see Mrs. P introducing Whitley to Olivia and Justin.

I came up and grabbed Olivia's arm. "I need to talk to you—now."

Olivia looked around, and her face blushed. "Um…Layton, can it wait? I mean—"

"No, you started it, and I'm finishing it."

I glanced at Justin, and he seemed like he wanted to say something, but he didn't. I glanced at Whitley, and she had a terrified look on her face.

"Fine! If you'll excuse me…" Olivia yanked her arm from my hand.

She made her way up to the house, and I followed behind her. As soon as the kitchen door shut, she attempted to kiss me, but I pushed her away.

"What in the fuck are you doing? Are you purposely trying to mess with my head, Liv?"

She started laughing. "Oh Christ, Layton. I've just missed you, that's all. You were always such a good fuck." She licked her lips.

I looked away from her and saw Whitley glaring back at the house.

"What's your game?" I asked Olivia, never taking my eyes off of Whitley.

"My game? What do you mean?"

"You left me for one of my best friends the day after my brother died. I haven't heard from you for months, and now, you see me, and you grab my dick and tell me you want a romp in the sack with me. What's your game?"

I watched as Whitley continued to stare at the house. For one brief moment, I saw concern all over her face.

Concern for me? Or for Olivia? Does she think I'm going to hurt Olivia?

I slowly turned around and saw Olivia glaring out toward Whitley. "Who is she?"

Holy shit, she's jealous of CG.

"It's none of your goddamn business who she is."

Olivia's head snapped over, and she studied me. "The hell it isn't. She's talking to my aunt. What does she want with my aunt? She's probably just using you to get close to my aunt for her money. That girl is trouble, Layton."

I threw my head back and laughed. "You don't even know who she is!"

Olivia turned and shook her head. "Don't be desperate, Layton. It's so unbecoming of a Southern gentleman. Go ahead and screw the local barmaid, but don't bring your tramps around to meet my aunt and uncle. You got me?"

What a bitch. How did I ever love her?

I turned to walk back out the door, but then Olivia grabbed my arm.

"Did you hear me? I mean it, Layton. Don't test me."

"Oh, fuck off, Olivia. Who I fuck and who I don't fuck is none of your business anymore. As far as who is talking to your aunt, her name is Whitley, and she's new in town and starting a business. Your aunt met her the other day, and Whit's planning a party for Mrs. P."

Olivia stared out the window toward Whitley. "You fucking her?" she asked without looking back at me.

"I believe I already said that's none of your business."

She snapped her head and glared at me.

"But I'll answer you anyway. No, I'm not sleeping with her." I opened the door, walked out, and slammed it behind me.

I heard Olivia open the door, and she started following me. "Layton, I'm sorry. Please just let me explain."

I picked up my pace and made it over to Mrs. P, Justin, and Whitley. Whitley took one look at me and smiled slightly before glancing over my shoulder at Olivia.

"So, You're starting a party-planning business? Olivia said..

"You're starting a party-planning business?"

Mrs. P smiled and clapped her hands. "Yes! Yes, she is, and I'm her first client."

Whitley grinned and nodded. "Really? I mean, I can go over more ideas and things with you first—"

Mrs. P shook her head. "No! I like you, CG. You're exactly what this town needs—a breath of fresh air. And my party is going to be your debut."

"Oh, I promise you, I won't let you down!" Whitley peeked over toward me and smiled. "And it's Whitley. I don't really care for Layton's nickname for me."

I gave her my best smile, which caused her to look at me funny. I glanced at Olivia, and she had a pissed-off look on her face.

"Well, since my aunt is so fond of you, Whitley, I'm going to have to talk to you about planning my engagement party."

Holy fuck. All the air just left my lungs. I looked at Justin, who glanced at me and then quickly turned away. *They're getting married?*

"I'd love to—" Whitley started to say.

"You can't plan their engagement party, CG!" I practically yelled out.

Whitley turned and gave me the dirtiest look I'd ever gotten. "Excuse me? And why not, Layton?"

Ah hell. I didn't really know this girl all that well, but I could tell that was her pissed-off look.

"Yes, why not, Layton?" Olivia asked with a smirk.

What a bitch. I'll never let another woman in my heart again.

I looked between Whitley, Mrs. P, and Olivia. Justin started to walk away toward the barn.

Fucker.

"Um…I just meant you might not want to get in over your head and all since you're just starting out."

Olivia smiled and hooked her arm in Whitley's. "Nonsense. This will give you the exposure you need, darlin'. Say you'll do it. Please!"

Whitley smiled at Olivia and then at Mrs. P, who had the fakest smile on her face I'd ever seen. She knew just as much as I did that Olivia was doing this on purpose.

The moment Whitley turned to me, our eyes met, and her smile faded, but it quickly came back.

"I have a few things to read over. I'll meet you back in my truck, Miss Reynolds." I gave her a weak smile.

She nodded and turned away.

I gave Mrs. P a kiss good-bye on the cheek and excused myself.

"Good-bye, Layton. I hope to see you soon!" Olivia called out.

I completely ignored her. I made my way around the house and back to my truck.

By the time I got into my truck, I felt like I was struggling to get a breath. *She's getting married.*

My cell phone started ringing, causing me to jump. I picked it up and saw it was Reed. "Yeah?"

"Dude, guess who in the hell is in town?"

I sucked in a breath of air, still trying to get my breathing under control. "Who?"

"Kevin!"

A smile played across my face. Kevin had been my brother's best friend from high school. They had served in the Marine Corps together.

"No shit. He's home on leave?"

"Yep, and he and a few other guys are heading to Joe's tonight. What do you say? Welcome-home party?"

I put my head back on the seat. I knew Misty would be working tonight. I didn't really want to see her again, but I needed to talk to her. Plus, I hadn't seen Kevin since Mike's funeral.

"Yeah, I need a few beers. I've had a shit-filled afternoon."

Reed laughed. "He's in!" He sounded as if he'd turned away from the phone, talking to someone else, and then his voice came back clear over the line. "Awesome, dude. See you at nine."

I looked up and saw Whitley and Mrs. P talking as they headed toward my truck. I looked to see if Olivia was with them, but it was just the two of them. I watched as Mrs. P said something to Whitley, causing her to laugh. I couldn't help but grin. She had the most beautiful smile I'd ever seen. Her eyes actually seemed to sparkle when she smiled. Her hands were flying everywhere as she talked.

Shit, that would drive me crazy.

She glanced up and caught me watching her. She crinkled her nose, and I had to laugh. All she had to do was look at me, and I pissed her off.

As they got closer, I jumped out of the truck, walked around to the passenger side, and opened the door for her. I heard Whitley tell Mrs. P that she would come back out in a few days to work on ideas for the party, and then they said their good-byes. When Whitley turned, she glanced at me and hopped up into the truck.

I shut the door and said good-bye again to Mrs. P.

"Layton, I'm sorry for what Olivia did. You have to know, she was just a bit jealous from seeing you with another girl. I'll explain to her who Whitley is. I'm sorry Olivia hurt you."

I smiled slightly. "Mrs. P, I highly doubt Liv is jealous from seeing me with another girl. After all, she's the one who left me, remember? No need to explain who CG is. It's none of Liv's business." I gave her a wink, and I started walking around to the driver's side.

Mrs. P called out, "Layton, stop teasing that girl! She hates that nickname you've given her."

I smiled and tipped my hat at her before jumping into the truck. I looked over at a very happy girl sitting next to me.

She looks good in my truck. It's a perfect fit.

Shit! Shit! Shit! Don't even, Layton.

"Okay, CG, let's get you home, shall we? Where do you live?"

"Jesus Christ, stop calling me that, you asshole! And how dare you embarrass me like that in front of a potential client. Are you insane? Do you know what planning her engagement party means for me?"

I threw my truck into reverse and glared at her before hitting the gas pedal. "Yeah, I know exactly what the hell it means."

I hit the pedal so hard that her head snapped back. I'd never wanted to leave that house so much in my entire life. I just needed to get drunk and forget this day even happened.

"I'll stop by Jack's, so you can get whatever you need out of your car."

She was staring out the window and didn't answer.

"Whitley, I'm going to stop by Jack's garage first. Then, where do I need to go?"

Nothing.

When I reached over and tugged her arm, she jerked away from me.

"Jesus, are you okay?" I asked.

She turned and looked scared to death. "Um…yeah, I'm sorry. I guess I was lost in a memory. What did you say?"

"Would you like me to stop by Jack's garage to get what you need out of your car? I'm not sure how long he'll have it. I'm sure he doesn't keep fancy car parts on hand," I said with a wink as I watched her holding her cell phone up.

"Ha-ha. That's fine. Oh, yes! I have a signal!"

She hit a number on her phone, and all I heard was another girl on the other end, going off in a high-pitched voice.

Whitley looked at me and smiled. "Hey, Court. So sorry, Lollipop. My car broke down in the middle of Bumfuck, Egypt, and I had to ride a horse back to this cowboy's house. Then, he called a tow truck and brought me to my appointment. No, in his truck. Um…"

She turned and looked at me. Her face was red, and the blush covering her cheeks caused me to smile.

"Yes. Uh…really? Right now, Courtney?" She sighed as she looked toward the window, and then she tried to talk softly. "I don't know…ugh. Oh. My. God! Nine! Are you happy, you bitch?"

Jesus…is she rating me? And if she is, why the hell am I a nine and not a ten?

"Yes, a real one. Yep." She glanced back and looked down at my feet. "Yes, Court…the whole package."

I started laughing. "Are you seriously talking about me while I'm sitting right here next to you?"

Whitley shrugged her shoulders and gave me a smirk.

Yep, she's from New York all right.

"Listen, I have to stop and pick up some things that I left in my car, and then Layton is going to drop me off at home. Will you be there?" She let out a sigh. "You're joking, right?"

She peeked back at me with a funny look. The way she smashed her lips together and frowned had me adjusting myself. I'd never been so attracted to a girl I couldn't stand to be around.

What in the hell is wrong with me?

"Listen, I'll just talk to you when I get home okay?" She ended the call and glared at me. "Don't go thinking I was talking about you being all hot and everything. Courtney is obsessed with real cowboys. That's all."

I glanced over at her and smiled. "Okay."

"I mean, really…I hardly even know you, and to be honest, you've gotten on my nerves more than anyone ever has in my entire life."

"Wow. Nice way to pay me back for helping you out today."

She snapped her head over at me. I stopped at a Stop sign and looked at her. Our eyes met again, and I swore I couldn't pull myself away from her. Something about her drove me totally insane. One minute, I couldn't wait to get away from her, and the next, I wanted to know more about her.

Zedd's "Clarity" started to play on the radio as I pulled my gaze from hers and took off driving. We both reached down to turn it up. Our hands bumped, and the shock that ran up my arm startled me.

Shit. I just need this girl out of my truck. With any luck, I'll only run into her every now and then.

"I'm so sorry. It's your truck. I just, um…I just like this song."

I gave her a half-smile and reached back down to turn it up.

⤙⤙⤙⤙⤙⤙⤙⤙⤙

Whitley had gotten a few items out of her car, and she was back in my truck, giving me directions to her house.

"You live in the center of town?" I asked her as I turned down Sandstone Street.

"Yeah. When I told my father I wanted to move to Llano, he flew here and looked at property. There was a house right on the river that he fell in love with. He sent me pictures, and I loved it, too. So, my parents bought it for me with the plan that I would pay them back."

She gave me the address.

"You live in the old Peabody house? That place is beautiful."

She smiled as she tilted her head and looked at me.

Jesus, I like when she looks at me like that.

"Yes, it is beautiful. My dream has always been to buy an older home and restore it. I fell in love with the sandstone. I love that house."

"It's a good thing since your dad picked it out." I pulled up and parked in front of her house. "Why didn't you come down with him? That's a lot of trust you put in your dad to let him pick out your house!"

Her smile faded, and her eyes filled with sadness. "I, um…I had some things to take care of in New York City." She gave me a slight smile.

I knew it. She's from New York City.

I nodded. "Gotcha. Well, Miss Reynolds, it has been…an experience, meeting and getting to know you."

She tried to look pissed but ended up laughing. "Are you going to be a Southern gentleman and help me carry this stuff inside, so my neurotic friend can eye you up properly? She's been dying to see a real cowboy," she said as her eyes moved up and down my body.

I laughed and jumped out of the truck. I grabbed two boxes while she carried a few other items. As we walked up to the front door, I could already see the changes she'd made to the house. She had added potted plants, and the landscaping in front of the house was amazing.

"You painted the front door red. I like it with that stained glass," I said.

She turned and gave me a proud smile. "Thank you. I've always wanted—"

The next thing I knew, the front door swung open, and I was looking at who I was guessing was Courtney. She smiled, and I couldn't help but look her up and down. She had on the shortest shorts I'd ever seen along with a Texas A&M T-shirt. She was about five feet five inches with blondish-red hair and sky-blue eyes. She was breathtaking but not as beautiful as Whitley.

She has nothing on my CG.

Wait—what? What in the hell is going on with me?

"Ah…" I stood there, just looking back and forth between them.

"Shit, Court, can you get the hell out of the way, so he can come in and drop off my stuff?"

Courtney smiled, and I swore I'd never been eye-fucked so openly before.

City girls.

She moved out of the way, and when Whitley walked by, she whispered something in her ear.

"Shut up, Lollipop. You're an ass."

I took a quick look around. The living room was in the process of being painted, and the wood floors were covered up, but I could tell they had been refinished.

"Layton, this is my best friend, Courtney. Court, this is Layton Morris."

Courtney flashed me a grin, and her eyes lit up. "My first official cowboy. It's a pleasure to meet you, Mr. Morris."

I laughed and shook my head. "Please call me Layton, and the pleasure is all mine."

They both peered at each other before turning back to look at me.

"Well, CG, it was a pleasure. Hope to see you around," I said with a wink.

"Yep, back at ya, cowboy." She gave me a wink back.

I smiled as I said, "Good-bye, ladies."

As I walked down the steps and toward my truck, I wanted to turn around and see if Whitley was watching me walk away.

Play it cool, Layton. You're not interested in her.

As I rounded my truck, I glanced back at the living room window. My heart jumped up into my throat when I saw Whitley standing by the window, watching me. She gave me a small smile and a quick wave. I waved back, jumped in my truck, and decided I'd have to maybe have that talk with Misty soon.

Ah hell, Layton, what are you doing? You don't even like this girl. You're not interested in getting caught up in that shit again.

I started my truck and pulled away, heading toward the bank.

→≫≫≫≫≫≫≫≫≫≫≪≪≪≪≪≪≪≪≪≪←

At the bank, I saw Richard and walked up to him to shake his hand. It was too bad the whole time Richard was talking to me, all I could do was see Whitley's green eyes looking into mine.

I needed to get her out of my head, just like I needed to get Liv out. I only knew one way to do that.

I pulled out my phone and sent Misty a text, asking if she could come back to my house tonight, while Richard took a quick phone call. I quickly received a reply.

Misty: YES! I thought you'd never ask! I was getting tired of fucking on the pool tables.

I sighed and put my phone back into my pocket. I ran my hands through my hair. *What in the hell am I doing?*

"Layton? Are you even listening to me?" Richard asked as he snapped his fingers in front of my face.

I looked up and smiled. "Yeah, sorry, Richard. I've got a lot on my mind."

"Well, you seem pretty preoccupied. Let's talk about this another time. It's a lot to take in, I know, Layton."

I nodded as I stood and held out my hand. "Thanks, Richard. I trust you to do what you think is the best. Invest it as you see fit."

"Layton, I'd like you to have an idea of what we're doing with your money."

I sucked in a deep breath. "It's my brother's money, not mine. Just keep doing what he wanted you to do with it. Honestly, I trust you." I said reaching my hand out toward Richard.

Richard took my hand and shook it. "Okay, I'll just keep investing it on the plan Mike and I had laid out."

I nodded again and gave him a forced smile.

Richard and I started to walk out, and as we got to the front door of the bank, it opened, and Whitley walked in. My heart immediately slammed in my chest, and I couldn't help it, but I smiled.

"CG, you couldn't stay away from me. I knew that would happen," I said with a wink.

She looked me up and down and rolled her eyes. Then, she walked past me and up to the teller, and Richard and I walked outside.

"You know Miss Reynolds?" Richard asked.

I laughed and nodded. "I had the pleasure of meeting her today and helping her out with something."

Richard sighed and ran his hand through his hair. "Girl is a tough cookie to break. I've been trying to ask her out for two weeks now, ever since she first walked into the bank. She's polite, but she just completely turns me down flat every time."

I was surprised at the surge of jealousy hitting me out of nowhere from hearing he'd asked Whitley out…and then I was surprised at how relieved I felt from knowing she'd told him no.

"Huh…well, honestly, dude, don't bother with this one. I think she hates men," I said.

"Really? She seems sweet."

I shook my head and looked back into the bank. "She's kind of a bitch."

Whitley walked out of the bank and smiled slightly at both of us.

"Later, CG," I called out after her as I watched her walking down the street toward her house.

"Fuck off, cowboy."

I smiled and tried not to start laughing. I turned and faced Richard with a serious look on my face as I shrugged. "See what I mean? B.I.T.C.H."

"Thanks, dude. At least I know that's a lost cause. See you later tonight at Joe's."

I shook Richard's hand. "Yep, see ya then."

I strolled back to my truck and got in. My heart was beating a mile a minute. I couldn't believe what I'd just done. Richard was a friend of mine.

Why did I just steer him away from Whitley?

Why do I have the feeling Whitley Reynolds is going to be a thorn in my side?

Damn girl with those green eyes.

FIVE

-≫≫≫≫≫≫≫≫≫≫≫≫≪≪≪≪≪≪≪≪≪≪≪≪-
Whitley

"So, today, while you were getting your first real client, I went to Ruby Cowgirl."

I rolled my eyes as I grabbed a Diet Coke out of the fridge. "Jesus, Court, you're gonna own everything they sell if you keep going there!"

Courtney jumped up from the sofa. "I did buy a really cute white dress in there. Anyway, the girl who works there invited me over to Fuel, the coffee house, for a cup of coffee. Guess what happened?"

I wasn't really in the mood for guessing games. Layton had me thrown for a loop, and my head was pounding. The moment I saw him, he had my stomach doing stupid flip-flops.

Why does he have to be such a jerk? A stupid, gorgeous, Southern cowboy jerk with a rocking body! No, it's good that he's a jerk. Keeps me uninterested.

"What, Court?"

"Come on, Whit, guess!"

I snapped my head over toward her. "Courtney, I've had a shit-filled day with the exception of picking up two new clients. I met one of the most annoying men I've ever encountered in my entire life today, and he wore my patience thin."

Courtney's mouth dropped open. "Holy shit. You like him!"

Wait—what? "What? Are you insane? Courtney, really? Do you think I want to get into a relationship with anyone? I mean, the last boyfriend I had just about killed me a few short weeks ago. I'm pretty sure I'm done with men."

Courtney rolled her eyes and shook her head. "Whatever. Believe what you want, Whit. You've got the hots for a cowboy named Layton."

I closed my eyes and just prayed she'd stop talking. I thought back to when Layton had grabbed my arm. All I had seen was Roger's face.

"Hello? Whit! Are you even listening to me?"

I opened my eyes and smiled. "Yeah, of course, I am."

"Okay, well, I guess that guy who works at the bank—what's his name? Richard?"

I sighed because I knew what was coming up. "Yes, I just ran into him and Layton."

A smile spread across Courtney's face. "Well, I ran into him at the coffee shop during lunch. He invited us to that bar on the square—Joe's. I guess one of his friends is home on leave. A Marine, Whit. A. Marine."

I started laughing. Courtney had a thing for military guys, guys who rode bikes, guys with tattoos. The list was endless.

"Court, you need to change jobs. I know you're looking for that perfect guy, like the ones in all those books you read, but you're never going to find him. He doesn't exist."

"Okay, first off, that's my job. It's so not fair to drag my job into my manhunt. I love being a freelance editor, Whit, you know that. Plus, my ass can live anywhere I want…hence, being able to pick up my life and move to Texas with you!"

"I know you love your job, but the whole reason you're not with anyone is because you keep comparing them to the men you've read about in those stupid stories."

"Gasp! I can't believe you called them stupid stories. I'm so not buying you a Kindle for Christmas. Hey, I get more pleasure from my books than anything. I love to read, and you should do it more often. It might give you some hope, Whit. Prince Charming is out there, babe. Don't give up."

"First off, you buy more books than anyone I know when your damn job is reading other people's books."

"That's different. I'm working when I read those. I need pleasure reading."

"Yeah, pleasure reading. How many vibrators have you gone through because you get turned-on by those books?" I placed my hands on my hips.

Courtney started laughing. "Oh my God. Are you jealous of my Kindle? You want a hot story, Whit? I'll recommend one to you. I'll even buy it in paperback for your ass."

I shook my head. "Puh-lease. No book would *ever* get me to the point where I needed to reach for a vibrator. *Ever!*"

The smile that spread across Courtney's face said it all.

Ah hell, I'm in trouble.

"One hundred bucks says I can get you reaching for one."

I stood there, staring at her. "No way."

"You're a chicken."

"I'm not a chicken, you bitch." I turned and walked toward the stairs.

"Two hundred then."

I stopped and looked at her. "You're really willing to put up two hundred bucks to see if a book will turn me on enough to need a vibrator?"

"Oh yeah. Just to prove your ass wrong. Baby girl, you have no idea what you've been missing out on during the last few years you spent with that asshole Roger."

Just the mention of his name caused a shudder to travel through my body. "Fine. One book. I'll read one book, and if it doesn't work, I don't ever want to hear about how hot your latest book boyfriend made you one night."

The smile on her face scared me slightly.

Oh dear God. What is she gonna have me read?

As I turned to head up the stairs, she called out, "Wait! What about tonight? Let's just go and have a few drinks. I'd kind of like to see a cowboy or two, Whit. *Please!*"

I really didn't want that Richard guy hitting on me all night, but I did want to relax a bit and grab a few beers. *Anything to keep my mind off of Roger and New York.*

"Fine, but I'm only going to stay for a couple of drinks."

"Yes! You're the best!"

The next thing I knew, she was flying past me and up the stairs.

"Jesus, what's the rush?"

She turned and looked at me like I was nuts. "I have work to do— shower, shave, search for an outfit, do my makeup and hair. My God, Whit, it takes work to get beautiful."

I shook my head. "Pesh, if they don't see you for how beautiful you are without going through all that shit, then fuck 'em."

"You can say that. You've given up on men for all eternity. I just want one good fuck. I haven't had sex in way too long."

My mouth dropped open as she turned and walked into her room.

"You're kidding, right, Court? Court?"

Oh God…she didn't just say she wanted to be fucked, did she? This is going to be one long night.

➤➤➤➤➤➤➤➤➤➤➤➤◄◄◄◄◄◄◄◄◄◄◄◄◄

Since Joe's was just a few blocks from our house, Courtney and I decided to walk.

When we had both stepped out in white dresses and cowboy boots, Courtney had insisted we do rock-paper-scissors to see who would have to change. I'd won, and she had changed into a cute pair of Miss Me jeans and a baby-blue sheer top.

As we strolled along the street, I glanced down at her boots. "When in the hell did you buy those?"

She stopped and looked at her boots. She peeked up at me and smiled. "These? Hell, I bought these the same day you told me we were moving to Texas. I needed an excuse to buy them, and you gave it to me."

I thought back to the day I'd checked out of the hospital. Courtney and I had gone to the apartment I shared with Roger to pack up my stuff, and we'd only taken the things I needed, leaving behind my favorite pair of cowboy boots. Really, they were the only pair I'd owned.

-»»»»»»»»»»»>)<(«««««««««««-

New York
A Few Weeks Earlier

As I opened the door to the apartment that I shared with Roger, my heart was pounding, my body ached, and my head had never hurt so much in my life. I knew Roger wouldn't be home, but I was still scared shitless. Courtney had told me she would meet me and help me get the items I needed.

Walking around the apartment, I looked around at everything. I couldn't care less about any of it. I stopped and picked up a picture of Roger and me on graduation night.

We look so happy. What happened to us? What did I do to make him treat me like this? I never could make him happy.

I jumped when I heard someone knocking on the door.

"Whit, it's me!" Courtney yelled.

I ran to the door, opened it, and pulled her inside.

"Shit, Court! Be quiet. He might have told one of the neighbors to call him if I came home early. We better move fast. We just need to grab the most important shit."

Courtney nodded. "Got it. I'll get your clothes, and you get your shoes."

She took off up the stairs, and I couldn't help but laugh at what she thought was important and what I thought was important.

I walked over to my desk and took important files I would need. I found some boxes and just started dumping files, photos and my laptop into them. I took a box up to Courtney and told her to grab all my stuff out of the bathroom.

By the time the closet and bathroom were empty, the home phone began ringing. We both stopped and stood still as we listened to it ring. Once it stopped, we looked at each other.

"Fuck!" we both said at the same time.

"Go, Court! Just start putting it all into your car. If we can't get it to fit in your Beemer, just leave it."

Courtney smiled. "Oh, honey, I went and bought myself a truck."

I stopped and turned to look at her. "What? When in the hell did you buy a truck?"

"Last night, after I left the hospital. I just stopped at the Toyota place and said I wanted the most loaded, tricked-out bitch they had."

I shook my head and started grabbing shit to take out to her truck.

By the time we were done, we had my clothes in the backseat and all the boxes in the bed of the truck. I ran up to the apartment one more time to take one last look around. I felt sick to my stomach, thinking of all the times I'd allowed him to treat me the way he had.

Never again. I'll never let another man ever lay one finger on me.

The phone started ringing again. I walked up to it and picked it up, but I didn't say a word.

"Hello? Whit? Baby, are you home already? Why didn't you tell me they'd released you early?"

I started shaking. I always knew he had the neighbors watching me, making sure I wasn't doing anything he wouldn't approve of.

I didn't say a word. I hung up the phone. I took the ring off my left finger and set it down next to the car keys. I picked up the picture of us at Martha's Vineyard from two years ago. I set it on the table and picked up the paperweight sitting next to it. I smashed it down on top of the picture, shattering the glass part of the frame.

"You thought you could break me into pieces that you could control. You thought you could beat me down to nothing…well, not anymore. You'll never control me again."

I turned and walked out, knowing I would never return to New York City again. I would never again let anyone tear me down like he had. As I walked into the elevator, memories of Roger, good and bad, flooded my mind. I'd always been so afraid I would let him down. Every day, I had done nothing but walk on eggshells around him…but not anymore.

As the door to the elevator opened, I exited, standing taller, as I walked with my head raised and a smile on my face. Tim, the doorman, grinned when he saw me walking up to him. I'd usually kept my head down and never looked at anyone.

"Miss Reynolds, you look like a new woman."

I smiled bigger. "I am, Tim. Today is the first day of my new life."

He nodded. "I'm glad to see you happy. You deserve it, Miss Reynolds. I hope you find happiness, and I hope it's far from here."

I stopped and looked at him, stunned by his response.

How many people knew?

I smiled and nodded before turning and walking up to Courtney's new truck.

After I got in and shut the door, she had the biggest smile on her face.

"All right, baby girl. Are you ready to get your country on?"

I started laughing as she handed me a Diet Coke.

She held up her drink to mine as she started to make a toast. "To leaving behind the past and starting a new life. To forgetting about asshole men who don't know a good thing when they see it."

"Amen! To being done. I'm done with being treated like I'm nothing because I am something."

"Fuck yeah, you are. Are we done here?"

I nodded. "Yes."

I picked up Court's iPod and found a song I'd put on there about six months ago. Once she took off driving, I hit the play button.

Courtney looked at me. "Hell yeah!"

We started singing along with Carrie Underwood's "Undo It," and I'd never felt so free in my life as we took off down the road to start my new life. We noticed people waving from the cars around us. Court kept waving back as we sang along to my new theme song.

"Wow! Who knew New Yorkers were so damn friendly? Sing it, Whit!"

As we headed up the road on our way to my parents' house, more and more people were honking and waving at us.

"My God, they act like they've never seen two hot girls singing in a truck!" Courtney said with a laugh.

Then, she looked in the rearview mirror. "Oh shit!"

The next thing I knew, Courtney was pulling over on the side of a bridge. She parked the truck, looked at me, and busted out laughing.

"What? What's so damn funny, Court? And why are we pulled over? Let's go. The farther we are away from him, the better."

She turned to me with tears running down her cheeks.

"Oh my God. Are you crying or laughing?"

She finally got herself under control enough to start talking. "Whit, all those people were honking and waving because they were trying to tell us that we had shit blowing out of the back of the truck!"

I turned and looked in the bed of the truck. All I saw were pads and tampons everywhere. I snapped my head back to Courtney, and we both busted out laughing.

"Oh. My. God! My pads and tampons were flying out of the truck!"

After we laughed for a good fifteen minutes, she started driving again. As Court pulled back out into traffic, the only thing she could say was, "That has to be a good sign of the happier times to come!"

We both lost it again and laughed practically all the way to upstate New York.

SIX

-➤➤➤➤➤➤➤➤➤➤➤➤➤❮❮❮❮❮❮❮❮❮❮❮❮❮❮-

LAYTON

I pulled up and parked a little ways down from Joe's. I wasn't sure how I felt about seeing Kevin. He would just be a reminder of what happened to Mike. I put my head on the steering wheel and just sat there for a minute.

Fuck, Mike. Why did you leave me? You promised me you'd be okay. You promised me, Mike.

I sat back and took in a deep breath. I regretted telling Reed I would come out tonight. I looked up and saw two girls walking, one in a short white dress and the other in jeans. I couldn't really see who they were because it was already dark, but one kind of looked familiar.

I jumped when someone started banging on my window. I turned and saw Bill Bishop standing outside my truck. I grabbed my hat and opened the door.

"Shit, dude. You scared the piss out of me," I said as I reached out for his hand.

"Layton fucking Morris. How in the hell have you been?"

I laughed as he grabbed me around the neck and pulled me closer.

Jesus, he's drunk already.

"How's Austin, Bill? You ready to move back to Llano?" I asked as we headed toward Joe's.

He shook his head and laughed. "Hell no, I don't want to move back. God, Layton, how do you take it? I'd want to leave and start a new life in a new town."

My smile faded for just a second. "Nah, I love it here. I love the country living, and I made a promise to my brother. I won't ever break that promise."

Bill looked over at me, and then he slapped the shit out of me on my back. "You're a stand-up guy, Layton. Now, come on, I need to get laid tonight. Please tell me this town has some new damn girls. I heard two knock-out beauties just moved here a few weeks ago."

I grabbed his arm and made him stop. "What? Who in the hell told you that? Who are they?"

Bill looked shocked when I started playing twenty questions.

"Um…Richard. He said they were new in town…city girls from…ah hell, where was it?"

"New York?"

Bill smiled and pointed his finger at me. "That's it. Richard said he's bound and determined to get in the pants of the one he has set his sights on. Guess she's been coming into the bank a lot. Richard just keeps talking about getting a piece."

The anger I was feeling was about to boil over. I grabbed Bill by the shirt and got in his face. "Don't fucking talk about her like that."

Bill glared at me and then pushed me away. "Jesus, Layton. What in the hell? Do you know this girl or something? If you got dibs, take it the fuck up with him."

I shook my head. *Motherfucker, what is wrong with me? I don't even like Whitley that way.*

"Ah hell, Bill, I'm sorry. My emotions are running crazy. I think I'm just nervous to see Kevin, and you know…all those memories."

Bill gave me a weak smile. "Dude, you need to get drunk and then get laid. Forget about all of it. Forget about Olivia. You don't need that shit."

"Yeah…I just need a drink. Let's go."

The closer we got to the bar, the more my heart started pounding. If I'd been walking alone, I would've turned and left.

As soon as we walked in, Thomas Rhett's song "Something to Do with My Hands" started playing. The hairs on my neck rose up, and I knew it was nerves from seeing Kevin. I took a quick look around.

Misty waved to me from behind the bar, and I gave her a weak smile. Out of the corner of my eye, I saw a white dress. I turned to see Whitley talking to Richard.

Fuck me. She looks amazing.

One more look around, and I saw Courtney standing at the bar, ordering drinks.

"Holy shit. Look at the blonde at the bar. I always did like girls with that blondish-red hair." Bill slapped me on the back again and smiled at me. "Sorry, dude. We'll have to catch up later."

I smiled and nodded. "Good luck with that one."

Bill smirked. "Shit, she'll be walking out with me in less than two hours, dude."

I watched as he walked toward Courtney, and then I glanced back over at Whitley. She was throwing her head back and laughing at something Richard was saying.

You don't like her, Layton. Who cares who she's talking to?

I walked up to the bar, and Misty came over to me with a shit-eating grin on her face.

"Hey, handsome," she said with a wink.

"Hey, girl. Looks like you got help tonight. You might even have time to spin around the dance floor with me."

She laughed and winked. "Oh, I want to take a spin a time or two but not on the dance floor. We still on for tonight?"

I wanted to tell Misty that what had happened those two times was just pure fun and nothing more, but then I'd gone off and invited her home with me tonight.

What in the hell was I thinking?

When the music changed, I turned and looked out toward the dance floor. Whitley was dancing with Richard and noticed me looking at her. I smiled slightly, and she looked away. That was when I saw Olivia dancing behind them. She was grinding her ass into Justin's dick as she smiled at me.

Fuck me.

I turned back and grinned as I leaned closer to Misty. "You bet that sweet ass we're still on."

She reached across the bar and kissed me. She let out a small moan as she bit on my lower lip. When she pulled back and walked away, I felt like shit. I had no feelings for this girl. All she was to me was just a fuck—and not even a good one at that.

She walked back and handed me a Dos Equis with a wink. "Reed and the rest of the guys are in the back."

I smiled as I thanked her and turned to walk away. I glanced quickly one more time at Whitley. She seemed like she was just trying to be nice to Richard by dancing with him. As I was walking by a table, I saw Courtney sitting there. I stopped and smiled down at her.

"You look like you're searching for someone or something," I said.

She smiled as she looked up at me. "A cowboy. You're the only fucking cowboy I've met since I've been in this damn town."

I laughed as I felt someone nudge me. I turned to see Richard smiling at me as Whitley sat down and grabbed the beer out of Courtney's hand. She practically downed it as she looked everywhere but at me.

"CG! You having fun?"

The look she shot me caused me to start laughing. I looked back over toward Courtney.

It's time to have a little bit of fun with the city girls.

"Courtney"—I flashed that smile I knew melted any girl's panties—"you want to meet some cowboys?"

Courtney lit up like a Christmas tree. "Fuck yeah. I do believe we just went over this, Layton dear."

I reached my hand down for her to take. "Well then, my dear, let's go meet some cowboys."

Whitley stood and reached for Courtney's arm. "No, I don't think that's a very good idea."

Courtney and I both looked at her. "Why not?" we asked at the same time.

Whitley peered between both of us. "Um…Courtney, really, you don't want to meet *his* friends."

The way she'd said *his* sounded like she was disgusted with me.

"Oh yeah, I do, Whit." Courtney turned back toward me and smiled as she held out her hand. "Show me the way, cowboy."

We started to walk toward the back. I turned around and winked at Whitley. She had her hands on her hips, and she looked so goddamn cute, being all pissed-off.

I turned back, and leaning down, I told Courtney, "Keep your panties on tight. These boys are nothing but a bunch of horny men, and one is fresh on leave from the Marines."

Her smile practically lit up the room. "Sweetheart, it's been so long since I got laid. I don't care how horny they are. They just better have functioning dicks."

I laughed as I shook my head. *I like this girl—feisty and tells it like it is.*

More women needed to be like her. I looked back to see Richard walking with Whitley. My smile faded, and I quickly turned back ahead. As we walked up closer to the table, I saw Reed and then Kevin. My heart started pounding, and it felt like my knees were about to give out.

"Layton, are you all right? Did you get dizzy or something?" Courtney asked.

I tried to give her a smile as I shook my head. "Nah, I think it's from not eating today."

"Holy motherfucking shit! It's Layton Morris. And the bastard brought us a friend." Kevin stood and made a beeline right toward Courtney.

Courtney smiled as she held out her hand, and Kevin kissed the back of it.

"Who is this beautiful creature?" Kevin looked Courtney up and down.

I turned around and reached for Whitley's hand. I was surprised when she took it, and she let me lead her to the front of me. The look that Richard had given me wasn't lost on me.

"My God, there are two beautiful creatures. Layton, what did I do to deserve this?" Kevin asked when he saw Whitley.

I smiled as I took in Kevin. He was as fit as ever. He was the same height and build as me. He'd always been known as the black stallion with the local girls. All the girls would go crazy for him. I didn't think I'd ever seen him with just one girl.

I introduced Whitley and Courtney to Kevin and explained to them that he was home on leave from the Marine Corps.

After talking for a few minutes, Reed finally noticed Whitley and Courtney. I knew it was going to be a long night when I saw his face light up as he looked them both up and down. I'd never in my life wanted to punch my best friend in the face before, but the way he was looking at them caused me to ball up my fists. He got up and walked over toward us.

Whitley was standing so close to me that I could smell her perfume. *Jesus, her scent is driving me fucking nuts.*

"So, are you the city girl Layton here rescued today?" Reed asked with a smile and a wink as he extended his hand.

Whitley shook Reed's hand. "The one and only." She gave a wink of her own.

I glanced over and noticed Courtney eyeing Reed up and down.

Reed could pretty much look at any girl, and she'd be his. Almost every girl at every bar we had gone to would tell him he looked exactly like Colin Farrell.

Reed started laughing. "Don't worry, Jack will take care of your car. He's the best. Welcome to Llano. What in the world made you want to move here?" he shouted over the music.

Whitley's smile faded for a quick second before she flashed that beautiful smile at him. "New town, new life."

Reed smiled and shook his head. "Folks normally say they want to leave Llano to start a new life."

Whitley winked. "To each his own."

"Amen, sister," Reed said.

I leaned over and said, "Whitley Reynolds, this is my best friend, Reed Moore."

Whitley grinned. "What? That's your name—Reed Moore?"

Reed gave her his big ole country-boy smile. "Yes, ma'am. You like to read, do you?"

Whitley threw her head back and laughed. "No, no, I really don't. I hate reading. Sorry."

Reed laughed as he turned his attention to Courtney. He stood there and just stared at her as she talked to Kevin.

Whitley leaned up, close to my ear. "If you were any kind of friend, cowboy, you would reach over and lift his jaw off the ground. He acts as if he's never seen a girl before."

I laughed as I looked at Reed practically drooling at the sight of Courtney.

"Courtney is going to *love* his name!" Whitley said with a giggle.

Her hot breath on my neck was driving me insane.

I rolled my eyes and shook my head. "God, he tries to use that to his advantage all the time. If a girl loves to read, he plays it up. Why will Courtney like it?"

Whitley turned and gave me an evil smile. "She's a freelance editor. She edits books for a living. She *loves* to read. It's her damn life. Her last name is Will. She is constantly saying, 'Oh, Courtney *will…*' It drives me nuts how she stresses the word *will*."

I laughed as I said, "No shit?"

"No shit!"

Kevin must have seen someone walking by who caught his attention because he excused himself from talking to Courtney. Courtney turned and smiled when she saw Reed standing there, and Whitley jumped into action.

"Courtney, this Layton's best friend, Reed," Whitley said with a huge grin on her face.

It was almost like she couldn't wait for Courtney to find out Reed's last name.

Reed reached out and shook Courtney's hand. "Reed Moore," he said with a smile.

Courtney's smile spread from ear to ear. "Oh, Courtney *Will*."

Both Whitley and I busted out laughing. Reed looked confused as hell and then laughed.

"Nice last name I have, huh?" he said with a wink.

Courtney nodded. "Especially for an editor whose job is to do nothing but read."

Reed started laughing. "Seriously, what's your last name?"

Courtney looked at him and tilted her head. "Will."

"Seriously? I thought you were being a smart-ass."

Courtney smiled and winked. "Oh, honey, trust me, you'll know when I'm being a smart-ass and when I'm not."

I leaned over and put my lips up against the back of Whitley's ear. "Looks like they're hitting it off just as well as we did."

She snapped her head around and slowly grinned. She was just about to say something when she glanced over my shoulder, and her smile faded for a brief second.

I felt someone put a hand on my upper back and move it down to my ass. Lady Antebellum's "Dancin' Away with My Heart" started playing.

Misty got in between Whitley and me. "Hey, babe. I'm on a break. Dance with me."

I smiled down at Misty and nodded. I looked back at Whitley, who was looking Misty up and down.

"Excuse me, CG," I said with a wink.

Whitley smirked and gave me the finger before turning and walking back to her table. Courtney followed behind, and Bill trailed her.

I took Misty's hand and led her to the dance floor. Then, I watched as Bill somehow got Courtney to dance with his drunken ass. I glanced around the dance floor and saw Olivia dancing with Justin. He was holding her

tightly up against his body as she rested her head on his chest. I pulled Misty close to me and started dancing.

"God, Layton. It feels so good to be in your arms," Misty said.

I couldn't even answer her. I kept staring at Olivia. I watched as she looked up at Justin, and he leaned down and kissed her. I wanted nothing more than to look away, but I couldn't. I just kept torturing myself by staring at them.

Then, I saw Kevin, and I closed my eyes. All I could see was Mike laughing and loving life as he twirled Jen around on the dance floor. They'd had so many dreams. They were meant to be together. Now, she was alone with their five-year-old daughter, Kate.

He left us.

My heart started pounding, and I felt like I couldn't breathe. I looked back at Olivia, who was still kissing Justin. Kevin was dancing with some girl I'd seen around, but I had no idea who she was. Courtney was dancing with Bill, and she actually looked like she was enjoying herself.

Then, my eyes caught those beautiful green ones.

Is she watching me dance?

She slowly looked away as Richard walked up and sat down to talk to her.

The music changed, and "What About Love" by Austin Mahone started playing. Olivia turned and began grinding her ass into Justin. I looked away as I pulled Misty closer. As she peeked up at me, I tilted her chin up, and I kissed her. The moan she let out moved through my whole body. When I closed my eyes, green eyes were all I could see.

Whitley's eyes are so beautiful.

I moved my hands down and grabbed Misty's ass as I started grinding into her.

"Layton…"

The sound of Misty's voice brought me out of my daydream. She turned around and started dancing closer to me. I moved my hands up and down her body.

I need to forget.

I leaned down toward Misty's ear. "Can you leave early?"

She spun around and captured my lips with hers as she reached around and grabbed the back of my neck. "Buck already said I could leave early. Take me home and fuck me, Layton."

I smiled as my dick jumped. I pulled her closer to me and pushed my dick into her stomach. In that moment, I looked up to see Whitley staring at us. I instantly pushed Misty away from me. I felt like a total fucking asshole.

"Layton, did you hear me? I can leave now. I'm excited to finally fuck you in a bed. I can do so much more than on a pool table."

I watched as Richard held out his hand, and Whitley took it. They made their way to the dance floor as Flo Rida's "Right Round" started.

Misty jumped up and down. "Oh my God, I love this song!"

I glanced over toward Olivia. She and Justin were leaving the dance floor and heading for the door.

Fuck.

When I looked back at Whitley, I almost fell over.

Jesus Christ, can she move her hips any more?

I felt Misty dancing all around me, but I couldn't move. I just stood there, watching Whitley.

Courtney ended up near Whitley. They started talking while they were dancing with Bill and Richard. Fuckers were enjoying this dance too much. When I saw Richard put his hands on Whitley's hips and move them up and down, I wanted to go and pull him away from her.

"Layton? Who in the hell are you looking at?" Misty asked.

I looked down at Misty and shook my head. "Nobody, babe. Nobody."

I grabbed Misty and pulled her closer to me as I lost myself to the song and the feel of her body up against mine. The one thing Misty was good at was making me forget everyone and everything.

I closed my eyes as I moved my hands up and down her body while I dreamed I was dancing with someone else.

SEVEN

->>>>>>>>>>>><<<<<<<<<<<<-

Whitley

I couldn't help myself. I couldn't tear my eyes away from Layton dancing with that girl.

Who in the hell is she? A girlfriend? I swear he said he didn't have a girlfriend.

After the Flo Rida song was over, I told Richard I was tired and thirsty. A slower song came on, and I watched as Layton danced, practically fucking whoever this girl was on the dance floor.

Jesus, get a room, for Pete's sake.

I looked away. I couldn't stand to watch them anymore. I caught Court looking at me.

She smiled and shook her head. "Jealous much, Whit?"

I gave her a dirty look as Richard asked us what we wanted to drink.

"Water, please," we both said.

Richard walked away as Bill sat down in between Court and me. I knew he was thinking he would get lucky tonight, and I was beginning to think Courtney had been serious about getting fucked. She had been hanging all over this guy.

Bill leaned over and whispered something in Courtney's ear. She smiled and shook her head. He said something else to her, and I heard her say, "Maybe next time."

Bill got up and made his way over to Richard as he was walking back to the table with our water. Richard started laughing and shuffled around Bill. He handed us the waters and sat down.

"Your friend just totally crushed my friend's dreams. Please tell me you won't crush mine."

Ugh. What a corny-ass line.

I looked up and saw Layton kissing that girl.

Stupid men. I hate them all.

"Richard, who is Layton, um…dancing with? If you can call that dancing," I said with sarcasm oozing out.

Richard looked out toward the dance floor. "Oh, that's Misty. She's a bartender here and has been after Layton for years. He just recently hooked up with her. Layton is only using her for sex, just a way to forget all his problems. He doesn't even like her."

My heart felt like it dropped into my stomach for some reason. "Forget his problems?" I raised my eyebrows.

"Yeah, six months ago, Layton's brother died in Afghanistan. He was set to get out of the Marine Corps. He was on his last tour and only had less than four days before he was supposed to head back to the States."

I looked at Layton, and my heart broke in two. "Oh my God. How terrible."

"Yeah, it really fucked Layton up. Mike was all he had…well, besides Olivia. Their mother had passed away, and then their dad had left them to fend for themselves, all alone, in some fucked-up conditions. Mike was a few years older, and after graduation, he joined the Marines, so Layton could go to Texas A&M and concentrate on getting their ranch going. He made a promise to Mike that he would always follow their dreams of raising cattle and racehorses. Really, the racehorses were kind of Mike's thing, just like their old man. Layton did it just because he knew how much Mike loved it. When Mike would come home from leave, they'd spend all their time with either cattle or horses. They did everything together."

I shook my head. "Poor Layton. That…that just breaks my heart."

I looked back out at Layton. The way he was moving his hands up and down Misty's body was starting to bother me and piss me off. And *that* pissed me off even more.

"Wait—did you say Mike was all he had besides Olivia? Do you mean Olivia, Mrs. Pierceson's niece?" I asked.

"Yep. She left him the day after Mike died," Richard said.

I brought my hand up and covered my mouth. "What?"

"That's not the worst of it. She left Layton for one of his best friends, Justin. Justin, Layton, and Reed used to do everything together when Layton wasn't with Mike. They had been best friends since…well, hell, since like first grade, all three of them."

I felt like I was going to be sick. It wasn't like I cared for Layton that much. He was sometimes an ass, but my God, this was just so terrible. I felt so bad.

"You want to dance?" Richard asked.

I shook my head. "Nah, I'm really tired and just need to rest for a bit before dancing again."

He got up. "I'm going to go talk to a few friends then." He gave me a weak smile and headed off to the other side of the bar.

I looked around for Layton and Misty. I couldn't find them on the dance floor anymore. Then, I saw them. Misty was leaning on the bar, talking to the bartender and smiling. She jumped down off the bar, and Layton grabbed her hand.

I watched as they walked out the door. For some reason, I felt insanely jealous.

Fuck! Why do I even feel this way? I don't even like him!

I stood up and said to Courtney, "I'm ready to leave."

"Wait—what? Oh, come on, Whit. I was having fun, dick-teasing this Bill guy. It might actually be more fun than having sex," she said with a wink.

"I need to leave. I'm tired, and my head is pounding."

Courtney grabbed her purse and sighed. "Fine, party pooper. Let's go home."

I started to walk away. I couldn't believe how mad I was.

What in the hell is wrong with me?

I felt like I wanted to just haul off and punch someone.

Stupid Layton Morris.

I stormed off, away from Courtney, and I made my way toward the door. When I went to walk out, the door opened, and I ran smack into Layton.

"Shit, CG, watch where you're going, sweetheart. I damn near knocked you over," he said with that drop-dead smile of his.

What an asshole! How dare he call me sweetheart after he was practically fucking that girl on the dance floor!

"Fuck off, you jerk." I tried to walk around him.

"Whitley, I was only kidding. Are you okay?"

I looked out the door and saw Misty standing there, waiting on Layton.

"Do all the cowboys in Texas take home slutty bartenders and fuck them to forget their problems? Real classy. Not what I was expecting from a—what did you call yourself earlier? Oh yeah, a Southern gentleman. Ha. That's a fucking joke."

Oh my God! Why did I just say that?

"Whitley!" Courtney said as she grabbed my arm. "Sorry, Layton. I think she's had too much to drink."

I pulled my arm out of Courtney's hand. "No, I haven't, Court."

I glared at Layton, and then I instantly regretted my words when I saw the hurt in his eyes—those beautiful blue eyes of his that I could so get lost in.

Ugh, those stupid eyes.

Then, he slowly let a smile play across his face. "No, Whitley, only the fucked-up cowboys who want to forget everything for a little bit take home slutty bartenders to fuck the memories away. Are all New Yorkers such nosy bitches?"

I pushed him away from me and started to walk out the door. "Fuck off, asshole." I looked over at Misty as she gave me a shit-eating grin. "Enjoy it, sweetheart. He's only using you for sex. Like all men, he's an asshole who only thinks with his dick."

Her smile faded, and I saw her look over my shoulder. I kept walking, but I turned around quickly and saw Layton standing there, watching me.

Fuck! Fuck! Fuck! Why did I just do that? He's been nothing but nice to me since I met him. Okay, maybe not nice all the time, but he's been a gentleman, and I just acted like a total bitch!

Courtney reached for my arm, and once we got a bit farther away, she stopped and spun me around to face her. "Holy shit, Whit. What in the hell was that all about? How many beers did you have? And what did that guy ever do to you that caused you to be such a bitch toward him?"

I felt tears stinging my eyes. I shook my head. "I don't know, Court. I don't know what happened. Something just snapped. Oh my God. I can't believe I said that. I'll never be able to show my face to him ever again." I put my hand up to my mouth and started crying.

"Oh, honey, it's okay. You've had so much going on that maybe Richard telling you Layton was using that girl just for sex pushed you over the edge. Whit, you can tell me all you want that you can't stand the guy, but I can tell you like him. Maybe you don't want to take him home and have your wicked way with him, but you do like him. I think you might have gotten a tad bit jealous."

I stood there and just looked at my best friend. I wiped the tears away from my eyes and put my hands on my hips. I knew she was right, but no way was I admitting any feelings for Layton Morris.

"Bullshit. That's just bullshit. I'm not the least bit jealous because I would never look at him that way."

Courtney raised her eyebrow and looked at me like I was a five-year-old lying to her mother.

I rolled my eyes and started walking again. "Ugh. I'm going home. I'm tired, I drank too much, and I hadn't even wanted to go out in the first place."

We walked up to the traffic light, and Layton's truck pulled up. He rolled down the window and gave me a weak smile.

"Why don't you let me drive y'all home?" he said with that stupid sexy accent of his.

I looked in the truck and didn't see Misty in the front seat.

Is she in the backseat? In another car? What in the hell?

Oh my God, my head. How much did I have to drink?

I began walking across the street, and Courtney followed.

"No, thanks. We don't have far to go, and I need the fresh air. Go on and enjoy the rest of your night," I called over my shoulder.

I was so pissed that I felt my whole body shaking.

I hate him! I hate him so much that I just want to scream. I can't believe I ever let anyone treat me the way he did.

"Whitley, I'm just trying to be nice. Don't be such a bitch," he said.

I stopped in the middle of the street and balled up my fists. I instantly heard Roger saying the same thing to me—*Don't be such a bitch, Squeak.*

"Ah...Layton, maybe you better just head on home." Courtney walked up and stood in front of me. "Whit, babe, I think you had a bit too much to drink, and—"

"How can you call me a bitch, you asshole? You don't even know me! You know what? You're a jerk, so just leave me alone."

I turned and started walking again. I could hear Courtney talking to Layton, and I didn't even care what she was saying. I wanted to get out of these stupid new boots I'd bought and crawl into a hot bath. I wanted to forget about seeing him kissing her and touching her and how it had driven me to act like this insane person I was being right now. I just wanted to forget everything.

I heard Courtney coming up behind me. As I made my way up to the front door of our house, I felt tears burning my eyes. I unlocked the door and started for the stairs.

"Whitley."

It only took the sound of Court's voice for me to break down. I sat down on the stairs and began crying.

"Oh God..." I couldn't get any other words out of my mouth. I just cried hysterically.

Courtney sat down next me and just held me in her arms as I sobbed.

"He took the best of me, Court. He took everything from me."

She moved her hand up and down my back. "Shh...I know, baby. I know."

"He broke me down so much that I don't even know who I am anymore," I said in between sobs.

"I know, honey, but he no longer has any power over you," Court said.

"That's just it. He does. He holds so much power in my world. It's unreal. It's like every little thing that happens triggers something. He's always in the back of my head. I find myself looking over my shoulder, Courtney, waiting...waiting for him to find me and get pissed-off and teach me another one of his damn lessons. What if *he's* just like that, too?"

Courtney pulled back and looked at me, confused. "What if who's just like that?"

I didn't even realize I had said that. "Nobody."

"Whit, were you referring to Layton?"

I pulled slightly away from her. "I don't like him, Court."

Oh God. What in the hell is going on with me? I'm so confused.

Courtney got up and knelt down in front of me. "Look at me, Whit. Not all guys are like Roger. Whitley...you don't have to be afraid to fall in love with someone, baby."

I shook my head. "No…I can't…I can't open my heart up like that ever again." My whole body began to tremble.

They're all the same—all of them.

"Whit—"

I stood and started to cry again. "You don't understand, Courtney. If I wore the wrong outfit, he'd hit me. If I told him to fuck off, he'd push me on the ground and kick me until I told him I was sorry. If I talked to another man, he'd drag me around the house by my hair."

I watched as Courtney put her hands up to her mouth as she began crying.

"Don't you see? Layton is just another man who uses women. They're all the same." I turned and walked up the stairs. I just needed to sit in a hot bath.

"Whitley…" Courtney ran up the stairs after me.

Right before I got to my room, she grabbed my arm.

"I'm sorry." Tears were rolling down her face. "If I had any idea of what he was doing to you, I-I would have…"

I pulled her into my arms. "Oh, Lollipop, please don't do that to yourself. How would you know when I pushed everyone away from me?" I stepped back and wiped the tears from her face. "Hey. What about that book that was going to have me reaching for my vibrator? And by the way, I don't even own one."

Courtney slowly smiled. "Um…you do now. I bought one for you before we left New York. I was saving it for your birthday, but I think this is more important."

I smiled and shook my head. "Court…you bought me a fucking vibrator? Oh. My. God. I don't know whether to kiss you or slap the shit out of you!"

She jumped up and down and turned to run to her bedroom. "Wait—don't go in the bath yet! Give me a second," she called over her shoulder.

I took a deep breath and leaned against the wall. I closed my eyes, and all I could see was Layton and his drop-dead smile.

Those beautiful blue eyes—what would it be like to make love to him and look into those eyes?

I snapped my eyes open and tried to shake the image from my head.

What in the hell, Whitley? Snap the hell out of it. You. Do. Not. Like. Him.

Courtney came running down the hallway and skidded to a stop. The smile on her face caused me to laugh.

God, I love this girl.

"Okay, now, this is my Kindle. You know how much I love my Kindle, Whit."

I nodded and winked at her. "Yep, I know Court. You've already given me the warning about your Kindle."

She slowly started to hand me the Kindle. When I reached for it, she pulled it back.

"Wait—I can't let you take it into the bathroom. I'll put it on your bed. I'll open it up to the book you need to read."

I laughed as I rolled my eyes.

I used her Kindle once to read a book while we had been on vacation. Sitting by the pool, I had been bored out of my mind. She'd just finished reading some fifty shades of more fucked-up men.

"Okay, Lollipop, just put it on my bed." I turned to walk into the bathroom. "Wait—what is it called, and what is it about?"

Courtney turned around and gave me her evil little smile. "The name of the book is *Knight and Play*. And you're gonna have to read it to see what it's about."

I just looked at her. "Bitch."

She laughed as she walked into my room. "You know you love me. I have fresh new batteries in your B.O.B!" She winked as she spun around and headed back down the hallway before stopping and turning to me again. "Hey, Whitley?" she asked with a serious face.

"Yeah?"

"Give Layton a chance. I know what he was doing tonight with that girl seems like a fucked-up thing, but…just don't put him in the same category as Roger. Okay?"

I smiled and nodded.

"Enjoy your bath."

I walked into the bathroom, and I closed the door. Leaning against it, I put my head back on it and sighed. I closed my eyes, and all I could see was Layton and his amazing eyes…and body…and smile.

Fuck it. I'm taking a shower and getting to that damn book!

EIGHT

-≫≫≫≫≫≫≫≫≫≫≫≫≪≪≪≪≪≪≪≪≪≪≪≪≪-

LAYTON

I couldn't get what Whitley had said out of my mind. I sat on the side of the road in my truck, dreading going home to an empty house. My phone started to ring—again.

Misty.

"Fuck!" I said as I let the call go to voice mail.

I'd never seen anyone so pissed-off as she had been when I'd told her I was going home alone. She'd called me every name in the book.

There was no way I was taking Misty home to fuck after what Whitley had said. A part of me was upset that Whitley even knew about Misty and me. I was going to find out which fucking friend of mine had spilled the beans.

My phone went off again. This time, I answered it.

"Layton! What in the fuck? I thought there was something between us. Who was that bitch who talked shit to me outside of Joe's? What did she say to you to make you change your mind?"

I took a deep breath. "Listen, Misty, I was going to talk to you anyway. Honey, it was fun, but I'm not looking to get involved with anyone, and it's really not very fair of me to string you along like I was. I just needed—"

I heard her laugh over the phone.

"You just needed, what, Layton? A good fuck?"

Ah, shit—if she only knew she wasn't even a good fuck. She was just someone to erase the memories for a bit.

"Something like that, Misty."

"You know what, Layton? I thought you were a nice guy. I didn't think you were like all the other guys out there, only looking for a piece of ass. I really liked you."

I put my head on the back of my seat and closed my eyes. I hated doing what I was about to do, but it was the only thing I could think of to get her to walk away from me.

"Well, Misty, it looks like you had me all wrong. It was fun, but I'm just not interested."

"Wow. That's what I get after a few great nights together, Layton?"

I sighed as I looked behind me to the deserted country road before pulling out. "We fucked on a pool table twice, Misty. It wasn't earth-shattering, and I'm pretty damn sure I wasn't the first guy you fucked there."

I heard her suck in a breath of air.

"Fuck you, Layton Morris. You're nothing but a prick. Don't ever call me again."

I threw my cell phone down on the passenger side seat and slammed the steering wheel.

Fuck! Fuck! Fuck! Why did you leave me, Mike? It fucked everything up.

On the way home, all I could think about was why Whitley had been so pissed-off at me.

Was she jealous because I was leaving with Misty?

No way.

She'd acted like she couldn't stand to be around me. One minute, I'd thought she was pretty cool, and then the next, she had been a total bitch.

Yeah, I don't need any more of that shit in my life. I'm done with women. They're all fucked-up, and they don't know what in the hell they want.

By the time I got home and in my house, I was exhausted. I started to walk toward my bedroom when I heard someone. I stopped and stood there, listening.

Snoring? Is someone snoring? Who in the hell is in my house?

I walked into the living room and turned on the light. I couldn't believe what I was seeing.

"Kevin?" I walked up and saw Kevin passed out on my sofa and then noticed Reed passed out in my recliner. "Reed?"

Reed opened his eyes and stretched while he yawned. "Hey, dude. Where in the fuck have you been? You left without telling anyone."

I just stood there, staring at him. I shook my head and looked back at Kevin, who was now starting to wake up.

"How in the hell did you get into my house, you asshole?"

Reed looked at me funny. "You gave me a key months ago, dude."

Motherfucker. I forgot I'd given him a key right after Mike had died, only to appease everyone who thought I was going to hurt myself after Mike's death and Olivia leaving me.

"The alarm?"

"Dude, I've watched your fucking dogs when you went out of town. You told me your code. What in the hell, Layton?"

"What if I had brought someone back here with me? And I've got two of my damn friends fucking sleeping in my living room?"

Reed stood and laughed. "Yeah, like you'd bring someone like Misty back to your house. Don't think so, Layton. You're not that kind of guy."

Shit. Now, I really feel like a royal asshole. "You still haven't answered me. Why are you both in my house, asleep in my living room?" I crossed my arms over my chest.

Kevin stood and smiled as he walked over and slapped me on the back. "Dude, I wanted to get up and take a ride on the ranch before it got too hot. It makes me feel closer to Mike, ya know?"

My heart slammed in my chest. "Fine. I'm exhausted, and I've had to deal with not only one crazy woman today but three, so if y'all will excuse me, I'm going to bed. Help yourself to the guest bedrooms or stay out here. I don't care." I turned and started back toward my bedroom.

"Hey, Layton, speaking of women, what's with Whitley and Courtney? They open, or you got dibs on one?" Kevin asked.

I turned around to see Reed staring at Kevin.

"What? Which one are you interested in, dude?" Reed asked as he looked at Kevin.

Oh, fucking great. First, Richard, and now, these two.

Kevin smiled and looked at Reed. "Which one are you interested in?"

Reed quickly looked at me and then back at Kevin. "Fuck…neither one. I mean, I think Layton here has got his eye on Whitley, and Courtney seems like a snobby dick-tease from what Bill said."

Wait—what?

Kevin glanced at me and then back toward Reed. He threw his head back and laughed. "Dude, I'm interested in the dick-tease. That long blonde hair of hers had me hard all night."

I noticed Reed tense up. *Interesting.*

I turned and walked away. "For the record, I don't have my eye on Whitley. I'm not interested in dealing with women and all their fucking problems, their neediness, and just their damn moods in general."

I heard both Kevin and Reed laugh.

Right before I shut my door, Kevin called out, "Okay, dude, you keep telling yourself that."

→≫≫≫≫≫≫≫≫≫≫≫≪≪≪≪≪≪≪≪≪≪≪≪←

I walked out of the bathroom with a towel wrapped around my waist. I was so damn tired, but I knew I wouldn't sleep well if I hadn't taken a shower before bed.

As I bent over to pick up my jeans, I heard my phone go off. I reached into my pocket and took it out. I had a few text messages. I swiped my finger over the screen and tapped on the Messages icon. My heart started beating when I saw I had two messages from Olivia. Then, I noticed that I also had one from Whitley.

I tapped Olivia's message and closed my eyes before reading it.

> *Olivia: Layton, I'm really worried about you. I saw how you were hanging all over Misty. Baby, please don't do this to yourself. Let's talk. I'll be up late. Call me.*

> *Olivia: Baby, please…I really need to talk to you. Seeing you today did something to me. I miss you, Layton. I just want to talk to you. Call me as soon as you can. I still love you, Layton. I always will, baby.*

I dropped the phone to the floor, sat down on the bed, and placed my face into my hands as I began to cry.

Why is she doing this to me? And just when I felt like I was getting over her. Why is she doing this?

I wasn't sure how long I'd sat there and just cried like a pansy-ass. I leaned down and picked up my phone. I was just about to tap on Olivia's message to reply when I remembered Whitley had sent a text also. I backed out of Olivia's message and opened up Whitley's. For some reason, my heart started beating faster at the idea of her sending me a text.

She probably just texted to call me an asshole again. Either that, or she is going to tell me to fuck off again. I should have never given her my cell number on the paper that had Jacks number on it.

> *Whitley: Hey, Layton, it's Whitley. I know it's late, and I hope this doesn't wake you up. If it does, then shit, I'm so sorry. Anywho, I just wanted to say I'm so sorry for the way I acted earlier. I'm not really sure what in the hell came over me. What you do and whom you do it with is none of my business. You were so kind to me today…well, for the most part, you were kind to me…and for me to have acted like that was a real bitch move. I just wanted to say I'm sorry. I hope you'll forgive my brass, New York–bitch attitude.*

I couldn't help but smile at her message. I read it again and shook my head.

Damn that girl is cute as a button. She's the only girl who has ever driven me insane with anger and lust at the same damn time.

Lust? Oh no, Layton. Don't even go there. Whitley is just…CG. That's all. Totally not interested.

I hit the screen, and my keyboard popped up. I smiled as I began typing my reply to Whitley.

> *Layton: Hey, CG. You're up late, girl. I thought women liked to get their beauty sleep, and here you are, texting me at three in the morning. And please…don't apologize for speaking the truth.*

I hit Send, and I started to get up to get some boxer shorts when my phone chimed again. I smiled when I saw Whitley's name.

> *Whitley: That's just a myth—that whole women-need-so-many-hours-for-their-beauty-sleep bullshit. It takes more than sleep to get me to look somewhat beautiful. I'm exhausted though, but I can't put down this fucking book that Courtney is forcing me to read. Have I mentioned that I hate reading?*

I laughed as I read her reply. I quickly opened my top drawer, pulled out a pair of boxers, and slipped them on. I walked over and plugged my phone in. I crawled into bed and then started to type back my reply.

> *Layton: Trust me, CG, you don't need anything to make you beautiful. You're naturally beautiful. So, tell me…how exactly is Courtney forcing you to read this book? It must be good if you can't put it down.*

I paused for a second before hitting Send. After sending it, I sat there, like an idiot, hoping she would text back. I closed my eyes and felt myself drifting off to sleep. My phone beeped in my hand and scared the shit out of me.

> *Whitley: Well, where do I start? First, thank you for the sweet compliment. What do you want? That felt like you were kissing up for something. Second, Courtney and I made a bet. I don't like losing. Hence…I'm reading.*

> *Layton: Learn to take a compliment, CG. I know it's hard for you Northerners. I'm intrigued by this bet. What are the deets on it?*

> *Whitley: Sorry. Thank you, cowboy, for the compliment. You're not so bad on the eyes either, if we're being honest. As far as the bet goes…um…pass. I don't think you want to hear the details of it. It's kind of…embarrassing.*

> *Layton: Ah hell, Whit. Now, I have to know. Come on, tell me. I won't be able to sleep because I'll be thinking about it, and I need my beauty sleep.*

> *Whitley: LOL! Okay…but you have to promise to never utter a word of this to anyone. Promise?*

> *Layton: Promise and cross my heart!*

I sat up in bed and watched my phone, like an idiot. My phone beeped, and I just opened up the message. My smile faded when I saw it was a message from Olivia.

Olivia: I guess I'm not going to hear from you tonight. I'm going to bed. I hope you are okay. Please call me, Layton.

How does she do it? Right when I'm feeling good, she sucks it away. I hit Reply and started typing.

Layton: I'm exhausted, Olivia, and I don't really want to talk to you. What I do and who I do it with is none of your business. Worry about your fiancé. I'm sure he wouldn't like knowing you are texting your ex at three in the morning. I'm turning off my phone.

My phone beeped again with another message from Olivia.

Olivia: You're grumpy. I'll call you tomorrow, babe. Night!

What in the hell?

My phone went off again, and I opened up Whitley's text.

Whitley: Okay, well…Courtney thinks I'm crazy because I don't get pulled into this world of hers filled with books and book boyfriends. She bet she could give me a book to read that would have me…um…well, it would have me…shit. I don't even really know you, Layton!

I smiled because I could just picture the blush on her cheeks. I was just about to start typing my reply, but I thought this one needed to be told over the phone. Plus, for some reason, I really wanted to hear her voice, so I called her instead.

"Hello?" Whitley answered.

"Hey, I hope it's okay I called you, but I'm getting tired of typing."

Good excuse, Layton!

"Oh Christ, Layton! I can't tell you over the phone. It's embarrassing. Just forget I even brought up the book."

I smiled as I thought about her sitting in her bed. I wondered what kind of clothes she wore to sleep in. I pictured her in a T-shirt and panties.

Fuck. I had to adjust myself from just thinking about it. *Just friends, Layton.*

"Come on, CG. Just tell me. It can't be that bad."

She let out a sigh. "Fine. She bet me she could have me read a book that was so hot that I'd be reaching for a vibrator. There—I said it."

What in the fuck did she just say? Vibrator? Holy hell.

"Motherfucker, Whitley. I was not expecting that."

She let out a laugh. "I'm sorry, but you asked."

"So…has it?" I asked with a smile.

"What?"

"Has it?" I repeated, knowing damn well she'd heard me the first time.

"Has it, what?"

"The book, Whitley...has it turned you on enough to have you reaching for your vibrator?"

Oh my God. Just talking to her about this had me wanting to take myself in my own hand. *What in the hell is this girl doing to me?*

"I don't even own one!"

Damn.

"Courtney bought me one though and left it by the Kindle."

She's trying to kill me.

I had to pull the phone away and take a deep breath. "You still haven't answered me, Whit," I said, grinning.

"Do you really want to know, Layton?" she asked with a purr.

Yep...she's fucking trying to kill me. Act cool, Layton. You're not interested in her. Just friends...talking about...orgasms with vibrators.

I took a deep breath before answering. "Yeah, I'm curious."

"Well...it's getting pretty hot. I'm thinking I might have to...you know..."

"No, Whitley...tell me."

"Layton...this is starting to go somewhere two friends shouldn't go. Plus, we just met today. I think we're both tired...maybe a little lonely, too. I don't really want to hear you jacking yourself off over the phone."

I started choking and then laughed. "Holy shit, CG! Wow. You think pretty highly of yourself, don't you? How do you know I'd even be the slightest bit turned-on by you giving yourself an orgasm?"

"You wouldn't?"

"No...I wouldn't. I don't look at you like that, CG." I tried my best to adjust my growing dick.

"Oh, okay. Well...I was just about to start it up, but—"

"What?" I practically choked again on my own damn word.

"I was getting to a good part, but I think I'll close it up for the night."

Dead. I'm dead. She has succeeded in killing me.

I smiled as I decided to play right along with her. "Okay, well...I'll have to remember that you're a serious person when it comes to bets. Sleep good, CG."

Nothing. Silence.

"Whitley?"

"Um...yep...you, too, Layton."

I smiled bigger, trying hard not to laugh. "Night!"

"Um...good night, Layton. Thank you again for everything you did for me today. I really do appreciate it."

I could almost hear the smile in her voice.

"It was my pleasure, CG. Good night."

"Sweet dreams," she purred into the phone.

I hit End and set my phone down on the nightstand. Lying down again, I stared at the ceiling for a minute or two.

"Fuck!"

I jumped up and headed back to my bathroom and turned on my shower. I cursed Whitley Reynolds as I stepped into the freezing cold water.

-》》》》》》》》》》《《《《《《《《《《《《-

I swore I woke up with a goddamn smile on my face. I did nothing but dream of a stubborn, hardheaded, beautiful, green-eyed beauty last night. After I got dressed, I reached for my cell phone and headed to the kitchen where I could already hear Reed and Kevin arguing. It reminded me of Mike and me, and for one brief moment, I felt like my chest was being pushed in on me.

I glanced at my phone and saw a text message from Whitley. I smiled as I opened it up to read it.

> *Whitley: Good morning, Layton. Have a good day. I read that damn book until five thirty this morning. Thank you again for helping me yesterday.*

"Jesus, dude, what in the hell has you smiling with that damn goofy-ass grin?" Reed asked as toast popped up from the toaster.

I looked between both of them. There was no fucking way I was telling them about my conversation with Whitley. They'd just go off on me about how much I liked her...which I didn't.

"Nothing. So, what's the plan for today?" I grabbed the eggs out of the fridge and started to scramble them.

Kevin stood and cleaned off his plate. "I'm going to head out for a quick run, and then I'd really love to just spend a bit of time on the ranch."

I smiled as I looked at my brother's best friend. I knew losing Mike had been hard for him as well.

"You want to saddle up a few horses?" I glanced over toward Reed, who was looking down at his phone.

He looked up and grinned. "That sounds good to me, dude. Kev, you up for riding?"

Kevin smiled and nodded. "Give me a good thirty-minute run, y'all." He headed out the back door.

I turned back to cooking my eggs.

"Layton?"

I looked over my shoulder and smiled. "Reed?"

"Um...I don't know how to tell you this, but—"

I turned and stared at him. "What? Is something wrong?"

"Uh…Olivia sent me a text a few minutes ago. She said some bullshit about worrying about you. She asked me if I was going to see you today and if I could let her know where you would be. What do I say to her?"

My heart instantly fell to my stomach. "Just don't text her back."

"What the fuck is her deal? Why is she all of a sudden so worried about you? Bitch wasn't worried the night she walked out and left you."

I felt the anger starting to build inside me.

She left me when I needed her the most. All women are nothing but selfish bitches.

"I don't know what her deal is. She was texting me in the middle of the night last night. I just ignored her."

"Bill said she was pissed when she saw you with Misty."

"Do you think she's jealous?" A part of me hoped so.

"Fuck yes, she's jealous. From what I hear, Justin is getting sick of her high-maintenance attitude. He said she practically threw this idea of an engagement party at him yesterday. They hadn't even talked about one before."

"Really? Huh…yesterday, she sure jumped all over Whitley to organize it."

Reed stood, walked over to the sink, and rinsed off his plate. He turned and shook his head. "Layton, think about it. Olivia saw you with Whitley, right?"

"Yeah. Olivia asked who Whitley was right from the get-go." I put my eggs on my plate and sat down to eat.

"So, she sees you show up with this drop-dead gorgeous girl. Olivia has no idea who she is, so she starts thinking you're together. What a better way to get to know Whitley than to have her organize a fucking party. Olivia never was one to miss the little things. She probably got the idea for the engagement party just on the spot."

I sat there and thought back to yesterday. I smiled slightly. *So, Liv thinks something is going on with Whit and me. This could be fun.*

"Layton, I know you keep saying that you're not the least bit interested in Whitley, and that's cool. From the short amount of time I talked to her yesterday, she seems like a sweet girl. Her friend, on the other hand, is…well, I don't know what she is just yet. Annoying."

I let out a laugh.

"Just don't use Whitley to make Olivia jealous. I got the feeling that she's been hurt before from the little bit I caught from Courtney. Don't be a dick, okay?"

My smile faded as I sat there and looked at my best friend. Reed was about the same height as me. His brown hair was always messy, and his eyes were sometimes green and sometimes blue. I'd never understood how they changed colors. He'd said it depended on his mood. He was every girl's dream—good looks, built, and had a heart of gold.

He loved his job as a horticulturist, working for the Texas Parks and Wildlife Department. Of course, he loved helping me with the cattle and racehorses as well.

"Layton?" Reed asked, pulling me from my thoughts.

"Yeah…I mean, of course, I won't do that. Shit, Reed, I'm not that much of a dick. Whitley is a tad bit annoying, but overall, I like her…as a friend."

He smiled slightly. "Good. Just don't let Olivia get you down, dude. You finally seem like you're getting over her, and I haven't seen you walk into a room with a smile on your face, like earlier, in a long time. I just want you to be happy, Layton."

I smiled as I nodded. Reed was the only person in my life since Mike who had been there for me.

"Thanks, Reed, for everything. Thanks for never giving up on my crazy ass."

Reed laughed and turned to head out the back door. "You know it, buddy. I'm heading down to the main barn. I need to find a horse feisty enough to buck Kevin off."

I laughed as I turned and went back to eating my eggs. I got up and reached into the fridge. I grabbed the OJ and poured myself a glass. I sat down and grabbed my phone. I opened up Whit's text and hit Reply.

Layton: Good morning, CG. Did you finish the book?

I started to eat again when my phone rang. I didn't even bother to look at who was calling. I figured it was Whitley.

"Was it that good of a book?" I answered.

"What a way to answer the phone, babe."

The moment I heard her voice, my hands started to shake. "Olivia."

"Good morning to you, too. How did you sleep, babe?"

I swallowed hard and tried to catch my breath. *Why is she calling me?*

"I, um…I slept fine, Olivia. What do you want?"

"Layton, can't we move past the hurt and just be friends?"

I let out laugh. "It's hard to just be friends, Liv, when you grab my dick in a barn and tell me how much you miss me—and with your fiancé right around the corner."

"That was a mistake, Layton. I was just so excited to see you. I've missed you, baby. Have you missed me?"

"Yes." *Fuck!* I'd admitted it before I could even think about what she'd asked.

"What are you doing today? Maybe we could just meet and talk. I'm so sorry I threw the whole engagement party at you yesterday."

Whitley…

"No worries, Liv. You're getting married, and people have engagement parties all the time. Whitley will take good care of you, just like she will Mrs. P. She's great at what she does."

Holy shit! I haven't even known the girl for twenty-four hours, and I'm saying how great she is at her job!

I heard Olivia take a deep breath and slowly let it out. "Yes…Whitley, the girl from New York. I know Mimi is really looking forward to Whitley throwing her party, and she better take care of my aunt. So, tell me, Layton, how long have you known *Whitley*?"

Ah hell. Reed was right. Olivia was jealous of Whitley. *Time to have some fun.*

"Not too long, but she's quickly becoming a good friend. She's just someone to text and joke around with. She's a sweet girl, and I'm pretty sure Reed is hot for her friend, Courtney."

"Really? Were you texting her last night?"

"Yep," I said as I popped my P. *God, I'm such a girl.*

Kevin came in, grabbed his bag, and headed to the guest bathroom. "Give me two minutes, not going for a run after all."

"Who was that?" Olivia asked with frustration in her voice.

"Just Kevin. We're taking the horses out for a ride around the ranch this morning."

"Oh, okay. Well, I have to go get ready. I have a meeting in a bit with someone. Layton, are you sure we can't meet later? Please. Just for coffee. I really need to talk to you."

I really didn't want to say no, but all I could think about was Whitley. "Today's not a good day, Liv. Sorry."

"Soon then, okay?"

"Sure. I gotta go." I hit End.

Then, I got up, picked up my plate, and threw it into the sink. I was pissed at myself for using Whitley to make Olivia jealous.

I needed some fresh air. I needed to be closer to Mike.

I need you, Mike. I feel like I'm slowly losing control over everything.

As I walked out the back door, my cell phone went off.

>*Whitley: Haven't finished yet…almost done with it…but I can share this with you…I lost the bet ;) TTFN!*

Holy shit. The image of Whitley playing with herself with a vibrator almost brought me to my knees. I looked up and saw Reed walking up with Lucky and three horses.

I sent Whitley back a quick text.

>*Layton: Damn, girl. You read fast. I can't believe you're almost done with the book. And what in the hell does TTFN mean?*

I hit Send and started laughing. *What I wouldn't give to see her face when she reads my response.*

"There's that smile again! Someone or something sure is making you *smile* today, Layton," Reed said with a wink.

Lucky looked and grinned as he shook my hand.

"How are the horses looking, Lucky?"

"Good, but I wanted to talk to you, if I could. I got a lead on a horse in Kentucky."

I raised my eyebrows. "Oh yeah? Let's talk about it later?"

He handed me the reins on Trigger and smiled. "Oh, believe me, we will because I won't let you pass this one up."

Kevin came out, and we all got on the horses and took off. I felt a sense of peace wrap over my whole body. I always felt so close to Mike when I was on a horse and out on the ranch. I closed my eyes and felt the summer sun warming my face.

Reed and Kevin were going on and on about some club in Austin.

All I could see was green eyes staring back into mine.

When my phone went off, alerting me to a new text message, I almost dropped it when I tried to get it out of my back pocket. I slowed Trigger down, so I could open up Whitley's text.

Whitley: Ta Ta For Now. ;) Have a great day, cowboy.

I tried not to smile, but I couldn't help it.

Layton: Have a great day, CG.

I put my phone in my back pocket, and for the first time in months, I actually felt happy.

NINE

-➤➤➤➤➤➤➤➤➤➤➤➤❮❮❮❮❮❮❮❮❮❮❮❮❮-

Whitley

I looked at Layton's text message again and smiled.

What a jerk! He can't fool me. Telling him I used a vibrator on myself has to have affected him. He's just being a stubborn cowboy.

And I couldn't believe he hadn't known what TTFN meant.

I smiled again, and for the first time in years, I had butterflies in my stomach.

Oh hell no. Friends, Whitley. Only friends. No way in hell am I opening myself up to another controlling man.

My phone went off again. I read his simple reply, telling me to have a great day, and I actually believed I was going to.

"Holy fuck. Either you enjoyed the book, or you got laid last night— and not by B.O.B. Which one is it?"

I looked up at Courtney, who looked like she was about to step onto a red carpet.

"Jesus, where in the hell are you going, all dressed up like that?"

"To your appointment. Where else? If you want me to help you with your business, I'm going to have to actually see what in the hell it is you do. Plus, I want to scope this Olivia bitch out."

Ugh. Just the mention of her name caused my skin to crawl. The way she had looked at me last night had given me the creeps. For someone engaged to be married, she couldn't keep her eyes off of Layton all night.

"Okay. Well, I think it's great you want to go with me. Plus, I need to use your truck, and I don't think I could even drive that thing, but—"

"But, nothing! I'm coming."

I let out a laugh. "That's fine, but she lives in the middle of the country, and yesterday, I was so overdressed that it was unreal. Jeans and a shirt will do just fine," I said with a wink.

"Oh, can I wear my cowboy boots?"

"Sure! I'll wear mine, too."

She sat down and smiled. "Okay. Now, back to that huge-ass smile that was on your face when I walked in here. Spill it."

I smiled as I thought about Layton's playful side. He'd seemed so serious yesterday, so it was nice to see he had a bit of a fun side.

"It's nothing really."

"Did I win?" She wiggled her eyebrows up and down. "I got up at five fifteen and saw your lights on."

I smiled and felt the blush hit my cheeks.

"Holy shit! You used it, didn't you?"

"Well, oh my God, Court! How could I not? Those sex scenes were amazing, and then talking to Layton…"

Oh. Fuck.

Courtney jumped and damn near knocked her chair over. "What? Talking to Layton? When in the hell were you talking to Layton?" She put her hands up to her mouth and started laughing. "Tell me you didn't do that with him on the phone?"

What? "Oh my God! No, Courtney! I'm not a slut, for fuck's sake!"

She slowly dropped her hands down to her sides, and the smile on her face caused me to laugh.

"What?" I said.

"Oh, don't *what* me! You were talking to Layton last night? What were y'all talking about? Spill it, Whitley Ashley Reynolds."

I started to laugh.

Why am I feeling so giddy? You need to get yourself under control, Whitley. Now.

"Okay, will you calm the hell down if I tell you?"

She clapped her hands together and grinned from ear to ear. "No promises, but I will attempt to calm myself."

"Okay…well, last night, I was feeling really bad for what I'd said to him since he really was kind of like my hero yesterday. So, I sent him a text that just said I was sorry. We got to texting back and forth, and I kind of told him about—"

"About what? What!"

"The bet we made."

Courtney fell back in her seat. "Mother of all things good, you told him about the vibrator bet? Whitley…you damn tease!"

I couldn't help it. I started laughing. "Well, he was in such a playful mood, and I wanted to see how far he would take it."

"And?" She moved her whole body closer.

The look in her eyes almost had me pissing in my pants from laughing. "He was a perfect gentleman."

Her face dropped. "No. He didn't bite?"

I shook my head. "Nope. Bastard was cool as a cucumber. So, you see…he doesn't look at me in any other way but friendship—just like I look at him."

Courtney shook her head. "I'm…I'm so damn confused." She stood and started walking over to the coffee pot. "What in the hell is wrong with these Texas men? I mean, his damn friend Reed was the same way. I think I

could have pulled off my shirt and shook my titties in his face, and he wouldn't have budged."

I busted out laughing again. "Oh God, Court! Hey, do you like Reed? I loved his name. It was fitting for you."

She smiled and shook her head. "That's about the only thing appealing about him—his damn name."

I raised my eyebrows at her.

She let out a sigh. "Fine. He's hot as hell. My God, he looks like a young Colin Farrell. I bet he's good in bed." She wiggled her eyebrows up and down and grinned.

I stood and shook my head. "Come on, let's get ready to go. You're going to love Mrs. Pierceson. She is a hoot."

"Yes! Off to break my baby in on some good ole country roads!"

→≫≫≫≫≫≫≫≫≫≫≪≪≪≪≪≪≪≪≪≪≪←

As we pulled up to the Piercesons' gate, Courtney let out a gasp. "Mother of God, I thought my parents had money!"

I laughed. "I know, right? You should see Layton's place. My God, it's my dream home."

Courtney looked over and smiled as she raised her eyebrows.

"Stop it, Court!" I said with a giggle.

I couldn't believe how happy I was today. I knew it was because I was starting my new life, and I already had two jobs lined up. As much as Court had tried to say that it was because of my message fest with Layton last night, I knew that wasn't true.

Courtney pulled up and parked her truck next to a BMW. We both jumped out and started to make our way up to the house. The front door opened, and Olivia came walking out with the biggest, fakest smile I'd ever seen.

"I don't like her," Courtney said.

I smiled back at her and whispered, "Neither do I."

"Well, hello, Whitley! Who's your sidekick here?"

"Good morning, Olivia," I said. "This is my best friend and business partner, Courtney Will."

Olivia looked Court up and down, like she was a bug that needed to be stepped on and killed immediately. "Well, welcome, Courtney. My Justin and Aunt Mimi are in the study. Come on in, and follow me."

Olivia turned, and we both followed her into the house. Courtney spun around and gave me a look that caused me to choke from holding back a laugh.

Olivia glared at me. "Do you need some water?"

The way she was staring at me made my skin crawl. "Um…no, thank you. I just had a tickle in my throat."

She gave me a slight smile, turned, and kept walking. She stepped up to two huge double doors and opened them. I smiled when I saw Mrs. Pierceson sitting there with Justin. I glanced over toward Justin, who was practically eye-fucking Courtney.

Men—they are all the same.

Olivia cleared her throat, and that seemed to bring her fiancé back to his senses. "Mimi, Justin, this is Courtney Will, Whitley's best friend and business partner."

Justin stood and walked over to shake Court's hand while Mrs. Pierceson followed.

"How wonderful! Miss Will, how long have you been in the party-planning business? And please, girls, I would like for you both to call me Mimi," she said with such a sincere smile.

Courtney looked at me like she didn't know what to say. I just grinned and nodded.

"Well, honestly, Mimi, this is all very new to me. My real full-time job is working as a freelance editor."

"Really? How exciting. What types of books do you edit?"

Ah hell, here we go.

Courtney smiled big. "Most of it is contemporary romance, but I also edit paranormal and thrillers, and I have some nonfiction thrown in there every now and then," she said with a wink.

"You read books for a living?" Olivia asked with sarcasm oozing out of her mouth.

Court's smile faded for one brief second. "I do a little bit more than just read them. I love my job. Plus, I can work anywhere I want, and it allows me to do other things that interest me, like helping Whitley."

Mimi clapped her hands and laughed. "Oh, Courtney, you and I are going to have to talk later. I love to read, and I need some new smut."

Olivia turned to her aunt with a shocked look on her face.

Courtney laughed and nodded. "I'd love to."

Olivia sucked in a deep breath and slowly let it out. "Shall we get to planning the parties now?"

For the next hour, we talked about both parties. I made notes and wrote down ideas. I got the feeling that poor Justin was just going along with this to please Olivia. She seemed to have a hidden agenda behind this party, but I just couldn't put my finger on what it was.

I needed to make a trip into Austin—that was for sure. I'd been dying to go to Austin ever since Court and I had moved here. When I mentioned heading into Austin later to look for some items for Olivia's engagement party, I saw Court's eyes light up.

Olivia stood and smiled. "So, now that business is out of the way, I see you girls are dressed perfectly for pleasure."

Courtney and I glanced at each other.

I looked back at Olivia and gave her a weak smile. "What did you have in mind?"

Her fake-ass smile grew bigger. "Horseback riding, of course. You girls do know how to ride, right? I mean, I know y'all are from New York and all, but riding is so easy. Anyone can do it. I use to barrel race in high school."

I saw Courtney sit up straight, and I quickly looked at her and winked. I turned back to Olivia.

What a royal bitch! If she wants to play that way…well then, have at it, honey.

"Oh, well, you know, I've been around a horse or two in my life. We could certainly give it a try."

The Cheshire Cat smile spreading across Olivia's face just about had me gagging.

"Well then, let's go, ladies. Justin, Mimi, will you excuse us for some girl time?"

They both nodded.

"Girls, now, be careful and have fun," Mimi called out.

I asked Olivia, "Do you mind if I run to Courtney's truck to put my things away and grab my sunglasses?"

"Of course not. Do you remember how to get to the barn? I've already called down to the stables and had them saddle up some horses, so y'all don't have to worry about trying to do something you're not familiar with," she said with a shit-eating grin.

As Court and I walked to the truck, I was getting angrier by the second.

"Oh. My. God. Who in the hell does she think she is?" I balled my fists.

"How long are you planning on playing the we-are-stupid-city-folk role? 'Cause I really want to kick her in the teeth right about now." Courtney turned and looked over her shoulder.

I shook my head. "What a damn bitch. What in the hell did Layton *ever* see in her?"

"Beats me. Maybe the blonde hair, big tits, and blue eyes? Probably rocked his world in bed, too."

I stopped and just looked at her. "Really?"

"What? You asked, and I gave you my thoughts. If you don't want to hear my thoughts, don't ask me the question, bitch."

The whole way from the truck to the barn, I couldn't shake the image of Layton and Olivia together.

-➤➤➤➤➤➤➤➤➤➤➤➤➤➤❮❮❮❮❮❮❮❮❮❮❮❮❮❮❮-

We rode for about forty-five minutes, and even though I was pretty sure we were heading toward Layton's property, I couldn't be certain. I wasn't so great with directions. Courtney was playing the whole city-girl act to a tee.

"How are you girls doing?" Olivia asked with a smile as she looked over her shoulder at us.

"Doing great!" I called back.

Then, I heard male voices.

"Oh, wow! Looks like Layton is out riding with some friends," Olivia said with a slight smile.

She took off so fast that I had to hold my horse back from wanting to run right along with her horse.

Courtney trotted up next to me. "You get the feeling she knew he was going to be out riding?"

I had the sickest feeling in my stomach. "Yeah, I do. I also get the feeling she thinks she's going to embarrass us in front of them."

Courtney let out a gasp. "Fuck me. Why is he here?"

I looked over and saw Layton, Kevin, and Reed. My heart felt like it dropped into my stomach when I saw Layton.

"Who? Kevin or Reed?"

"Reed. Blah. He's such an asswipe."

I let out a laugh. "He's a nice guy, Court."

I watched as Olivia rode up and started talking to Layton. He seemed pissed. He looked over toward Court and me, and when our eyes met, my stomach started to flutter.

Stop it, Whitley—right now. You don't like him that way.

My breath was taken away by the smile he was giving me.

Good Lord, his smile is breathtaking—that dimple and those lips.

Courtney leaned closer to me and whispered, "Is it just me, or does his smile cause your panties to just melt?"

I snapped my head over and glared at her.

She laughed and winked. "Nope, it's clearly not just me!"

"Fuck off, Lollipop!"

"Lollipop?"

Courtney and I both turned to see the guys all riding up to us, and Reed was smiling.

Court's face turned fifty shades of red. "Yeah, it's a stupid nickname that Whitley gave me when we were little."

Reed smiled from ear to ear. "What's your favorite lollipop?"

Courtney smirked back. "Blow Pops."

Reed's smile faded. "Um…"

Courtney smiled and winked at him. She really was good at this shit.

When I glanced over toward Layton, I saw he was just staring at me. I smiled, and the smile he returned would have brought me to my knees if I had been standing.

"So, CG, you any good on that horse?" he asked with a wink.

I looked over at Olivia. The smile on her face answered all my earlier questions. She had known Layton and his friends would be out riding. She was trying to set me up to look like a stupid city girl from New York.

Okay, Whitley, time to reach in and pull out your inner cowgirl, and show this bitch she messed with the wrong girl.

I grinned. "I bet I could hold my own against you and your Thoroughbred."

Olivia, Kevin, and Reed all laughed.

"Oh hell, Layton, I believe she just challenged you and your horse," Kevin said.

Layton gave me a crooked smile that melted my heart completely. For the first time in years, I actually wanted to be with another man besides Roger.

Oh, for the love of God, Whitley, stop this. You don't want Layton.

I shifted in my seat and looked over at Courtney, and she smiled a wide-ass grin at me.

Layton laughed. "You want to race me, CG? You think you can keep up with me?"

I peeked at Olivia, who was now glaring at Layton. She clearly didn't like the fact that Layton was not only flirting with me, but he was also enjoying the little banter we had going back and forth.

So am I—more than I want to admit.

"Oh, cowboy, I'm sure I can do just about anything you can do…and do it just as well, if not better."

"You want to make that a bet?" Layton said as he looked over and winked at Courtney.

She busted out laughing, causing Reed, Kevin, and Olivia to all turn and look at her.

I couldn't help but smile as I remembered that I'd told him I didn't like to lose bets. "What's the bet?"

He looked around and then back toward me. "If I win, you have to sit in my deer stand with me, but I bet you won't last two hours. There's no talking, no moving, nothing until we see a buck walk up."

"I'm not killing a deer!" I said as my heart started pounding.

Layton threw his head back, laughing.

Damn it, I swear the feeling between my legs is going to drive me insane. Why do I want him so much?

Fuck! Don't let him do this to you, Whitley. He's only a friend.

"It's not even hunting season, CG. I win, and you have to sit with me in my stand until we see a deer. You win…and I'll let you decide what you want."

I smiled. I didn't really think my quarter horse was going to beat Layton's, so I pretty much knew I was going to lose. I was only playing this game to annoy Olivia.

Shit. How hard could it be to sit in a damn deer stand? I've seen at least fifteen deer a night in my front yard. I've so got this. Plus, it would drive Olivia nuts to know I'd be spending time alone with Layton in his deer stand. That's what the bitch gets.

"You're on. Where are we racing to?"

Layton turned and looked out in the open field. "You see the third oak tree down there—the largest one you can see from here?"

I glanced over toward where he was pointing and saw it. *Shit.* That had to be at least a half a mile away. I had no idea how this horse would run.

"Yep, I see it."

I walked the horse up next to Layton. I quickly glanced over at him, and his beautiful blue eyes captured mine. I couldn't even think. He seemed to be locked into our trance just as much as I was.

He smiled and leaned closer to me. "I know you're a fast reader, CG. I don't know how fast you are at self-satisfaction…yet."

My smile dropped, and I felt my cheeks blush. *I can't believe he just said that to me!*

"But let's see how fast you are on a horse." He winked, and reaching up, he tapped my nose with his finger.

When he touched me, I instantly felt a hot tingle travel throughout my body. *What in the hell? I can't let him do this to me. I will not fall for him.* I shook my head to clear my thoughts.

He laughed and winked at me.

That fucker knows what he just did to me!

"Get ready to eat my dust, asshole." I gave him a dirty look.

"On three then?" he asked with a wicked smile.

"On three."

As soon as Layton hit three, I kicked the shit out of my horse and took off. For most of the time, I stayed neck and neck with him. He looked over at me and smiled as he did something to his horse, and the next thing I knew, he was gone.

Holy shit! That's a fast horse.

By the time I reached the third oak tree, he was already there, waiting for me.

"Holy shit! Why is that horse not training for racing?" I tried my best to catch my breath from all the excitement.

He laughed and winked at me as he ran his hand up and down the neck of the chestnut Thoroughbred gelding. "Buck here is a retired winner. He actually won me close to a million dollars in the few races he was in."

My mouth dropped open. *Oh. My. God. He totally just played me.*

"You are such a jerk, Layton Morris. Ugh!" I turned the horse and started to head back toward everyone.

I heard him laughing behind me.

"Oh, come on, CG. You walked right into that one! Didn't I tell you I raised and had racehorses?"

I rolled my eyes. "Yes, you did tell me that, Layton."

He came up, riding his horse next to mine. "I'm impressed at how well you ride, Whitley. I think I'm going to have to change the meaning of CG from city girl to country girl," he said with a sweet smile.

I couldn't help but smile back at him. "Thank you. I actually love riding. I always have, and I've always been a cowgirl at heart."

Layton smiled. "Why do I get the impression that Olivia was surprised by the fact that you could ride?"

"Ha! Why do I get the impression that she *knew* you would be out riding, and somehow, she was trying to show me up?"

Layton's smile faded as he looked away. We rode for a bit in silence.

"What are you doing this evening?" I wasn't even sure why I had asked.

He let out a sigh and shook his head. "Heading into Austin. Kevin and Reed want to check out some club."

I snapped my head over to him. "Really? Court and I are going to Austin! I've never been. We're going to look at a few stores for Olivia's engagement party."

Layton's smile faded for one brief second before another one of his amazing, panty-melting, dimpled smiles returned.

His eyes lit up. "Can I take you out to dinner tonight in Austin?"

Jesus, between his eyes and that smile, he could drive a girl mad.

I smiled and nodded. "What about Courtney?"

"That was an open invitation for both of y'all," he said with a smirk.

For some reason, it disappointed me that he didn't want to spend time alone with just me. I grinned and looked away.

"What time are you planning on heading into Austin?" he asked.

I pulled out my cell phone and looked at it. "Probably around three. That way, we'll have a few hours to look around."

"Perfect. How about I call you around six? I have the perfect place to take y'all for dinner."

I heard Courtney laughing, so I looked up, and I saw Olivia glaring at Layton and me.

"Do me a favor, cowgirl?"

I smiled and looked at him. I loved hearing him call me that. "Of course."

"Don't mention Austin in front of Olivia, okay?"

I frowned and then gave him a small smile. "Okay. Wait—dress code for this place?"

He started to look me up and down, and I couldn't help it, but I licked my lips. The sight of him looking at me like that turned me on so damn much. His eyes landed on my lips, and I swore I heard him let out a small moan.

His eyes locked onto mine. "Don't change, cowgirl. You look beautiful. I mean, you look perfect."

I felt the blush instantly warm my cheeks. I looked away and grinned at Courtney. She winked and smiled back.

"So, Whitley, Courtney here enlightened us all about your riding experience," Olivia said, looking pissed.

I shrugged my shoulders. "I really need to head back now, Olivia. I have a ton of things to do to get ready for both parties."

She gave me a fake smile and turned to Layton. "Are you free later?"

Layton quickly gave Reed a look. It was almost like a keep-your-fucking-mouth-shut look.

"Sorry, Liv, guys' night out tonight. Maybe another day."

He turned and made his way back to the makeshift gate. I hadn't even noticed before how the three of them had gotten on to Mimi's property.

Courtney leaned over and whispered to me, "How in the hell did she know where they would be?"

I rolled my eyes. "Who in the hell knows? Her powers must be stronger than we thought!" I winked and turned the horse around.

We followed Olivia, and this time, we pretty much galloped all the way back to the barn.

Courtney and I said our good-byes and made our way to Courtney's truck. Once we got in and started to head down the driveway, we both busted out laughing.

"My God, she is the biggest bitch I've ever met in my life, and believe me when I say that I've met a lot of bitches," Courtney said.

I laughed as I shook my head. I was just about to tell Courtney the plans for this evening when I felt my phone go off in my pocket. I pulled it out and saw I had a text from Layton. My stomach did a little flutter.

Layton: Thank you for this morning. And last night. I haven't smiled this much in a long time.

Whitley: I could say the same thing. I'm looking forward to dinner.

Layton: Me, too, cowgirl.

I leaned my head back in the seat and closed my eyes.

"Spill it, Whit."

I looked over at my best friend and smiled. "Spill what?"

"That goofy-ass grin on your face. Who was the text from?"

"Layton."

"Really?"

"I guess they're going into Austin tonight to some club or something. He said he wanted to take you and me out to dinner. I asked him what to wear, and he told me not to change."

"Shit. Where exactly is he planning on taking us to dinner? Cheap bastard!"

I laughed so hard I almost peed my pants. "Let's just go home. I need to get some things together before we head into Austin."

"Is Reed going? God, please tell me he isn't going, too."

"Um…Layton mentioned both Reed and Kevin, and he did say it was a guys' night out, so I'm sure Reed will be with him."

"Ugh, shit! He gets on my nerves. He has no damn sense of humor."

"Court, I think he's just never met anyone like you before. I mean, did you see his face when you said Blow Pops were your favorite lollipop? I thought he was going to pass out!"

We both started laughing again.

Court started saying all this shit about Reed, and I couldn't stop laughing.

"Oh shit! I think I might have just peed in my pants!"

Courtney hit the brakes, and I was slammed back into my seat by the seat belt.

Fuck! My ribs were still killing me from when Roger had kicked them.

"What in the hell, Court!"

"Get out!"

I looked at her, shocked. "What?"

"Get the hell out of my truck, pissy-pants."

"Oh my God, you freak! I didn't really piss in my pants. You're insane, do you know that?"

"Sorry, I might have panicked just a little."

"A little, Court? More like a lot!"

We drove the rest of the way home almost in silence. I could tell she was deep in thought—about what, I didn't know. I thought back to my short ride with Layton on the horses. I wasn't sure what it was that had me thinking about him, but I couldn't get him out of my mind.

Maybe I shouldn't go to dinner with him?

Every time I was around him, I needed to remind myself that we were only friends.

Friends. Just friends. Nothing more…ever.

TEN
-»»»»»»»«««««««««-
LAYTON

I sat at my kitchen island and listened to Kevin and Reed talking. My mind kept drifting back to the horse race with Whitley. I hadn't been the least bit surprised she could ride as well as she had. I knew deep down inside she had a bit of a country girl in her. I smiled, thinking of the look on her face when I'd called her cowgirl and how she'd clearly enjoyed it.

"Layton? Hello? Earth to Layton?" Reed was snapping his damn fingers in my face.

I pushed his hands away and stood.

"What in the hell are you thinking about?" Reed asked.

"It's more like, *who* are you thinking about?" Kevin asked with a smile.

"I'm thinking about the horse Lucky talked to me about earlier. Looks like I'm going to Kentucky to buy me a new racehorse."

"Shit. I wish I were out of the corps. I'd totally go with you. That was the one thing I loved about Mike being…" Kevin stopped talking as he looked away and then back at me.

I smiled. "Kev, you can talk about him. I want to talk about him. He'll always be a part of our lives."

Kevin gave me a weak smile. "So, what are the plans for tonight? Hitting Austin, right?"

Reed jumped up. "Hell yeah! I already called Bill and Richard. They're in for heading to Austin."

I wanted to cringe when Reed had mentioned Richard. I hadn't asked Whitley about going to a club, but I figured with them being in Austin, they'd be up for it.

"Are they going?" I asked.

Reed just looked at me. "Hell yeah, they're going."

"Listen, I told Whitley I wanted to take her and Courtney out to dinner tonight since they're heading into Austin this afternoon to do some shopping for the parties she's planning."

I noticed Reed stand up a little straighter.

"Really?" Reed asked.

Kevin shook his head and laughed. "I'm gonna take off. Thanks for letting us crash and for the ride, Layton. I'll meet y'all in Austin. Reed, you riding with me or heading in yourself?"

Reed glanced back at me. "Nah, I think I'll drive in with Layton."

I tried not to smile, but I knew the only reason the fucker wanted to drive with me is because of Whitley and Courtney.

He better have his sights on the right fucking girl.

Shit! You're not interested in Whitley. She's only a friend. Only a friend, Layton, that's all.

"Okay, see y'all later." Kevin grabbed his bag and headed out the front door.

I turned back and looked at Reed. "Which one?"

"What?" he asked, looking confused.

"Which one of the girls do you have your sights on, Reed? Courtney or Whitley?"

He grinned that big ole grin of his. "I don't know what you mean. Dude, I don't have my sights on either one. Plus, it's pretty fucking clear you like Whitley. Olivia even saw it, and let me tell you, it drove her nuts. She was damn near chomping at the bit while y'all were just riding back slower than molasses after the race."

Well, that caught my attention. "Really? What did she say?"

"Layton, please don't do this to yourself."

"I just asked a question, Reed. What was she saying?"

He shrugged his shoulders. "I don't know. She was super pissed when Courtney told her Whitley's been riding for years. Then, she just kept making comments."

"Like, what kind of comments?" I wanted to grab him and shake it out of him.

"Dude, I don't fucking know. Shit like, why were y'all taking so long to get back and what in the hell were y'all talking about. Layton, please don't use Whitley. I like her. She seems really sweet. In a strange way, even Courtney is somewhat appealing."

"She's just a friend, Reed. I keep telling you that, and I've already told Olivia that. I can't help what Olivia thinks. Are you staying here or going home to change?"

He looked down toward the floor. "Layton, it's okay to move on. You know that, right? Mike would want you to be happy. And Olivia doesn't deserve your love."

I slapped him on the back and nodded. "I know he would, and I'm trying, Reed. I've only ever loved three people in my life since my mother died. Two of them left me, and I gave my heart and soul to Olivia. I just don't think I can give it to anyone else."

"Layton, you need someone to love. Everyone does. Just keep an open mind to it. That's all I'm saying. I see how you look at Whitley, and I see how she looks at you. You're both going to have to learn to let love back in."

"What do you mean? What do you know about Whitley?"

Reed looked everywhere but at me as he started stepping back and forth.

"Reed!" I yelled.

"Fuck! Fine, but you can't let her know that anyone knows. Please, Layton."

"I won't." My heart was beating a mile a minute.

"I don't know much, but I guess right when Whitley moved here, she went and saw Dr. Martin, and you know, Wes works there. Wes told me last night that Whitley had all kinds of bruises all over her body, including some really bad bruised ribs. She claimed she had been in a wreck, but Wes said it was classic abuse, and Dr. Martin questioned Whitley about it. I guess Whitley broke down and asked Dr. Martin not to tell a soul. She moved to Llano to get away from her ex and to start a new life."

My knees about buckled out from underneath me, and I felt sick to my stomach. "Why in the fuck is your sister telling you that, Reed? That's private information. Wes could get fired. Who in the hell else has she told?"

"Jesus, Layton! No one. The only reason she told me is because she saw me talking to Whitley, and Wes asked me to keep an eye on her and not to let her get hurt by some fuckwad. Wes was looking out for Whitley, Layton, that's all. Wes told me she talked to Whitley. She really liked her and was just worried about her."

I had to hold on to the counter. *Oh my God. What kind of an asshole would ever hit someone so amazing? Why would someone hit any woman at all?*

"Reed…" I grabbed a chair and sat down. I put my head in my hands. I wanted to throw up. "But…she's so headstrong. So…how could she ever let…how long?"

Reed shook his head. "I don't know. Wes thought she'd heard Whitley tell the doc they'd been together since high school."

"Fuck…that poor girl."

"Please, Layton, don't let her know you know. Wes could lose her job, and she instantly fell in love with Whitley's sweet personality. Wes just wants someone to look after her."

I nodded. "Of course…yeah, don't worry, Reed. I'll never bring it up to her." I needed some fresh air. I stood and started toward the back door. "I need some air."

"I'll be by in a little bit. Layton?"

I stopped and waited for him to talk.

"Are you okay?"

I nodded and walked out the door. The moment I got outside, I practically ran toward the barn. When I got into the barn, I fell to the ground.

All I could see was her beautiful green eyes looking into mine—so sweet and innocent and so damn beautiful. The thought of some asshole beating her had my blood boiling over. If I knew who this guy was and where to find him, I would get on a plane and go beat the fucker until he couldn't move.

"What am I supposed to do, Mike? I love Olivia…but Whitley has brought something out in me that I buried deep, so deep down inside. She makes me feel…happy…alive." I laughed as I shook my head. "I've only known her two damn days. What the hell is wrong with me? Help me, Mike. I can't take another woman hurting me. I won't let it happen."

I lay back and stared up at the ceiling of the barn. I closed my eyes and thought back to the day Mike and I had finished building this barn.

➤➤➤➤➤➤➤➤➤➤❯❮❮❮❮❮❮❮❮❮❮❮❮❮

Senior Year

"Someday, Layton, you're going to walk into this barn with the love of your life. You're going to raise a family here. Both of us are."

I laughed and smacked Mike on the back. "Dude, I've already brought Liv in here about twenty times while we've been building it."

Mike frowned and walked to the other side of the barn to start putting up the tools.

"Why don't you like Liv? I love her, Mike."

He slowly turned and smiled at me. "Layton, it doesn't really matter if I like Olivia or not."

"It does, Mike. It means everything to me. When we get married, I don't want my brother standing up next me, hating on the woman I'm about to marry."

Mike took a deep breath and rubbed the back of his neck with his hand. "Layton, she doesn't deserve you. She treats you like shit. I'm pretty sure she's fucked around on you, and I just don't trust her."

"Wow. Shit, Mike, you certainly didn't hold back. Olivia would never cheat on me—ever. You don't know her like I do. She's high-maintenance, yes, but I love her, and she loves me."

Mike grinned as he walked up to me and put his hand on my shoulder. "Then, that's all that matters, Layton. Just…please keep an open eye with her. I don't believe in my heart that she's the one for you. You've always had this dream of being with her. You've talked about her blonde hair and

blue eyes." He let out a gruff laugh. "Honestly, in my dreams, I see a beautiful brunette with stunning deep green eyes as the love of your life."

I threw my head back and laughed. "Fucker…you just described your damn fiancée! I don't think Jen would appreciate me moving in on her."

Mike laughed and shook his head. "I'm just saying, please don't rush into anything with Olivia. Get through school, we'll finish up the house, and then let's get our place up and running full speed. Keep your heart open, Layton. Keep it open for that one girl who's going to wake up something deep down inside of you."

⟶≫≫≫≫≫≫≫≫≫≫≫≫≫≪≪≪≪≪≪≪≪≪≪≪≪≪⟵

I pulled out my cell phone and sent a text to Whitley.

Layton: It's close to six. Y'all hungry?

Whitley: Yes! Done shopping, and I'm starving!

I sent her the address to where we were going to have dinner.

⟶≫≫≫≫≫≫≫≫≫≫≫≫≫≪≪≪≪≪≪≪≪≪≪≪≪≪⟵

"This is where you're taking them? Holy shit, dude. You do know that you've got thousands of dollars in your bank account, right?"

I turned around and looked at my favorite food trailer in Austin— Honky Tonk Hot Dogs.

"What? It's a must to eat at a food trailer when you come to Austin. They'll love it."

"They're from New York! Aren't fucking food trailers all over the place there?"

I smiled as I shook my head and pulled out my ringing cell phone. "Hello?"

"Um…Layton, it's Whitley. I don't think you gave me the right address. The place where we are walking up to is like a food trailer park."

I laughed as I looked up and saw them both girls walking toward us. Courtney had a huge smile on her face and was snapping pictures with her cell phone.

"It certainly looks like Courtney likes it," I said with a laugh.

The moment I saw the smile spread across Whitley's face, my heart started jumping around in my chest.

Why would anyone ever hurt such a beautiful soul?

I had to shake the image of her being hurt out of my head. I needed to push it back and wait until she was ready to tell me on her own.

Her eyes caught mine, and my smile grew bigger.

"I see you," she said with a giggle.

"I saw you first." I pulled my cell phone away and hit End.

When I looked over at Reed, he had his mouth hanging open.

"What in the hell is wrong with you?" I asked him.

He slowly shook his head. "Nothing."

"Honky Tonk Hot Dogs? This is where we're having dinner?" Whitley laughed.

I smiled as I leaned in and kissed her and then Courtney on their cheeks.

"Best hot dogs you'll ever have. I know how to treat the ladies," I said with a wink.

"Hey, Whitley, Courtney," Reed said as he smiled at Whitley, barely looking at Courtney.

"Hey, Reed!" Whitley said.

Courtney smiled and just nodded.

"I'm starving. What should I order?" Whitley hooked her arm through mine, and we made our way up to the trailer.

"Well, my favorite is the Jesse Dayton's Jumbo Deep-Fried Bacon 'n Brisket Oil Rig Dog. It's a jumbo dog wrapped in bacon, fried, and then topped with brisket, onions, jalapenos, barbeque sauce, and cheddar cheese. My mouth is watering just from talkin' about it." I smiled.

"Um…holy shit. I don't think I want to have a heart attack today," Courtney said.

I glanced down at Whitley, and her eyes were wide open.

"You eat all that on a hot dog?"

She scrunched up her nose in that cute way. I was overcome with an incredible desire to reach down and kiss her.

Shit! I need to not feel sorry for her. That's all this is. I know what happened to her, and I feel guilty. That's it. That's all this feeling is.

I just shrugged my shoulders.

"What are you getting, Reed?" Courtney asked.

"The Dallas Wayne Chili Mac Dog."

Courtney turned and looked at him. "Oh. My. God. That sounds gross! Eww, mac and cheese on a hot dog? What the hell is wrong with the water in Texas?"

Reed laughed and walked up to place his order. He turned around and motioned for Courtney to order. She ordered The Scott Dog, and Reed never once took his eyes off her.

After I ordered, I pulled Whitley up next to me. The moment she touched me, I felt a shock run up and down my body.

Holy shit! That hasn't happened in a long time.

The young girl behind the counter smiled at Whitley.

"What would you like, ma'am?"

"Well"—Whitley looked at the young girl's name tag—"Callie, I'll take an All-American Austin Honky Tonker with mustard and onions only." She turned and looked at me with a smile.

"Really, cowgirl? You're getting a normal hot dog?"

She smiled that drop-dead gorgeous smile of hers. "Yep! I'm just that boring."

➤➤➤➤➤➤➤➤➤➤➤❭❬❬❬❬❬❬❬❬❬❬❬❬❬

I'd never laughed so much as I did while we all sat there and ate our hot dogs. Reed and Courtney even seemed to be getting along—for now. He even got her to take a bite of his hot dog.

"Wow! That's actually really good!" Courtney said as she looked over at Whitley. "I never in my life thought I would say mac and cheese on a hot dog was good."

"I'll just take your word for it," Whitley said with a slight smile.

I got up and told everyone else to sit and relax while I cleaned off the table.

As I was walking back to the table, David Nail's "Whatever She's Got" started playing. I couldn't help but smile.

I walked up and stood in front of Whitley. "Does this cowgirl know how to two-step?"

When she looked up at me, I swore her eyes twinkled. They got more beautiful every time I peered into them.

She got up and took my hand. "Yes, she does."

I led her out to the makeshift dance floor where a few other people were dancing. I pulled her into me, and we took off two-stepping. She fit perfectly in my arms, and she smelled like heaven. She even danced like an angel.

"Where in the hell did you learn to two-step, Whitley?" I asked.

She pulled back a bit and smiled. "I told you, I'm a cowgirl at heart!"

I laughed as I pulled her back into me.

Dierks Bentley's "5-1-5-0" started playing, and I smiled as I twirled her around a few times.

"All right, let's see what you got, CG!"

As much as I tried to throw her off with twists, turns, spins, and dips, she kept up with me the whole time. By the time the song was over, she was smiling from ear to ear.

We walked back to the table, and right before we got there, she looked at me and said, "We should have made a bet."

I laughed and shook my head. There was just something about her, and I couldn't put my finger on it, but she sure knew how to make me smile.

"How would y'all like to go out with us? We're meeting Kevin and a few other guys at a club on Sixth Street."

Courtney smiled and said, "Yes!" at the same time Whitley said, "No!"

"Oh, come on, you party pooper! We're in Austin with two very handsome men. What more could you want?" Courtney said.

I noticed Reed smile when Courtney mentioned being with two handsome men.

"To finish my book!" Whitley quickly realized what she'd just said.

I leaned down and put my lips right up to her neck. The smell of her skin had my dick jumping. "Are you seriously picking your book over me, cowgirl?"

She quickly stepped away from me. "Um…"

I gave her my crooked smile, knowing damn well I'd just made her nervous.

"Whit…please! I so want to go out," Courtney said.

Whitley looked at Courtney, Reed, and then me.

"Oh God…fine. But just for a little bit. I don't want to be out late tonight, Court."

→≫≫≫≫≫≫≫≫≫≫≫≫≪≪≪≪≪≪≪≪≪≪≪≪←

I sat on the bar stool, watching Whitley dance again with Richard. I was beyond pissed. Plus, she'd been drinking like a fish. I wasn't sure what had happened, but for some reason, she was now acting like she was pissed at me. I sat there and finally finished the same beer I had been nursing since we'd gotten here a few hours ago.

I looked over toward Courtney, who was talking to some hipster asshole at the bar. Reed was out on the dance floor, dancing with some girl who I swore was not old enough to even be in the club.

I felt someone bump my shoulder.

"You haven't danced with Whitley at all, Layton," Courtney yelled over the music as she sat down on the bar stool next to me.

"She won't dance with me. Besides, I think she's pissed at me. Honestly, I'm totally fine with her dancing with Richard."

Lie. Nothing but a lie.

"Who was the pretty young blonde you danced with for four songs in a row when we first got here?" Courtney asked with one eyebrow raised.

"What? She's pissed because I danced with some girl? It's not like we're on a date, for Christ's sake."

She stood and looked at me. "Really? 'Cause the last time I checked, you fucking asked her to come out with you. The least you could have done was danced with her first before you took off and started grinding on some blonde. Maybe you were…" She stopped talking.

"Maybe I was, what?"

"Nothing. Never mind. I'm going to find Reed and make him dance with my ass." She stumbled off and walked right up to Reed on the dance floor.

He quickly took her into his arms and started dancing with her.

Good God. Who isn't drunk besides me?

Kristinia DeBarge's "Goodbye" started playing. Something happened with Whitley. I saw her down another beer, and the way she started dancing with Richard was just getting me more pissed-off.

I watched as his hands moved up and down her body. She wasn't facing him, and she started grinding her ass into his dick. I jumped up and walked out to the dance floor. I marched up to Richard and gave him a look. He just looked back at me.

"Move," I said.

"Fuck off, Layton." He went to turn back toward Whitley.

I grabbed him and pushed him away. "I said, move, asshole."

Richard held up his hands and backed away.

Whitley turned around and smiled when she saw me standing there. She inched closer to me and started to move with the beat. I put my hands on her hips and moved right along with her. She spun around and pushed herself into me.

My heart was beating so fast in my chest. She grabbed my hands and started to move them up and down her body. I felt my dick getting harder, and I didn't want her to feel it, but she just kept pushing herself into me. She stopped and turned around. Her eyes caught mine. She wrapped her arms around my neck as she slowly started dancing closer to me.

The song ended, and we just stood there.

"I want to kiss you, Layton."

My heart slammed in my chest.

She's drunk.

I leaned down and placed my lips to her ear. She let out the sweetest moan I'd ever heard.

"Honey…you're drunk. I think I need to take you home before you do something you're going to regret."

She pulled back away from me, and the tears in her eyes just about killed me.

She nodded. "Yeah…I guess so." She slowly turned and started to walk toward the bar where Courtney was standing and talking to Kevin and Reed.

Fuck me. She thinks I just turned down her kiss. Shit!

I walked up and took an assessment of everyone. Both Courtney and Whitley were drunk. Reed was halfway to drunk, and Kevin had been drinking water the whole night.

"Kevin, who did you come with?" I yelled above the music.

"I rode with Richard."

"Can you drive Courtney's truck back to her house?"

Courtney turned and looked at me. "Wait! I'm not ready to leave yet. I'm having so much fun."

"Court, I think I need to get Whitley home," I said.

Courtney turned and looked at Whitley. "Wait—why is she crying? What happened? Did you do something to hurt her, Layton?"

What? "No! I'd never hurt her. She wanted me to kiss her, and I told her I thought it was time to head home before she did something she would regret."

Courtney's face fell. "Um…I'll leave, too, but I'll ride with Kevin because if he does anything to my truck, I'll kick his ass."

Reed decided to ride with Kevin and Courtney.

I walked up to Whitley and gently took her by the arm as I leaned down to her ear. "Are you ready, honey?"

She pushed me away. "Don't call me honey, you asshole." She grabbed her purse and started toward the door.

By the time we got to my truck, she looked like she was about to get sick.

"Whit…honey, what all did you drink tonight?"

She shook her head and put her hand up to her mouth. "I don't know. Beer…and shots."

Shots? Who in the hell gave her shots?

I put my finger under her chin and brought her eyes up to look into mine. She was trashed.

"Whit, who gave you shots?"

"Um…I don't know, Layton. I can't remember."

"Whitley, I need you to try and remember. Did you know the person? Was it one of my friends? Or some guy you met tonight?"

"I don't remember. I feel sick."

Fuck! "Whitley! Try to remember!"

"I…um…I don't know."

"Who gave you the shots?" I shouted.

She jumped and looked at me. "I don't know, Roger! I don't fucking know! Oh God…I'm going to be sick."

I grabbed her, brought her over to the side of the truck, and held her hair back while she puked.

"Oh my God…oh God, please…make it stop, Layton. Please…"

It was killing me to hear her cry while she asked me to make it stop.

"Baby, I would if I could. We need to get all that alcohol out, honey. Keep throwing up if you have to."

Someone came walking up to me with baby wipes. I smiled as she handed them to me.

"Been there, done that!" she said with a wink.

I thanked her and pulled a few out.

Just when I thought Whitley couldn't puke any more, she started again.

"Oh God, I'm never gonna be able to eat a hot dog again!" she said in between her sobs.

I couldn't help it, but I had to laugh.

God, I love this girl.

Wait—what in the hell? No…I care about her as a friend, and that's all. I'll get her home, make sure she's okay, and then I'm out of there.

I needed to distance myself from her and fast.

I don't love her. I barely know her. No…it's impossible. I do not love her.

→≫≫≫≫≫≫≫≫≫≫≫≫✕≪≪≪≪≪≪≪≪≪≪≪←

I woke up to my phone ringing on the nightstand. I tried to move my arm, but Whitley was sleeping on it. I looked at her sleeping so peacefully.

Last night, I hadn't had the heart to leave her. By the time Kevin and Reed had gotten back with Courtney, she had passed out, and Kevin had carried her in and laid her down in her bed. Reed had covered her up, and I had been shocked when I saw him kiss her on the cheek and say good night to her. I had told them I was staying because Whitley kept getting sick, and I was worried about her.

My phone started ringing again. When I slid my arm out from underneath her, she rolled and put her head on my chest and started making little noises.

"Ah hell," I whispered as I reached for my phone. "Hello?"

"Layton, where in the hell are you?" Reed asked on the other end of the phone.

"What are you talking about? What time is it?"

"It's damn near ten. I'm sitting outside Lucky's office. Weren't we supposed to meet at ten thirty with the owners of that Thoroughbred you've been trying to buy for the last year?"

I flew up out of Whitley's bed. "Motherfucker! I totally forgot all about it. I'm still at Whitley's. Son of a bitch."

"Well, get your ass down here, Layton. You blow this, and Lucky won't ever train another one of your horses again."

I looked around. I was still in the same clothes I'd worn yesterday. "Reed, I'm still in my clothes from last night. And I smell like…" I tilted my head down and smelled my shirt. "Fuck, I smell like beer, vodka, and puke."

Reed started laughing. "Dude, don't you keep a spare set of clothes in your truck? Jump in the shower and then change."

"Jeans. I only have jeans. I need a shirt!" I started to make my way to Whitley's bathroom. I shut the door and turned on the shower.

"I'm on my way," Reed said.

"Great. I'm jumping in the shower now. See you in a few."

I stripped out of the clothes that smelled like a frat party gone bad and jumped into the hot water. I rinsed off and looked for a bar of soap.

Nothing.

Where in the hell is her soap?

I looked on the shelf behind me, and all I saw was an orange bottle. I picked it up and read it out loud, "Coconut Island Quench moisturizing body wash with coconut oil for soft, smooth-feeling skin." I looked around again. "What in the fuck is this shit? Where's her soap?"

After staring at the shelf for a good five minutes, willing a bar of Irish Spring to show up, I poured the damn coconut shit in my hand and rubbed it all over my body. I used her coconut shampoo in my hair as I decided I would be packing an emergency kit in my car, complete with soap and shampoo for men.

I jumped out of the shower and started drying off with her towel. I put the towel up to my nose, took a deep breath in, and smiled. It smelled like Whitley. I wrapped the towel around my waist and cracked open the door.

Whitley was still sound asleep. I ran out of the bedroom and down the stairs. Right before I got to the front door, Courtney stepped out of the kitchen, right in front of me.

I was going too fast. I couldn't stop, and I ran smack into her, which caused her to slam into the door.

"Shit!" we both called out at the same time.

She pushed me off of her and started yelling at me. "What in the fuck are you doing here? And, oh my God, why are you wrapped in a towel, looking hot as fucking hell? My eyes! Oh God, I need to wash them out."

I didn't know whether I should be happy that she had given me a compliment or worried because she was now screaming something about her eyes burning.

"Did you spill coffee in your eyes?" I asked her.

She stopped and looked at me. "Really, Layton? Good God." She moved past me and walked back into the kitchen. "What is wrong with you Texas boys? And why in the hell do you smell like coconut?"

There was a knock on the door, and I opened it to see Reed. I grabbed the shirt and the jeans he had gotten from my truck, and I headed back up the stairs.

"Court's in the kitchen. Chat for a second," I called over my shoulder.

I ran into Whitley's room and came to a stop when I saw her sleeping in bed.

She's so incredibly beautiful.

I walked up and looked down at her. She had a small smile on her face, and she was mumbling something. I bent over, trying to hear what she was saying.

"Layton...*please*..."

I stood back up and started walking backward.

She's dreaming about me. Shit. Shit. Shit.

I went to head into the bathroom, but then I stopped and turned back toward her. I slowly walked up to her, bent down, and lightly brushed my lips against hers.

Motherfucker...her lips are so soft. I want more.

"Hmm...Layton."

I smiled, knowing I was the one in her dreams.

When I stood back up, she opened her eyes. She instantly smiled and then looked me up and down.

"Am I dreaming that you're standing next to my bed...wearing nothing but a towel?"

I let out a laugh. "Nope. I'm really standing here next to your bed in a towel."

She smiled slightly and then raised her eyebrow. "Why?" Then, she sat up quickly. "Oh my God! Did we—"

"No! Jesus, Whitley, I would never take advantage of you like that. We're friends, for Christ's sake."

She fell back down to her pillow and grabbed her head. "Oh...my...God...I feel like shit," she whispered.

"Give me two seconds, honey." I turned and ran into her bathroom. I slipped on the jeans and the clean shirt Reed had brought me.

I heard my phone go off with a text message, but I ignored it as I walked out of the bathroom and up to her.

"Layton, why are you here? And why are you half-naked?" she asked.

I leaned down and brushed the hair away from her beautiful green eyes. "Honey, you were so drunk last night that I had to bring you home. You actually threw up...a lot," I said with a wink.

"No…that's impossible. I only had a few beers." She rubbed her temples.

"Whitley…can I ask you something?"

"Sure, of course."

"Who is Roger?"

Her eyes snapped open, and she looked at me with fear in her eyes. "Why?"

"Well, you told me someone had given you shots to drink, and when I was trying to find out who it was, you got angry with me and called me Roger."

The moment I saw the tears welling up in her eyes, I hated myself for asking. I already had a feeling who it was—the fucker who had beaten her.

I really want to kill that motherfucker for hurting her.

"He's no one, and I'm so sorry. You're nothing like him, Layton. *Nothing.*"

I smiled, leaned over, and kissed her forehead. "I have to go. I have a meeting. What are you doing a week from today?"

The smile spreading across her face caused my stomach to drop. I wanted to make her smile like that always.

In a friendship kind of way.

"Um…I think I'm free," she said with a wink.

I stood and laughed. "Good. You're going to pay up on our bet."

She sat up and shook her head. "Wait! What? You mean the deer stand?"

I turned and grabbed my phone, keys, and wallet off of her nightstand. "Yep. I'm leaving tomorrow for Kentucky to look at a racehorse, and I won't be back until Wednesday afternoon."

I opened up the text message waiting for me. It was from Kevin, and I started to read it.

Son of a bitch. I'm going to kill that asshole.

"Layton? Did you hear me?"

I looked down at her, still sitting up in bed. "Sorry, cowgirl…I've got to go. I'm already so late for a meeting. Next Thursday? Keep it open for me?"

She smiled and nodded before I started to leave her room.

"Hey! Layton?"

I turned and looked at her.

"Thank you so much for bringing me home and taking care of me. I'm really lucky to have you as a friend," she said with a slight smile on her face.

Yep…friends. Friends only.

"Always, Whit. Bye, sweetheart. Have a good week."

As I walked down the stairs, my heart started hurting. I didn't want to leave her. I wanted to spend the day with her and make sure she was all right and felt better. I wanted to take her to the ranch and baby her.

Fuck, this is not good. I can't get attached to her.

My phone went off again, and it was another message from Kevin. When I read it, I got even angrier.

"Reed! Let's go!" I called out as I opened the front door and made my way to my truck.

Reed came running out behind me. "Finally. Dude, we only have a few minutes to get there."

"I'm going to be a little late. I need you to start the meeting and just tell them I'm held up with another meeting. I will be ten minutes late."

Reed grabbed my arm and pulled me to a stop. "What? Jesus, Layton, I know about cattle, but I don't know shit about racehorses." He made a face as he leaned in to smell me. "You smell like…a girl!"

I rolled my eyes at him. "Just small talk, Reed. You're good at that shit."

I jumped into my truck, started it, and rolled down the window.

"Layton, what in the world is more important than this?"

"Richard was the one giving shots to Whitley. This morning, he told Kevin that he had tried to get her drunk. I guess he wanted to hook up with her last night."

Reed shook his head. "What a fucking asshole. What are you going to do?"

I smiled and put the truck in drive. "I'm simply going to ask that he stay away from Whitley."

I hit the gas and headed toward the bank.

⋙⋙⋙⋙⋙⋘⋘⋘⋘⋘⋘

I walked into the bank and saw Richard talking to one of the tellers. *Bastard.*

I walked up and tapped him on the shoulder.

He turned around and smiled. "Hey, dude, where did you go last night? Everyone left."

"Did you give all those shots to Whitley?"

His smile faded a little. "Uh…I might have given her one or two to, um…loosen her up some."

I reached back, and before he even knew what was happening, I punched him. His head snapped back, and he lost his balance. I watched him tumble to the ground.

"Oh my God, Layton! What are you doing?" Susie yelled from behind the counter.

I bent down and grabbed him by his shirt. "You ever try something like that with her again, and I'll do more than just punch you. Do I make myself clear, Richard?"

He wiped the blood from his mouth as he just stared at me.

"Do I make myself clear, Richard?" I asked again.

"Yeah, Layton…crystal clear."

I pushed him back down and stood. "Sorry, Susie, I didn't mean to cause trouble."

I walked out of the bank as I made a vow that I would never let another man hurt Whitley. I'd rather die than see her hurt.

ELEVEN

-≫≫≫≫≫≫≫≫≫≫≫≪≪≪≪≪≪≪≪≪≪≪-

Whitley

I'd been sitting at the same table since six this morning, just staring at my notebook. Courtney was editing a book at home, and I needed to get out, so I told her I was heading to Fuel for a bit.

I tried to concentrate on work, but my thoughts were all over the place today. After two hours of sitting here, my mind was blank. I pretty much had Mimi's party planned. She was so easy to please, and I'd had so much fun with her this week while we had been planning the party.

Olivia's engagement party was another story. Every idea I'd given to her, she had turned down. I was beginning to think she hated me. No matter what I'd said, she'd turned her nose up to it.

Bitch! It's a damn engagement party in Llano, Texas, not New York City.

I threw my pen down and closed my eyes. That was when I saw his eyes…and felt his lips on mine. I brought my fingers up to my lips and lightly touched them. At first, I thought I had dreamed he kissed me, but the more I thought about it, the more real it became. The fact that he'd stayed with me through that night made the butterflies take off in my stomach.

The way he called me honey, cowgirl, and sweetheart made me feel so special. No one had ever called me things like that, except for my dad.

I opened my eyes and thought about Layton holding me while we'd danced.

Damn it! I really wish I could remember what it was like to have him sleeping next to me.

Damn it all to hell, Whitley. Stop this! He even said…we are friends. We're just friends.

I shook my head to clear my thoughts of Layton. It was easier said than done. He was coming home tonight, and all I could think about was our bet. I couldn't wait to see him, just to be near him.

While he had been in Kentucky, we'd talked on the phone every night, and we'd texted at least ten times during each day. And now, I was sitting here, counting down the hours until I could see him.

Ugh! This has to stop. I'm done with men, including those who have incredibly sexy bodies, irresistible lips, and breathtaking smiles. Oh, that dimple—paralyzingly handsome Layton Morris.

Maybe I should tell him I can't make it tomorrow.

When I looked up, I saw Richard walking in. I raised my hand and waved at him. He took one look at me and quickly hustled up to the counter. He'd been avoiding me for almost a week now. I'd gone into the bank once, and he'd actually gotten up and walked to the back.

I remembered we had danced a lot at that club in Austin. I kind of even remembered doing a little dirty dancing with him, but every time I tried to remember anything else, I could only see Layton turning down my kiss and then me puking outside of the club. I still cringed when I thought about calling Layton by Roger's name.

I picked up my pen and started making notes about Olivia's party. Just when I finally got my thoughts redirected, my phone started to ring. I glanced down and saw Layton's name. I almost fell out of the chair when I reached for it.

"Hello?"

"Hey, cowgirl! Did you miss me?" he asked with that sexy-ass Southern drawl of his.

Oh good Lord, I really need to stop thinking about him like this. He only wants to be friends, Whit.

"Um, I'm sorry. Who is this?" I tried to hold in my giggle.

"It's Layton!" he said, sounding offended.

I started laughing.

"You bitch! And here, I brought you back a present."

I sat up straight. "A present? Really? Layton, I *love* presents! I'm sorry! I totally knew it was you. I was kidding."

"You're gonna have to make it up to me now."

I couldn't help it, but I smiled with excitement. "Oh yeah? Like how?" My heart was beating a mile a minute.

"Have lunch with me today?"

"Are you home? I thought you weren't getting home until later this evening."

He laughed, and I felt my stomach doing crazy flips from the sound of his laughter.

"I missed my new best friend, so I came home a day early. I got in late last night."

His new best friend? Wow. He is really making sure that I know we are nothing more than friends. Fine by me.

"You just want to win that bet a day early, don't you?" I started packing up my things.

He laughed again and then sucked in a deep breath.

Holy shit…the tingling this man gives me between my legs is not anywhere near the friend zone.

"Yep, I totally want to win this bet! You up for it today?"

I took a deep breath. *Am I really going to do this? Could I do this?*

Yes, I totally can because I don't want another man in my life…at least not now.

"What time do you want me at your house?" I asked before I lost the nerve.

"Have you gotten your car back?"

"Yep. It runs great. Thank you again by the way."

"I didn't do anything but call the tow truck."

I smiled and stood as I started to put my laptop in its case. "Well, thank you for calling the tow truck."

"You're welcome, honey. How about you head out in about an hour? Will that work? I'll pack us a picnic, and we can eat at one of my favorite places on the ranch."

I sat back down in the chair. I couldn't catch my breath.

Oh my God. If he does this for just his friends, how in the hell must he treat someone he dates? He's probably unbelievably romantic.

"That sounds amazing, Layton. I'll be there in about an hour."

"See you soon, cowgirl."

I could practically hear the smile in his voice.

"Okay, bye."

I hit End and flew up out of the chair. I grabbed everything in one scoop. Even though I just lived a few blocks from the coffee shop, I was thanking God that I'd driven there this morning.

→⟩⟩⟩⟩⟩⟩⟩⟩⟩⟩⟩⟩⟩⟨⟨⟨⟨⟨⟨⟨⟨⟨⟨⟨⟨⟨⟨←

I flew into the house and dropped everything on the sofa before turning and running up stairs.

"What in the hell, Whit? Where's the fire?" Courtney yelled.

"I'm leaving for a few hours," I called down.

Do I have time to shower?

It would take me a good twenty minutes to get to his place. I still needed to change, put makeup on—

Oh shit! I have to shave!

After I quickly shaved my legs, I grabbed a pair of jeans. I figured if I was going to be sitting in a deer stand, I better have on jeans. I threw on a T-shirt and pulled my hair back into a ponytail.

"You better get a change of clothes," Courtney said.

I looked up and saw her standing in the doorway, watching my craziness.

"What? Why? And how do you know where I'm even going?"

She threw her head back and laughed. "Please, Whitley, I'm not stupid. Obviously, Layton's back and calling in his bet. Should you, um…take care of yourself before you go?" She nodded toward the drawer holding the vibrator.

I stopped dead in my tracks. "Oh. My. God. You have problems! You have serious problems, Court. Gesh…oh wow. I can't even believe you would go there."

She started laughing as she walked in and up to my closet. She pulled out a white sundress that we'd bought the day before yesterday at Ruby Cowgirls. Then, she walked over to my dresser drawer and pulled out a pair of white lace panties with a matching bra.

I just stood there, staring at her. "Why the fuck do you think I need a change of underwear?"

"Oh, Whitley, you should always carry a change of clothes with you. *Always*. I know y'all are just going to hang out at the ranch, but what if you decide to go somewhere for dinner? A girl can never be too ready to spend an evening with her, um…*friend*."

"Did you just say y'all?"

Courtney rolled her eyes and walked out of my bedroom. I finished getting ready. Then, I grabbed my things and threw them into my bag. I glanced down and saw the dress.

"Ah hell."

I grabbed the dress, panties, and bra and placed them in my bag as well.

A girl can never have too many outfit options!

➤≫≫≫≫≫≫≫≫≫≫❌≪≪≪≪≪≪≪≪≪≪≪◆

I sucked in a deep breath at the sight of Layton's house. I would never get tired of looking at his place. It was breathtaking. I grabbed my bag and purse out of the backseat and made my way to the front porch. I'd already buzzed him to let me through the gate, so he knew I was here. Right before I walked up the steps, he opened the front door.

Holy mother of all things good, he's trying to kill me.

He was dressed in a tight-ass gray T-shirt, jeans, and boots. The smile on his face almost knocked me off my feet.

"Hey, cowgirl! Look at you, dressing very appropriately, I see, for our little bet."

I laughed and shook my head. I pushed his shoulder back as I made my way into his house.

"Jesus, I forgot how beautiful it is in here. I'd never want to leave if this was my house." I turned back to him and smiled.

"Yeah? You'd like living way out here in the country?"

I laughed and nodded. "I've already put an offer in on fifty acres about three miles from here. I actually found it a few days after we'd moved here, but they've been dicking around with me. I'm just waiting to hear back."

"No shit?" He had a serious look on his face.

I smiled and winked at him. "No shit. So, I'm ready to get this bet going. How long do I have to stay in the stand?"

He gave me that damn crooked-ass grin of his. "Two hours. If you can last two hours, you win."

I bit down on my lower lip and thought about this. "What happens if I make it to the end of the two hours? Do I win something?"

He threw his head back and laughed as he started to walk toward the kitchen. "My respect isn't good enough?"

"Sorry, but no. I want something else."

He turned and looked at me. "I'll give you your surprise this evening instead of tomorrow."

I smiled and bit down on my lip again. His smile faded as he walked up to me.

He used his thumb to pull my lip out from between my teeth. "Don't do that, Whit." He spun around and started toward the refrigerator.

My lip was on fire from where he'd touched it. I'd never thought just a simple touch would drive me insane.

Damn you, Layton Morris!

He pulled something out and slipped it into a picnic basket. "You ready?"

With the way I nodded, I felt like a high school girl going on her first date.

Jesus, Whitley, calm the hell down!

-》》》》》》》》》》》《《《《《《《《《《《《-

We drove through the pastures in Layton's Jeep until he found his perfect spot. It was an open field looking out to the hill country. I jumped out of the Jeep and just stood there, staring at the horses in the pasture.

"I've never seen anything so beautiful in my life," I barely said.

He walked up and stopped next to me. "I have."

I turned to look at him. He stared out at the horses for another few seconds before turning and winking at me.

What or who is he talking about?

Probably Olivia.

He pulled out a blanket and laid it down on the ground while I grabbed the picnic basket. I sat down with the basket as he smiled and nodded for me to open it. When I did, I busted out laughing.

I reached in and grabbed the container of chicken nuggets from Chick-fil-A. "Layton, how did you even remember I said I loved these?"

"I make it my business to pay attention to what people like, what they love. Besides, when we were talking on the phone the other day, I promised you that I'd buy you a shitload of Chick-fil-A nuggets. When you said you had eaten there and had died and gone to heaven, I knew I had to bring some home to you."

"You big at keeping promises?" I asked with a laugh.

His smile faded, and he looked out toward the horses. "Yes, I am. I never go back on my promises—*ever*."

I could almost feel his pain. My heart broke for him, and I was wondering what in the world he was thinking about. I wanted so badly to ask him about his brother, but I didn't.

"Well, I'm glad. These nuggets are so good, especially cold! I would have never thought they would be good cold."

He looked back at me and smiled, but I saw the hurt in his eyes.

We ate in silence until he clapped his hands, scaring the shit out of me.

"Time to hit the stand, sweetheart!" he said with a wink.

I jumped up and started to clean up our picnic. After I was done, I hopped up into the Jeep and sat there, waiting for him. I turned, and he was just standing there, staring at me.

"What?"

"Babe, the stand is right there."

He pointed to a giant deer stand that I hadn't even noticed was there.

"Holy shit, you want me to climb up that?" I just looked at him.

He smiled and nodded.

"How high is that, Layton?"

"It's just ten feet, Whit, that's all."

"Ten feet! Layton, I'm afraid of heights!"

He walked up to me and grabbed my hand. He led me over toward the stand. The whole way there, he rubbed his thumb up and down along my index finger, and the butterflies in my stomach were going crazy. I wasn't sure if it was from the idea of being that high or the fact that he was holding my hand or a combination of both.

After he got me to climb up, I got settled into a seat. He sat down and then reached into his back pocket.

"Here—now, the outfit is complete." He put a camouflage hat on me.

When I laughed and pulled it down, my hand brushed against his. The look in his eyes told me he felt the same thing I felt every time we touched.

I sat there for a good forty minutes, perfectly still, and it was killing me.

Come on, you stupid bucks! I see you every damn night in my front yard. Where in the hell are you?

Layton reached over and put his hand on my leg. I looked down to see I was swinging my legs.

Shit!

After another fifteen minutes went by, he slowly turned and looked at me. I peeked up at him, and he laughed.

"Jesus, Whit...stop humming!" he whispered.

"Oh shit, am I?"

"Yeah, you are."

I smiled. "Sorry, I thought I was being quiet."

With his finger, he pulled my chin to look me in the eyes. "Honey, stop sniffling, too."

"But my nose is running."

"Let it run," he whispered.

"Eww, gross, Layton. I'm not letting my nose run." I shuddered at the thought and turned away from him. I quickly wiped my nose and prayed it would stop running.

Why in the hell is it running in the middle of July anyway?

I glanced over at his watch.

Yes! It's almost been two hours, and I haven't asked to get down yet.

I slowly looked back out the window, and I saw a huge buck walking up. It was beautiful, the most breathtaking creature I'd ever seen. I counted really quickly. It was a big twelve point. *He is huge.* As he got closer, I felt the excitement building. He walked right up toward us, and when he glanced up, I swore he looked me right in the eyes. I let out a gasp and brought my hands up to my mouth. The buck snorted and ran off.

Oh...shit.

I turned to see Layton glaring at me.

He was shaking his head. "If I'd been hunting, do you know how pissed-off I'd be right now?"

I felt the heat move across my cheeks. "Oops."

His mouth dropped open. "Oops? That's all you've got? You're never going hunting with me—*ever.* That was a heavy twelve point, Whit. A twelve point!"

"Yeah, I counted. He was big!" I smiled.

My smile quickly faded as he took his hands and rubbed them down his face.

"Oh, for Christ's sake, Layton. It's not even hunting season. Why are you getting all upset?"

"Let's go." He started to make his way down the ladder as he mumbled something about it being a huge, heavy twelve point that would look awesome on his wall.

108

I went to get down, and I froze. "Um…Layton…"

Then, it started pouring right as Layton was helping me down and out of the stand.

I glanced over at him as he drove the Jeep in the rain. He looked so damn handsome when he was mad. I looked away and giggled. He didn't think I had noticed the three times he'd placed his hands on my ass to help guide me down from the stand.

Something caught my eye, and I spun around to look at it. "Wait! Layton, stop!"

He came to a stop and looked at me.

"There's an old house back there. Can we go look at it?"

His face turned white as a ghost. "I haven't been to that house in years, Whitley."

"Oh, come on! Please? I want an adventure!"

"Driving in the rain isn't adventurous enough for you?" he asked with a small smile.

"Nope," I said.

He started to turn around, and we made our way up to the house. After he stopped, I jumped out of the Jeep and about slipped and busted my ass in the mud.

Thank God I brought the change of clothes Courtney had insisted I bring.

I had barely seen the house from the road. As I walked up to it, I could tell it was unfinished. It was a white clapboard house with a tin roof. It would have made a darling ranch house if the owners had only finished it.

I walked up onto the porch and pushed open the door. The inside was filled with old torn-up furniture.

"Please don't go in."

I turned and saw Layton standing in the yard. He looked gutted. I quickly stepped back out of house and shut the door. I glanced to my right and saw two chairs sitting on the porch.

My eyes caught the carving in the wooden rail—*Layton and Mike*. There was a date, but I couldn't make it out.

No…oh God, no.

My head snapped over to Layton. Our eyes met, and I knew it wasn't rain on his face. I walked down and took him into my arms.

He lost it and started crying. I'd never in my life seen a grown man cry.

"They both left us…he left us all alone. He never came back."

Oh God. Who is he talking about? His parents?

"Shh…it's okay. I'm here, Layton. I promise I'll never leave you. I promise."

He held me tighter in his arms. I brought my hand up and started to caress the back of his head.

"Mike did the best he could. He went into the fucking military, so I could go to college, and it cost him his life."

He began to cry harder, and my heart had never hurt so much in my life.

"He left me…alone. Everyone leaves me."

After a few minutes, he pulled away and began to walk toward the house. I saw a sign that said outhouse with an arrow pointing out into a field. I got a sick feeling in my chest.

He walked up and sat down on the porch. "I've never brought anyone here, not even Olivia."

I walked up and sat next to him. For a few minutes, we stayed like that, sitting in silence.

"My father started building this house for my mom. Then, she got cancer and died. He had to get out of the house where he'd lived with her, so he moved us out here after she'd passed away. I guess he thought this would be better, but all it did was remind him of her. *We* reminded him of her. He told us he was going out of town to look at a racehorse." He smiled as he looked at me.

"Besides the cattle, that was his thing—racehorses. It was Mike's thing, too. My dad was damn good at it, and he had the eye for a winning horse. Our dad would send money every year for the property taxes, but we never got anything extra. One day, we got a letter in the mail. My dad had signed the ranch over to us. Mike used it as motivation. He got a few jobs, and we bought cattle and slowly started saving up our money. Then, a lawyer pulled up one day when we were standing right here on these steps, trying to decide what to do with the house. Mike's high school friend Mitch, the foreman who had been working for my dad since he was practically in high school, had told him where to find us. All the lawyer did was walk up to us and hand Mike an envelope. That was it."

My heart started pounding.

"Mike opened it, and there was a check in it for half a million dollars. Turns out our dad was better at racehorse pickin' than we thought." He let out a gruff laugh.

"In the note, my dad said he wanted us to start building the best cattle ranch in Llano. He sent us the money for that, yet he'd let his two sons live in a house with no running water or heat or air conditioning, leaving us to totally fend for ourselves. I was already in my freshman year at A&M, and Mike was a few years into the Marine Corps when we received the money."

I took a deep breath and slowly let it out. "Layton, I'm so sorry."

He turned and looked at me. "Please don't feel sorry for me, Whit. I have more money now than I know what to do with. Mike took the money, and he invested it well. Then, he made even more money with our horses. My side of the business has always been the cattle. The horses were always Mike's thing. Before he left for the Marines, he made me promise him that if anything ever happened to him, I would keep up with the racehorses and keep his dream alive."

"I'm sorry you lost your brother, but do you know how proud he would be of you?"

He stared out into the pasture and smiled. "I hope so."

I could see how being here was tearing him apart. I stood and reached my hand out for him. "Ready to let go?"

He looked at me funny. "Let go?"

"Yep, I think it's time you let go of the anger and the hurt. It's time to let it go, Layton."

He stood and took my hand as he smiled at me.

We walked back to the Jeep, and he didn't say a word. He started rubbing his thumb up and down my index finger again, and I felt like I was going to combust. He held my hand up and helped me into the Jeep. He started to walk around the Jeep, and then he stopped and slowly turned around. He stared at the house. He stood there for a good three minutes before he finally turned and got into the driver's side of the Jeep.

"Thank you, Whitley." He gave me that drop-dead gorgeous smile of his.

I smiled. "Always."

"Let's have some fun, shall we?" He wiggled his eyebrows up and down.

I had a strange feeling that his idea of fun was going to be very different from mine.

TWELVE

-⟫⟫⟫⟫⟫⟫⟫⟫⟩⟨⟨⟨⟨⟨⟨⟨⟨⟨⟨⟨-

LAYTON

I turned up the radio, and Whitley started singing along to the songs.

Why in the hell is her voice turning me on so much? I don't know.

She was soaking wet and looked more beautiful than ever. I loved the fact that she didn't even care that she was soaked. I wasn't even paying attention to where I was going on the ranch. I kept looking at her, watching her dance in her seat.

She threw her head back and let the rain just fall onto her face.

I think she's trying to kill me! Fuck, I really wish she'd stop doing that. It is fucking hot as hell.

I stopped the Jeep and sat back. "Shit!" I hit the steering wheel.

She looked over at me, confused. "What's wrong?"

"I think something just happened to the front passenger side tire."

"Really? Like what?"

"Not sure…I felt a pop. Did you not feel it?" I said, trying to hold back my smile.

"Nope."

"Will you do me a favor? I'm going to slowly start driving. Will you lean out and take a look at the tire? Tell me if everything looks okay."

She nodded as she grabbed on to the bar. She leaned out the side of the Jeep. "Okay…ready."

I smiled and gunned it while I held the brake down. Mud flew up everywhere, and she let out a scream that I was sure Mimi and her husband Frank would hear.

I let off the gas and looked over toward her. She was covered in mud. "Oops. Sorry."

Her mouth dropped open, and she balled up her fists. "You asshole! My eyes are burning from the mud in them, you fuckwad!"

I lost it and started laughing. I laughed so hard that I was pretty sure I'd snorted once or twice.

Whitley jumped out and began walking away.

"Where are you going?" I called after her.

"As far away from you as I can get!"

She turned and walked backward as she shot me the finger with both hands. Then, she dropped out of sight.

I jumped out of the Jeep and ran over to her.

"Shit! Oh shit! Oh my God…shit!" She cried out over and over as she held on to her ankle.

"Sweetheart, what's wrong? Whit, what's wrong?" I dropped to my knees.

She looked up at me, and the next thing I knew, I had a handful of mud in my face. She smeared it all over my face and down my neck. She started laughing, but then she quickly stopped when I looked at her.

"You better run," I said, glaring at her.

"What?" She jumped up and started to run.

I gave her a good thirty-second head start before I went after her. She kept looking back at me, laughing. She ran up to a group of oaks.

"You think a few trees are going to stop me?" I asked with a sly smile.

"Layton, let's just call a truce, okay? Truce 'cause I'm itching all over. I really need to get this mud off of me."

I shook my head. "Oh no, Miss Reynolds. Payback is a bitch."

"Wait! You got mud on me first! I was paying you back."

I acted like I was going to run to the left and then made a sharp move to the right. She screamed and tried to go left, but then she slipped. I ran up to her, picked her up, and threw her over my shoulder. I looked up and saw we were near the hunter's cabin. There was a tank right around the bend next to the cabin.

Oh yeah, her ass is going in the tank.

"Layton, put me down! Layton! Oh. My. God. No, Layton, no! Where are you taking me?"

She must have seen the tank because she started kicking and screaming.

"Scream all you want, honey. No one can hear you!" I laughed.

"Mimi! Frank!" she yelled out. "I know sound travels in the country."

"Whit, it's pouring. No one can hear you."

I smacked her ass, and she let out another scream.

"You're crazy! Layton, please…I'll do anything."

I walked up to the edge of the tank and saw a snake. *Shit. She lucked out!*

I turned around and saw a huge mud puddle. I started walking toward the cabin.

"Oh, thank God! I thought you were going to throw me in the tank."

"I was…but I saw a snake."

She started screaming and kicking again. "Oh my God! Put me down! I just want to go back to the house. I want down, Layton! Now!"

"You want down?"

"Yes! Right now, you asshole!"

"Okay then." I dropped her right into the mud puddle.

The look on her face and the scream she let out were priceless.

I couldn't help but laugh. "Shit, I really wish I had a camera right now."

I turned to walk toward the cabin, and then I felt her jump onto my back. She was pulling with all her might to get me to go backward.

"Aww, you're so cute, thinking you could pull me—"

The next thing I knew, she reached around and grabbed my dick. I lost my wits long enough for her to pull me back and jump on top of me in the mud puddle. She grabbed handfuls of mud and rubbed it all over me. I was pretty sure I had enough mud in my nose to build a small house. I grabbed her arms, flipped her over, and crawled on top of her. She was kicking and screaming, and then she stopped instantly.

"Do you give up?" I asked her as I tried to catch my breath.

Her face was white as a ghost. "I think you should get off of me now."

I tilted my head with a questioning look. She bit down on her lower lip, and I immediately felt my rock-hard dick pressed against her stomach.

Fuck! Fuck! Fuck! Friends, Layton. Friends don't get hard-ons for other friends.

"Shit! Sorry, Whit. It's just…you grabbed me and—"

She started to push me away. "It's okay."

I helped her up, and she started screaming again.

"Oh God! Get it off!"

I looked at her, confused. "Get what off?"

"Layton, they're crawling all over me and biting me!"

With one look at her, I saw she had red ants all over her. I grabbed her hand and ran over to the water hose. I turned it on and started to hose her off as she began stripping out of her clothes right in front of me.

Jesus Christ, I've never seen such a perfect body before in my life.

She had on black lace boy shorts with a black lace bra.

"Shit! Ouch, you little fucking bastards!" She threw her clothes off to the side and grabbed the hose. She washed her whole body down.

I just stood there and watched her. My dick couldn't possibly get any harder. I turned and walked onto the porch. I reached up for the spare key and opened the door. Mike and I had always kept an extra change of clothes in the cabin. I walked over toward the sink and quickly stripped out of my clothes. I washed the mud off of me, and then I grabbed a towel, dried off, and wrapped the towel around my waist.

I hadn't been in the cabin since last hunting season—*with Mike.*

I was just about to change into a clean T-shirt and jeans when I looked up and saw a soaking wet and crying Whitley standing in the doorway.

My heart broke in two from just seeing her cry. "Honey…"

She ran up to me and jumped into my arms as she cried hysterically.

I ran my hand down her hair and tried to get her to calm down. "Sweetheart, are you okay?"

She shook her head and buried her face into my chest.

I reached down and made her look up at me. "Are you hurt somewhere?"

She shook her head. "I…I…" She bit down on her damn lower lip again. "I threw my clothes right back into the mud puddle, and the ant bites are itching, and I…" She took a deep breath and tried to calm down. "I don't have any clothes to wear now!"

She started to cry again, and it was everything I could do not to laugh. I held her for a minute or two before I reached over and grabbed another towel. I took the towel and started to dry her off. I dried off her back…then her arms…stomach…down one leg and up another.

I took in her perfect body, and I wanted nothing more than to touch her. I slowly stood back up and looked into her eyes. The look in her eyes told me she wanted me just as much as I wanted her. I leaned down and brushed my lips gently against hers. She let out the softest, sweetest moan I'd ever heard.

What am I doing? I don't want or need this. I can't be hurt again.

I pulled back just a bit. "I'm sorry." I took a step away from her.

She reached out, took the towel, and wrapped it around her body. I walked over to the dresser and pulled out a Texas A&M T-shirt and a pair of sweats. I handed them to her and turned away, so she could get dressed.

"Please keep your bra and panties on, Whit."

"Why? They're soaking wet."

"If I know you have no bra or panties on under my clothes, I'm not sure how I'll react."

"Oh," she said in such a sweet and innocent way. "Okay."

When she touched my shoulder, I jumped and spun around to face her.

"Sorry. I'm, uh…I'm done." She looked down at the floor. "I'll wait in the Jeep for you." She turned and walked toward the door.

I wanted to call out for her to stop. I wanted to take her in my arms and make love to her so bad that it almost hurt.

She opened the door and shut it behind her.

I sat down on the bed and tried to catch my breath. I shook my head and tried to clear the image of her standing in front of me. I tried to erase the look in her eyes. I closed my eyes and saw Olivia and me making love on this very bed. I could never make love to Whitley for the first time in this bed. She deserved so much better than that.

She deserves so much better than me. I need to distance myself from her.

I was starting to fall for her, fast and hard, and that was the last thing I wanted to do.

Then, I heard a truck pull up, and someone started talking. I quickly got changed and headed outside. I locked up the cabin and put the key back above the door. I rounded the corner and saw Mitch, my ranch foreman, talking to Whitley.

The next thing I knew, she was running around to the passenger side of his truck and getting in. Mitch started to drive off, but I stepped in front of his truck. He quickly slammed on the brakes. I looked directly at Whitley, who appeared to be on the verge of tears. I walked up to Mitch's window, and he rolled it down. He looked pissed-off.

"Layton."

"Mitch." I looked over at Whitley. "Where are you going, Whitley? And why are you in my foreman's truck?"

"I, um…I just need to get back, and he pulled up, so…I'm just going to head back to your house, if that's okay. I just need to leave."

I looked at the hurt in her eyes. *Is it hurt or fear?*

I smiled and nodded. "Okay, I'll be up there right away. I just have to go back to the Jeep."

She nodded and tried to smile. "Yep…okay."

I looked at Mitch. "Thanks, Mitch."

He gave me a nod and rolled up the window. I stood there and watched as he drove off with her.

My heart started pounding, and I felt sick to my stomach.

Why does it feel like she's leaving me? She promised me she wouldn't leave me—ever.

THIRTEEN

Whitley

I jumped out of Mitch's truck and thanked him. I practically ran up the back steps into Layton's house. I shut the door, ran through the kitchen, and grabbed my bag and purse. I headed toward the door. I needed to leave and leave right now.

"Oh God! How could I be so stupid? What's wrong with me? I can't believe I actually wanted him to kiss me...I wanted him to...*oh God*!" I started to make my way out when I stopped dead in my tracks.

I saw the picture of Mike and Layton on the fireplace mantel.

I promised him. I promised him I'd never leave him.

I closed my eyes for a few seconds before I turned around and started walking down the hallway, looking for Layton's bedroom to take a shower and put on dry clothes. I slowly opened a door and saw it was the master bedroom. I walked in and put my hand up to my mouth.

It was amazing. There was a huge king-size bed with a beautiful solid wood bedframe. The matching dressers were incredible. The walls had been painted a blue-silver color, and the bedding matched it perfectly. The pictures on the walls were all hand-painted country scenes.

"My God...it's so serene in here," I said to myself.

I glanced over and saw a nook with two giant oversized chairs. I thought about how comfortable it would be to sit there and read a book.

Ah hell...I sound like Courtney now.

I walked up, opened a door, and prayed it was his bathroom.

Nope.

"Holy shit. This is bigger than my whole bedroom."

I walked into the completely empty walk-in closet. I backed out and looked across the room to another door. I walked over and opened it.

It was filled with Layton's clothes. I walked in and ran my hand along all his shirts. I pulled one up to my nose and took a deep breath in.

"Oh Jesus," I whispered as I closed my eyes. It smelled just like him.

I turned, stepped out of the closet, and shut the door behind me.

I made my way over to a set of double doors. When I opened them, I let out a gasp. "Who in the hell decorated this house?"

The first thing I noticed was the oversized tub surrounded by sandstone rock. Then, I looked over to the huge walk-in shower made of travertine in a matching color. The cabinets looked like pieces of furniture, and both sinks were copper with faucets that looked like little wells. I smiled because it all screamed Layton.

And me. This is exactly how I would have wanted this bathroom.

It was spotless.

Does he even use this bathroom?

I pulled the wet Texas A&M T-shirt off and threw it to the floor. I unclasped my bra and tossed it on top of his T-shirt. I took the sweatpants off and kicked them away from me as I reached in to turn on the shower. The heat from the water felt heavenly. I stood there, staring at the water falling down.

I'm falling in love with him. I'm totally falling in love with him, and I can't keep denying it.

The moment I felt his hand move down my back, I smiled. When he leaned down and kissed my neck, every nerve in my body started going crazy.

He put his lips up to my ear and whispered, "I was so afraid you were going to leave me."

I turned around and looked into his eyes. The way our eyes held on to each other caused me to catch my breath. It felt like every fear I'd ever had just melted away from the way he was looking at me. Every doubt about myself was instantly gone. I felt…healed.

I smiled as I whispered, "I promised you I'd never leave you."

He reached his hand up and brushed the back of it down the side of my face. "When you first met me, Whitley, I was so damaged. I had a broken heart that was still bleeding. When I look into your eyes…I feel…like my heart is healing."

Oh my God, he just said the same thing I'd thought.

"I feel…meaning in my life. I see a purpose again. Today, at the old ranch house, you literally healed my broken heart. I just need to know more about you. I can barely breathe when I leave your side." He bent down and brushed his lips against mine.

My whole body trembled with his every touch.

"I think about you constantly, Whitley. I wonder what you're doing, what you're thinking about, and who you're thinking about. I want to take away all of the hurt…all of the fear…I see in your eyes. I want you to lose yourself in my love."

Oh my.

My knees were giving out on me. He reached around me and held me up as he moved his lips down my neck. I'd never in my life felt so on fire…so desperate for another person's touch.

I tried to talk, but nothing came out. His lips traveled down my body until he found my breasts. He fondled my one breast and nipple while he took the other into his mouth.

"Oh God…" I threw my head back as my whole body trembled.

He slowly moved his lips down my stomach. I'd never had a man treat my body with such…adoration.

"I can't get close enough to you, Whitley."

My breathing started to pick up, and I grabbed his hair to keep myself from falling. As his lips moved farther down, his fingers slipped beneath my panties. The feeling that shot through my body was amazing. It was like nothing I'd ever experienced before.

He slowly started to slip off my panties. The trail of sensations he left with his fingers on my skin was more than I could stand. I was barely able to pick up my feet to get the panties off.

Then, I felt his lips on my upper thigh, and I ran my hands through his hair as I threw my head back again and moaned.

"Layton…"

I'd never let Roger give me oral sex—*ever*. At first, I'd practically begged him to, but he'd said it was dirty. Then, toward the end, he'd wanted to, but I couldn't bear the thought of his lips down there.

Layton kissed me all the way up my leg and ended right above my clit. I wanted to grab his face and make him touch me with his lips, but he slowly stood up. He cupped my face with his hands, and leaning down, he kissed me with so much passion and love that I wanted to cry.

He slowly backed me into the shower. He pushed me up against the wall, and all I could think of was how jealous Courtney was going to be. All she ever talked about was shower sex and how she wanted it.

When I didn't think we could kiss any longer and when I was in desperate need of air, he pulled his lips from mine. He gently bit down on my lower lip, and I let a moan slip from my mouth.

"Whitley," he whispered against my lips, "I want to get to know every inch of your body. I want to make nothing but memories with you. Every day. Every minute. Every second." He gently kissed me in between his words.

I'd never experienced such passion in my life. "Layton…I…I…"

His smile caused my stomach to drop.

Oh good God, I've never felt like this before. I love him.

"Tell me, Whit…tell me, baby."

He placed both hands on my face and brought me in for another kiss. I was slowly losing myself to him. I never wanted this moment to ever end.

I slowly pulled away and looked into his eyes. "I love you, Layton. I tried to fight it, but…I want to be with you every second of the day. I want…I want you to…" I felt tears burning my eyes.

Can I do this? Can I open myself up to another man again? Can I trust that he'll love me and never hurt me?

He slowly smiled as he reached around my body and lifted me up.

"You want me to, what, Whitley? Love you? Because I've loved you since the moment I saw you standing next to your car, since the moment your beautiful green eyes looked into mine. The moment I heard your sweet voice talk to me, I knew deep down inside that I would love you forever."

I buried my face into his neck and cried.

I wasn't sure how long he held me while I cried. He gently put me down and reached for the soap. He began to wash every inch of my body. He turned me around and placed my hands on the shower wall.

Everywhere he touched left tingles. The way he was washing me was almost as sensual as having sex. I didn't want him to stop. I'd never felt this intimate with another person in my entire life.

Then, his hands began to wash my hair.

"Feels…so…good." I could hardly talk.

After he rinsed my hair and body off, he reached over and shut off the water. I didn't even care that we hadn't had knock-my-socks-off wall sex in the shower. He'd just knocked my fucking socks off by washing me and giving every square inch of my body attention.

He took my hand and led me out of the shower. Reaching into a cabinet, he pulled out a towel. He looked down at me and smiled the most breathtaking smile I'd ever seen. His eyes sparkled, and his dimple—

My God, I feel weak in the knees.

I slowly smiled back as he let out a small laugh. He wrapped me up in the towel, and then he quickly grabbed another one and dried himself off. I looked up and down his perfect body. I knew he worked out every day, but holy hell, he was amazing.

He had a tattoo on his side of the U.S. Marine Corps symbol with Mike's name on it. Under that was another name—Kate.

Who in the hell is Kate? And why is her name on his body?

I pulled my eyes away from her name and looked into his eyes.

He smiled and gave me a wink. "Kate's my niece, Mike's daughter."

What?

I started to shake my head as tears began burning my eyes. "I didn't…oh my God. How old is she?" My heart instantly hurt for this little girl who had lost her daddy. *I can't even imagine.*

He smiled and placed his hand on my face. "She's five. Don't cry, baby."

I slowly put my hands over my mouth. "Oh, Layton."

He shook his head as he slowly unwrapped the towel from my body. "Only happy tears and memories tonight, honey." He stepped back and looked my body up and down.

I instantly started to blush.

"Don't be shy about your body, Whitley. You're breathtaking, the most beautiful thing I've ever laid my eyes on." He reached down, scooped me up, and carried me into his bedroom.

Just when I didn't think he could make the butterflies in my stomach any crazier, he did something else that made them take off into flight. He gently put me down and then crawled onto the bed.

"I've never in my life wanted someone as much as I want you, Whitley. I'm almost unable to breathe because I want to be inside you so badly."

My chest started heaving up and down. "I need you, Layton," I barely whispered.

I did need him. I needed him to make me forget every bruise caused by a man who had never truly loved me. I needed him to make me feel whole again. I needed him to make love to me. In that moment, I realized that Roger had never made love to me. He'd simply fucked me.

Layton slowly started to kiss my stomach, and as he moved his burning kisses up my body, he ran his hand up and down my leg. By the time his lips met mine, I felt like I was going to scream.

Jesus...touch me, for Christ's sake!

"Layton, please!" I practically willed him to touch me as I pushed my hips up to him, pleading for him.

I felt him smile against my neck.

"I've dreamed of this, Whitley, for the last week and a half. I don't want to rush."

I wanted to scream. As much as I loved how slow he was going, I needed to feel him closer to me. I needed to feel him inside me.

He brushed his lips against my neck and then captured my lips again.

"I'm going to make sweet love to you now, baby."

Oh God. "Yes," I whispered as I felt his hand move up my leg.

The moment he touched me, my whole body jerked.

"Oh God!"

I was so afraid I was going to come the moment he touched me. He slowly rubbed his thumb against my clit.

"Oh God, Layton."

Right before he placed his finger inside me, he kissed me with so much passion that I started to cry. Then, he slid two more fingers in, and my hips jerked up. He moved his hand in such a way that I felt like I was floating on a cloud of pleasure.

He pulled back slightly, and against my lips, he said, "Oh, baby...you're so wet."

"I want you inside me, Layton," I said as I breathed heavily.

He started moving his hand faster. I swore I could feel the build-up starting from my toes. It was moving up my body, and I grabbed his arm as I moved my hips faster.

Then, he pulled his hand away.

Wait! What is he doing? Why did he stop?

My head was spinning, and I was so confused. Then, I felt him on top of me and our eyes met.

"I want to be inside you the first time you come."

"Yes," I whispered.

"Condom?" he asked.

"I'm on the pill, and I've only ever been with Roger. I was actually tested not long ago when I, um…when I found out he had been cheating. They all came back clean."

Layton smiled as he looked at me. "I've always used a condom, even with Olivia."

I just stared at him. "Always?"

He nodded and smiled.

"So, I'm kind of, like, your first?" I crinkled up my nose and let out a giggle.

"Yeah, baby, you are, and I pray to God I last at least a minute."

I smiled and put my hands on his back. He teased me for a few minutes as I felt his dick just barely enter me before he pulled out.

"Oh God, Layton…you're gonna kill me."

He smiled and shook his head. "I'm so afraid I'm gonna lose it, Whit. I don't want this feeling to stop. It feels like heaven."

I slowly moved my fingertips up and down his back as he began to move again. He leaned down and brushed his tongue over my lips, and I let out a soft moan. I opened my mouth to him, and he slowly slipped his tongue inside. The way our tongues danced together was amazing. I pulled away and threw my head back as he pushed himself oh-so slowly inside me.

I let out a gasp, and he instantly stopped moving.

"Am I hurting you?"

"Don't stop! Feels so good…please don't stop."

I moved my hands to his ass and pulled him closer to me.

Oh my Lord…he is huge.

But I didn't really have much to compare him to since I'd only ever been with Roger.

He pushed more and let out a moan that traveled through my whole body.

"Jesus…you feel incredible," he whispered against my ear. "Whitley…"

"Layton, it feels so good, so amazingly good."

He moved his lips to mine and kissed me as he made such passionate love to me. I was feeling something I'd never felt before. The way he was

moving in and out of me felt like pure heaven. He was so gentle, but at the same time, he gave me so much pleasure.

Then, I felt the build-up.

Oh yes! Oh dear Lord...what is happening? This has never felt so amazing. Never.

"Layton...Oh God, don't stop! I'm..." I couldn't even finish talking.

The orgasm swept over my body so fast and hard that all I could do was call out his name. I grabbed his ass as he started to move faster, harder.

"Yes!" I called out.

Just when I thought I was coming down from my orgasm, another one hit when he started to call out my name.

Oh God.

I almost needed him to stop. It was so intense.

"I can't...Oh my God, Layton..."

My whole body was vibrating as he slowly came to a stop. It almost felt like I was still coming.

"Oh my God, I've never experienced anything so incredible in my entire life."

I could hardly breathe, and the heat of his breaths on my neck was starting to drive me crazy.

Motherfucker! I want him again! What is wrong with me?

I'd just had two of the most intense orgasms of my life, and my body was being a greedy bitch!

"Whitley," he whispered.

He started to kiss my neck and then down my chest to my stomach. He got up and went into the bathroom. I was finally starting to return to Earth when I felt a warm washcloth. He was cleaning me. I closed my eyes and relaxed with each gentle stroke.

Before I even knew what was happening, I felt his tongue on my clit, and then his fingers slipped inside me.

"Jesus, Layton! I can't! My body can't take it."

Holy motherfucking shit. It feels...amazing.

"Oh...Layton...that feels...oh God...oh God, Layton...not again!"

I arched my body as he sucked on my clit, and then he hit it with his tongue at just the right pressure, throwing me over the edge, as I called out his name.

He was lying on top of me again, and this time, he was kissing my nipple. He was trying to kill me with incredible, amazing, rock-my-world sex.

"I'm going to go rinse out my mouth, baby."

I had my eyes closed, and all I could manage was, "Mmmkay."

He laughed, and I felt the bed move as he got up and made his way into his bathroom. My body slowly started to relax like I'd never relaxed before. I felt him crawl back onto the bed.

Then, he pulled me next to him. "Sleep, my beautiful cowgirl," he whispered as he stroked my arm up and down.

"Layton?"

"Yeah, baby?"

"I'm not dreaming, am I?" I turned toward him, and I looked up into his eyes.

He smiled that drop-my-panties smile at me. "If you're dreaming, then I'm also dreaming, and I don't ever want to wake up."

"I've never in my life experienced such amazing orgasms. I think I might have actually felt the Earth shake."

Layton laughed and brought me closer to him. He leaned down and kissed the back of my neck. "Neither have I, Whit. It almost felt like it was my first time. It felt so fucking good."

I smiled and felt myself drifting off into a dream. I was pretty sure I said his name as I fell deeper into my dream.

FOURTEEN

LAYTON

I instantly woke up in a cold sweat. I'd been dreaming of Mike. In my dream, he'd told me how I'd finally found the love of my life and how happy he was that I wasn't sad anymore.

I glanced down at the beautiful woman in my arms, and I smiled.

We'd only known each other for such a short amount of time, but she was my everything. There wasn't anything I wouldn't do for this girl. The way she made me feel…was amazing. My heart felt like it was whole again.

I was finally looking at the other half of me. I was able to open my heart and let someone in—someone I wanted to be with more than I needed the air I breathed, someone I wanted to be with forever.

She moved, and I rolled right along with her. She lay on her side, so I pulled her in close to me. She felt so perfect in my arms. I smiled as I thought about how she had fallen apart three times for me. I had never been able to do that with Olivia. She'd just wanted to fuck and get it over with. With Whitley, we'd made love—sweet, slow love.

I had a feeling she'd never had oral sex…at least I was hoping she hadn't. I wanted to be the first who had done that for her, not that motherfucker ex of hers.

What a stupid fucker, not to see what an amazing woman she is.

"I'll always protect you, Whit. I'll never let anyone ever hurt you, cowgirl."

She let out a small moan and pushed her ass into me. I instantly felt my dick coming back up. I knew she was exhausted, but I needed her. I needed to feel the love pouring out of her and into me, and I wanted to pour my love into her.

I moved back some and rolled her over. I moved my hand up and down her side. Her body shuddered, and I smiled. I loved what my touch did to her.

I leaned down and whispered in her ear, "Whitley…baby, wake up."

She let out another soft, small moan that traveled through my whole body.

Shit, the way she makes me feel is unreal.

She slowly opened her eyes and smiled that beautiful smile of hers.

"Layton," she whispered, "touch me. Love me."

I moved my hand down and slowly put two fingers inside her.

Fuck me, she's so wet.

I started to move my fingers in and out. Reaching down, she grabbed my hand and stopped me from moving. She pushed me off of her, and the next thing I knew, she was straddling me.

"Can I be on top?" She raised her eyebrows.

I smiled, and she smiled back at me.

"Baby, that's one thing you never have to ask."

"Really? I want to make you come with me on top."

Jesus. She acts like she's never been on top before. Has she?

That fucker probably didn't want her to have control over anything.

God, I want to kill him.

"Layton?" she said almost in a whisper.

"Yeah, baby?"

"I've, um…I've never been on top before, so I'm not sure I'll be able to make you come."

My heart broke in two. I sat up, grabbed her, and pulled her closer to me. I brought her lips to mine and kissed her as sweetly and softly as I could.

"Just move, Whit…you can't do anything wrong, baby. Do what makes you feel good, and it will make me feel good also."

She started off slowly as she moved her tongue along my bottom lip. I opened my mouth up to her, and she slipped her tongue inside. Instantly, I was lost in her kiss as I held her to me. Then, the way she was moving started feeling so damn good. I let go of her and fell back on the bed.

"Does it feel good?" she asked as she moved up and down so damn slow.

"Whit…it feels like fucking heaven. Faster, baby."

The look in her eyes caused me to suck in a breath. Her eyes got a fire in them, and she started going faster and harder. I closed my eyes to concentrate on not coming too soon. When I opened my eyes, she had her head thrown back, and she was touching her breast.

Motherfucker…I'm gonna come soon…please, Whit…hurry.

"Whitley, baby…God, it feels so good. You look so fucking hot, touching yourself."

Her head snapped forward, and she smiled at me. She slowly moved her other hand down and touched her clit as she continued to play with her nipple.

"Fuck." I felt myself about to lose it. "Son of a bitch, Whitley…I'm gonna come, but I want you to come…"

She moved faster.

"Oh God, Layton…I'm going to come…Layton! Ah…"

I could actually feel her squeezing on my dick.

Holy shit, this is unreal.

I called out her name as I had probably the most intense orgasm of my life. It felt like I was pouring everything I had into her. It lasted forever.

She finally collapsed onto my chest, and we both tried desperately to catch our breath.

"I've...never...done...anything...like...that...before..." she said in between each breath.

I smiled and wrapped my arms around her. She got up and off of me and then lay down next to me.

I needed to tell her how I felt. I needed her to know. "I love you, Whitley. Please don't ever leave me."

She rolled over and put her chin on my chest. She looked into my eyes. "I love you, too, Layton. Please don't ever hurt me."

Shit. I felt tears building in my eyes. I squeezed them shut and vowed that I'd never, as long as I took a breath, let anyone hurt her. I'd kill them before I let them hurt her.

I opened my eyes and smiled at her. "I'll never hurt you, baby. I promise."

→≫≫≫≫≫≫≫≫≫≪≪≪≪≪≪≪≪≪≪≪←

While in the kitchen, I looked at my cell phone and saw missed text messages from Olivia.

Fuck...why won't she leave me alone? She's getting married, for fuck's sake.

I had also missed a text from Reed, saying he'd run into Courtney at the coffee shop, and his message went on and on about what a bitch she was. I laughed and shook my head.

I poured a cup of coffee and then a small glass of orange juice. I placed it all on a tray.

I'd gotten up and made breakfast tacos for Whitley and me. I'd watched her sleep for about an hour this morning. The small little noises she'd made had driven me insane with lust. It had taken everything out of me not to wake her up and make love to her again.

I closed my eyes, and I could feel her hands on my body. My dick instantly jumped. I laughed as I shook my head and headed back to my room with our coffee, juice, and tacos.

I glanced over to the picture that Mike had sent me right before he died. It was a Robert Tew quote.

> "THE FUTURE NEEDS YOUR
> ATTENTION RIGHT NOW.
> IT HAS SOMETHING BEAUTIFUL
> TO OFFER YOU, BUT FIRST...
> YOU MUST LET GO OF THE PAST
> IN ORDER TO RECEIVE IT."

It was almost like Mike had known Whitley would be coming into my life. He had given me hints. Even in my dreams, he had tried to tell me about her.

My doorbell rang, and I stopped dead in my tracks.

Who in the hell is here? I'm not expecting anyone.

Both dogs started barking, and I tried to get them to be quiet.

I set the tray down on the entryway table and walked to the door as the doorbell rang again.

"I'm coming! Fuck, give me a damn minute."

It had to be Mitch—only he would bother me this early on a Friday morning.

I unlocked the door and pulled it open. "What the hell, Mi—"

Olivia was standing in front of me. She smiled that smile that used to bring me to my knees.

Now, it did nothing to me, not a damn thing.

"What are you doing here, Liv?" I asked.

Her smile dropped. She shook her head and started to push past me. She walked in and shooed the dogs away.

"Well, I had something very important to talk to my party planner about, and I tried calling her all last night and this morning. Then, I ran into her overly talkative friend slash *business partner*"—she said with air quotes—"at the coffee shop this morning. Ugh, she was arguing with Reed about some stupid fucking tree."

I had to smile, thinking about Reed and Court arguing about trees.

I wonder if Courtney knows what he does for a living. I'll have to ask Whit.

I grinned, thinking about my sleeping beauty waiting in bed for me.

"Um, hello? Layton, I'm trying to talk to you!"

I looked up and shook my head. "Sorry."

I saw her glance down, and she frowned at the tray of food. Her head snapped up, and she glared at me.

"Do you have company?" She stood there, staring at me.

Whit had pulled her car around back, so Olivia probably hadn't seen it when she pulled up.

"Yes, I do. So, if you don't have a real need for anything, Olivia, I'm going to ask that you go."

At first, she looked pissed. Then, I saw tears building in her eyes. She put her face in her hands as she sat down and started crying.

My first reaction was to run to her and hold her in my arms. Then, I thought of Whitley saying, *Please don't ever hurt me.*

I took a deep breath, leaned against the door, and waited for Olivia to finish her show. I wasn't falling for her games anymore. The only thing I wanted was for her to leave, so I could get back to the love of my life waiting for me, naked, in my bed.

The love of my life.

I truly did love her. I loved her so much that it almost hurt. I'd never imagined I could fall in love with someone so hard and so fast.

"Layton, are you even paying attention?"

I glanced up at Olivia. "Oh, sorry, Liv."

"I'm having second thoughts about marrying Justin."

Nothing—I felt nothing for Olivia.

"Oh yeah? Why's that, Liv?"

She looked at me and gave me a small smile. "He's not you. He could never be you, Layton. Please, please can we just maybe go for a ride or something? I really need you right now."

I pushed myself off the wall. "Is that so? Kind of like when I really needed you after my brother died, and instead of being there, you walked out on me?"

She started to shake her head. "No! Layton, I didn't want to leave. It was just...you were so upset, and so...I don't know. It was like a part of you was missing, and it scared me. I didn't know how to deal with that."

"A part of me was missing, Liv. A big part of me is still missing. All I needed you to do was stay with me, hold me, and show me you loved me to prove I wasn't alone in this fucked-up world."

She started to walk toward me. "I can do that now, Layton. I promise you, I'll never leave you again. I promise. Just please...give me another chance. I'm begging you. I've loved you since we were young kids. Layton...please."

She went to reach out for me, and I put my hand up.

"Stop. Just stop this, Olivia. We were never in love."

She shook her head. "Don't say that, Layton."

"We weren't in love. We were in lust, Liv. I thought I loved you, but someone has taught me what real love is. She has totally opened up her heart and soul to me, and she trusts me to take care of her, to love her with no conditions. I can't even stand the thought of being away from her for

more than five minutes. My heart stops when she walks into a room or when she smiles at me. When I hear her laugh, I just want to make her laugh more because it makes me feel so happy."

Olivia rolled her eyes and shook her head. "Oh, please, Layton. Did you fuck her last night? You know that's all this is, don't you, baby? She's just another girl who you've taken to bed to try and forget about me. But, baby, I'm here now. We can be together. I know what I had, and I'm ready to take it back."

I felt heat rising in my body. "Don't you ever talk about Whitley like that again."

"So, it's Whitley who's here. For Christ's sake, Layton, you barely know that girl. I don't trust her anyway. She's hiding something. I don't think this is a good idea, baby. Come on, you go tell her to pack up her shit and leave, and then let's go for a ride."

I just stood there, listening to her crazy talk. "Get out."

"I know how hard the last six months have been, Layton, but I'm here now, baby."

I let out a long sigh. "Get the fuck out of my house right now, Olivia."

Her mouth dropped open. "Excuse me?"

"You heard me. I want you to leave my house, and so help me God, if I ever see or hear of you talking to Whitley in any negative sort of way or if I find out you're digging into her life, I'll make you pay for it. I love her, and I'll do whatever it takes to protect her. Do you understand me?"

"You're insane, do you know that? You don't know a damn thing about this girl. She's only after you for your money, Layton! How can you say you love her? You've only known her for, what? Two weeks?"

I turned and opened the door. "Get the hell out of my house, and go back to Justin, Olivia. You two were made for each other."

She squared off her shoulders and started out the door, but then she stopped right in front of me. "You don't know what you're walking away from here."

I laughed and gave her a wink. "Oh, the hell I don't. I know exactly what I'm walking away from. Just like I know what I'm walking toward—happiness and love."

She turned and walked away. "Good luck with that."

I shut the door and turned to see Whitley standing there with both dogs lying at her feet. She was leaning up against the doorjamb, wearing nothing but one of my T-shirts.

I instantly smiled and shook my head. "Damn, Whit, you sure look good in my shirt."

The smile that spread across her face made my legs shake and my stomach drop.

Shit, I love this girl standing in front of me.

She slowly started making her way over to me. "This shirt sure feels good on me."

I smiled wider. "Oh yeah? I bet it would feel even better if you took it off."

She threw her head back and laughed. She glanced down at the tray and then back up at me.

"You hungry, babe? It's probably all cold now."

She moved up to me and placed her hands on my chest. The moment she touched me, I felt electricity move through my body.

She looked up at me with those beautiful deep green eyes that just sparkled. "I'm hungry...but not for food." She raised her eyebrows.

I literally felt my stomach do a flip. Reaching down, I picked her up and made my way back toward my bedroom. I walked past the bed and went straight into the bathroom. I set her down on the bench and turned on the shower.

"I need to take a shower," I said with a wink. I glanced down and saw her rubbing her legs together.

Fuck me. I want her so damn bad.

She bit down on her lower lip, and something in me snapped. I walked up and grabbed her, pulling her up to me.

I placed my hands on her face and looked into her eyes. "Whitley, you drive me crazy. How do you do this? How do you make me feel so insane?"

She smiled slightly. "Layton, I want you so much that I can't even breathe."

I pulled the T-shirt over her head and picked her up. She wrapped her legs around me and started kissing me with so much passion that I could feel it pouring into my body from hers. Our tongues explored each other, and she let out a moan.

I walked into the shower and pushed her against the wall. I slammed my dick inside her.

"Oh God...yes!" she called out.

Last night had been all about love. Now, it was all about passion.

"Harder, Layton...please...I just need to feel only you."

I bit down on her lower lip and sucked on it as I pumped faster and harder into her body. I felt her getting tighter around my dick, and I almost wanted to stop just to make this last longer.

"Oh God! Layton, I'm going to come," she said as the water cascaded down her face.

"Whitley...oh God, baby, it feels so fucking good."

I felt myself pouring into her as she called out my name over and over. I swore I could feel every ounce of me, down to the last drop, spill into her body.

I stood there, holding her against the shower wall, both of us trying desperately to catch our breaths.

"Whitley…for so long, I've been standing in the rain…withering away. I just wanted to forget everything. I did things, things I'm not proud of."

She wrapped her arms around me tighter. I swore I thought I heard her crying.

"The moment you walked into my life, I knew you were what I'd been looking for. I knew you were the one who would save me from this broken shell of a man I had become. Please, baby…have faith in me, and I promise you, I'll love you forever."

I slowly let her slide down my body. I pushed her hair away and cupped her face in my hands. The tears were running down her cheeks, mixing with the hot water.

"Layton, he broke me so badly, and I've been so afraid to ever open my heart again. I never thought I would feel this way, but you…" She started crying harder.

My heart was breaking for her.

"You told me last night I healed you, but you healed me just as much. I love you, Layton. I'll love you forever, too."

I slammed my lips to hers as I picked up her wet body. I reached over, turned off the water, and brought her to the bed. I gently laid her down and crawled on top of her.

The moment I entered her body, I felt all the anger, fear, and doubt just leave my body. Our wet bodies moved together in sync. It wasn't long before we were both calling out each other's names again.

She was my angel who had been sent to me from Mike. I felt it so strongly. I knew Mike had sent her to me.

I pulled her next to me and held on to her as tightly as I could.

I was finally happy, finally at peace.

FIFTEEN

➤➤➤➤➤➤➤➤➤➤➤➤➤➤◄◄◄◄◄◄◄◄◄◄◄◄◄◄

Whitley

I opened my eyes when I heard Layton's cell phone going off.

Oh shit! Courtney is probably freaking out. I never called her.

"Hey, Lucky, there better be a damn good reason you're calling me. You interrupted the pure heaven I've been in."

I smiled as I pulled the covers up and over my mouth to giggle.

Oh my God! I can't believe this is happening to me. I swore off men. I was never going to fall in love again, but Layton…he loves me. I feel it in my heart.

I'd never felt like this with Roger, not even in the beginning. It had never felt so…powerful, so full of magic and love.

Layton sat up and smiled. "He's here? No shit? How the fuck did they get him here so fast?"

He? Who in the hell is Layton talking about?

"We'll be down in a few minutes. Yes…don't run him until I get there."

A horse—he must be talking about the horse he went to see last week.

He hung up the phone and leaned down toward me with the biggest smile on his face. He gently brushed his lips against mine, and I let out a slow, low moan. He pulled slightly away and kept his eyes closed.

"How is it even possible I could want you so badly again?"

I laughed as I ran my index finger down the side of his face. He opened his eyes, and I let out a gasp when I saw his beautiful blue eyes looking into mine.

I could barely talk. "Layton," I whispered, "is it even possible to fall so madly in love with someone like this?"

He smiled that crooked smile of his, and I swore his eyes sparkled as he glanced down at my lips and then back into my eyes.

"Yes," he whispered. "You wanna go see a horse?"

I laughed and nodded. "Yes! I want to be wherever you are."

He reached down and kissed my nose. He jumped up and walked over toward his closet before turning back to look at me. "Your clothes?"

"I have spare clothes in my car," I said with a wink.

He returned my wink with a panty-melting smile as he grabbed a pair of jeans and put them on. For some reason, the idea of him going commando

turned me on even more. He walked out of his closet with flip-flops, and I fell back onto the pillow and moaned.

Holy shit. He makes fucking flip-flops look sexy as hell. A cowboy in damn flip-flops! Oh God, what is he doing to me?

I slowly moved my hand down and touched myself.

What in the hell is wrong with me?

I had such a damn pulsing feeling between my legs. I just needed it to stop.

How is it possible to have this much sex yet still be so damn horny?

"Whitley?"

I looked up at him. "Hmm?"

"Are you feeling on yourself? Baby, I think you're trying to put me in the hospital. I've been pleasantly surprised at my stamina, but damn, baby."

"I just…I've never had such a need for someone before in my life. Just watching you turns me on and…" I moved my hand faster.

Oh my God, I can't even believe what I'm doing!

I closed my eyes and tilted my head back. The next thing I knew, the covers were off of me, and I felt Layton's hot breath. One touch of his tongue on my clit, and I lost it. I grabbed the sheets, and all I could do was ride out one of the most intense orgasms I'd ever had. He slid his fingers into me, and I felt another one coming on just as the first one was ending.

I started to shake my head. "Oh. My. God. I can't take another one. I can't!"

He moved his tongue faster and did something with his fingers that just sent me over the edge. I bucked my hips and started calling out his name.

He moved his kisses up my body. When he put his lips to my neck, he whispered, "I love it when you come and hearing you call out my name, Whit."

I finally came back to Earth and looked into his eyes. "I don't know what came over me. I'm so embarrassed." I pulled the pillow over my head.

He laughed and pushed it out of the way. "Whitley, that was one of the hottest fucking things I've ever seen. You can do that anytime you want!"

I felt the heat in my face as he moved the back of his hand down my face.

"Nothing is more beautiful than your face…with that rose color in your cheeks." He jumped up and adjusted himself. "Now, I'm going out to your car. Behave while I'm gone." He started to walk off.

I called out, "My clothes are in a pale blue gym bag in the trunk!"

The moment he opened the door, both dogs came running in, and they jumped on the bed before he yelled and told them to follow him.

I laid there for a minute or two before remembering Courtney.

"Fuck!" I jumped up, wrapped the blanket around me, and set out for my phone.

I had twenty-seven missed calls, thirty-two text messages, and five voice mails—all from Court.

Oh shit. I took a deep breath and hit her number.

"Where in the fuck have you been? Do you know how worried I've been, you bitch?"

"Lollipop, I'm so sorry!"

"Oh, oh, don't you even Lollipop my ass. I've gone mad, wondering what in the hell happened to you. You better start talking, and you better tell me you got laid, or I'm going to be even more pissed!"

I walked back into Layton's bedroom and sat down on the bed.

Where in the hell do I start?

"Courtney…"

"Oh. My. God. Is he big?"

"What? That's really what you're gonna ask me, Court? If he's big?"

"Um…hell yeah, that's my first question. I bet he is. He looks like he is well-off in that area. I mean, from the bulge I've seen in his tight-ass Wranglers."

My mouth dropped open, and I let out a sigh. "Okay, first off, you're *never* allowed to look at that again—ever. Off-limits. Second, yeah, he is."

"Ah hell! I knew it! How many times?"

"Um…I don't even remember. But I had wall sex…in the shower!"

"You cunt! I hate you."

"Oh my God, Court! That was so mean. I can't believe you just called me that." I giggled.

"Really, Whit? You swear off men, and then you go off and have mad, passionate sex with one of the best-looking guys I've ever laid my eyes on. I'm totally hating on you right now. I just want to have sex. I'd take bad sex at this point. Maybe I should ask Reed."

I lost it and laughed. "Courtney! You're so mean. Reed is a sweetheart."

"He's a pussy. Do you know what I found out this morning? He's a horticulturist. He screws around with flowers and shit!"

Wow, I didn't see that one coming.

"See? Even you're in shock. He should be like a cop or something with that hot body of his. He didn't take it too lightly this morning when I called him a tree-loving, cultivating-plant pussy."

My mouth dropped open, and I just sat there. She so liked him. It was unreal.

"We argued for a good twenty minutes about a damn tree. I've never in my life had anyone get under my skin as much as he does. But forget about plant-pussy. I want to know everything!"

"Okay, well, he's an amazing lover, and when I say amazing, I mean ah-may-zing. I'm totally in—"

I glanced up and saw Layton leaning against the doorjamb, smiling at me.

I stopped talking and smiled at him. He was holding my bag, and I looked his body up and down. His hair looked like he'd just had a good fucking. His smile was beyond beautiful, and the look in his eyes was filled with passion.

"You're totally in, what? Whit? Hello? Holy hell, you can't just stop mid-sentence like that."

"Um…" I barely said as I couldn't pull my eyes from him.

He dropped the bag and walked up to me. I smiled as he knelt down in front of me.

He took the phone out of my hand. "Hey, Court," he said.

Layton laughed at whatever Courtney had said to him. "Sweetheart, she's gonna have to call you later."

He pulled the phone away from his ear, and I could hear Courtney. "Wait! Layton—"

He hit End and tossed my phone onto the bed. Then, he put his hand behind my neck as he brought my lips to his, and he kissed me so gently and sweetly.

He pulled back slightly and smiled. "I so want to make love to you again, but I think I've exhausted my dick."

I let out a giggle. "I've never had so much sex in such a short amount of time in my life."

"Come on, babe. I want to show you something, and I have your surprise." He stood and pulled me up with him.

I looked at his massive chest and placed both hands on him as the blanket fell away from me. His body was beyond perfect. I didn't think I would ever get tired of looking at it.

"Jesus, Whit, I gotta go finish getting dressed." He looked my body up and down and licked his lips.

I didn't know what came over me, but I had the intense urge to drop to my knees and take him into my mouth. He turned and walked away before I could. I took a deep breath and closed my eyes.

Jesus, Whitley…calm the hell down…you ho!

"Here, babe."

I opened my eyes to see him holding my bag. I took it, and I gave him a wink. "Give me five minutes."

He smiled and nodded. "I'll meet you in the kitchen."

I turned and took off into his massive bathroom. I looked at the shower and blushed at the intense sex we'd had in there, earlier this morning. I'd never been fucked against a wall, and that was exactly what had happened. He'd made my body feel so alive. It was hotter than hell, and it was something I surely wanted to do again.

It was hard to believe that twenty-four hours ago, I had fought my feelings for him so hard.

No longer. All I wanted to do was be in his arms—forever.

-》》》》》》》》》》》《《《《《《《《《《《《-

Layton held on to my hand and rubbed it up and down with his thumb, making the butterflies go crazy in my stomach.

"Where are we going?" I asked.

He was driving on the road that went through his whole ranch. We had just driven by the main stables, and I was shocked at how massive it was.

He smiled. "To the track."

"The track?"

He glanced at me and nodded.

"You have a racetrack on your property?"

He laughed. "Yep, it's a small quarter-mile track that Mike put in about three years ago."

"Wow."

How much money did they make off their horses anyway?

"Mike was just like our old man. He knew his horses. Since we were in high school, he made me save every damn dime I'd made, and he would use half of it on the races. He always at least doubled it."

It's like he's reading my mind.

He glanced over and smiled at me. "What made a girl from New York move to the small town of Llano?"

I laughed and shook my head. "I've wanted to move to Texas since I was in high school. One day, my dad met this guy at the racetrack, and he talked about his hometown in Texas. My dad instantly connected with him, and needless to say, they became fast friends, especially after my father won over a hundred and fifty thousand dollars on the races just from listening to this guy. Oh man, did he know his racehorses. We saw him a number of times after that, and each time, my dad made a ton of money. Nothing like that first day though!"

I smiled, remembering back to the first time we had met him. Fast-Track Jack was his name. He had the bluest of blue eyes and a dimple on his cheek. I remembered being slightly in awe over how good-looking he was. Even my mother had leaned over to tell me she'd had to fan herself from the heat coming from the guy. I briefly closed my eyes and pictured that day.

Layton laughed. "Damn, sounds like he knew his shit. What town was he from in Texas?"

I snapped my eyes open, and my heart started pounding.

Oh my God. The man I remembered looked exactly like...Layton.

"Um...Llano. He was from Llano."

I was looking at Layton, and his smile faded. He stopped the truck, put it in park, and looked at me.

"What was his name?"

My chest started moving up and down. "Fast-Track Jack. I mean, his name was Jack, but that's what the guys at the track called him."

I watched as all the color drained from Layton's face.

"Layton..."

He turned and looked straight ahead. We sat there for a good five minutes in silence.

"I know now why he had to leave."

I shook my head, confused. "Your dad? You know why he left you and Mike?"

He looked back at me and smiled slightly. "He had to leave me in order for you to find me."

I felt tears building in my eyes. "Oh, Layton."

I unbuckled my seat belt and crawled over onto his lap. My lips found his, and I ran my fingers through his hair as he moved his hand up my dress.

"Whitley, my father led you to me." His kisses quickly turned more passionate.

I felt him moving his seat back as I pulled my lips from his.

"Layton...Oh God...Layton," I whispered.

I watched him unbuckle his pants, and I sat up slightly, so he could pull them down and expose himself to me. I lifted my dress and pushed my panties over, so I could sit down on him.

"Oh. My. God," I said as I sank down onto him, feeling him fill my body.

I didn't even want to move. I just wanted to feel him inside me. I was so damn sore from all the sex, but I didn't care.

"God, Whit...baby, I need you to move."

I slowly started moving up and down, feeling him go in and out of my body. He pulled down the top of my dress and buried his face into my chest as I threw my head back.

"Baby, are you sore?" He placed kiss after kiss along my neck and chest.

"It's okay...feels so good," I said in between pants.

I couldn't get enough of him. I wanted him to be buried so deep inside me. I felt myself trying to go faster and harder. I needed more of him.

I was totally blaming this behavior on Courtney and that damn erotica book she'd had me read.

"God, Layton...I can't get enough of you! I need you...so...much."

"Faster, baby…go faster," he said, breathing deeply.

I moved as fast as I could, feeling his dick pounding into me. Each movement was better than the last. I started to feel that familiar build-up, and I prepared myself for another intense orgasm.

"Oh God, Layton…I'm about to come!"

Wait—is that a horn honking?

"Whit…"

I started going faster.

Fuck, he's hitting something.

"Um…Whit…"

There's the horn again.

Layton grabbed my hips and stopped me from moving.

I snapped my eyes open and looked at him. "Layton! I was just about to come!"

He smiled the cutest damn smile ever. "Whitley…Reed's behind us."

I looked up and out Layton's back window.

Oh. My. God. "Where's the closest rock?" I whispered.

I flew off of Layton and into the passenger seat as he pulled his pants up and started laughing.

"Holy shit! I just had public sex!" I whispered.

He laughed harder. "Baby, he can't hear you. Why are you whispering?"

I looked over and hit him on the shoulder. "I'm never going to be able to look at Reed again." I let out a gasp. "What if he tells Courtney?"

Layton put the truck into drive and started driving. He rolled down his window, stuck out his hand, and gave a wave.

"Why in the hell would he tell Courtney?"

I shook my head to clear my thoughts. "Damn you, Courtney, and damn that book! It's that stupid book's fault. It turned me into a horny-horn dog!"

Layton looked at me and smiled. "Well, I'd kind of like to think it's me, babe, that's turned you into a—what did you call it? A horny-horn dog?"

I looked over at the man that drove me crazy and insane. "Oh, trust me, it's your damn fault, too!"

SIXTEEN

→≫≫≫≫≫≫≫≫≫≫≫≫≪≪≪≪≪≪≪≪≪≪≪≪←

LAYTON

I glanced over at Whitley as the blush on her cheeks got deeper by the second.

Good Lord, I've never wanted someone so much in my life.

I can't believe it was my dad who had led her here, led her to me, just when I needed her more than the air I breathe.

As we got closer to the track, I could see her moving around in her seat. I reached over, grabbed her hand, and brought it up to my lips.

"Whit, don't worry. He probably didn't even see what we were doing," I said with a slight smile.

I knew damn well that Reed had seen everything though.

"Do you think?" she asked with the cutest damn look on her face.

I wanted so damn bad for her to finish what she'd started a few minutes ago.

"Yeah. He didn't see anything. Don't worry." I smiled and gave her a wink. "Here we are!" I pulled up and parked behind Lucky's horse trailer.

"I still can't believe you have a damn track on your property," Whitley said.

"It's not very big, but it gives the horses the practice they need when they're here."

I jumped out of the truck and jogged around to open up her door as Reed was pulling up. I glanced over at him, and I could tell by the smile on his face that he knew exactly what we had been up to.

I helped Whitley out and took her hand. We started to make our way over toward Lucky and my new horse.

"Is that the horse you bought in Kentucky?" Whitley walked up to the bay Thoroughbred horse I'd bought just a few days ago. "Oh my gosh, he's beautiful, Layton! I love bay horses. They're my favorite. What is he? About sixteen hands? He looks fast as hell."

Well, I'll be damned. The girl knows her horses, too. She's so damn perfect in every way.

I smiled as I glanced over toward Lucky, who was trying to hold back a grin. I knew he instantly loved Whitley.

Beautiful and smart, too.

She was moving her hand up and down each leg and checking out every part of him.

"Sixteen on the dot. And yes, he's fast as hell." I walked up and put my hands on my new baby boy.

"What's his name?" Whitley asked with a smile.

I smiled. "Blazin' Dreams."

Whitley turned back and pulled his face down to hers. If I hadn't known any better, I would say they were both looking into each other's souls.

"Blaze. I like that name. It fits you." She moved her hand up and down between his eyes.

My heart swelled up about ten times its normal size, watching her with Blaze.

Christ almighty, this girl is too good to be true. Now, if she ends up knowing her shit about cattle, I'm going to marry her tomorrow.

I hadn't even noticed Reed walking up.

"You must have a magical touch. I've never seen a horse so calm before," Reed said, smiling at Whitley.

Whitley threw her head up and looked over at Reed, who winked at her. Her cheeks instantly turned red.

She slowly let a smile play across her face. "It's all in the hands. The more gentle and attentive, the more you get from them."

Reed's smile dropped, and I busted out laughing. I walked up, took her into my arms, and turned her to face me.

"Do you want to see what a fifty-thousand-dollar racehorse feels like between your legs?"

Whitley glanced down at the dress she was wearing. Then, she looked at my boots.

"Can I wear your boots?" she asked with a slight smile.

Fuck yeah. I love her more and more.

Whitley ended up riding Blaze all the way back to the stables. Lucky had decided to keep him at my ranch instead of taking him to his place. That was fine by me. Whitley had instantly fallen in love with Blaze, and I wanted to keep that smile on her face for as long as I could.

I pulled up, parked, and jumped out of my truck. I just leaned against it, watching Whitley take care of Blaze. She had the saddle off in no time flat. I watched as she brushed out his coat and then picked up each foot and picked out his hooves. I was getting turned-on more and more from just

watching her with the horse. I couldn't wait to give her the surprise I had gotten her.

She took Blaze by the lead rope and walked him around for a bit before handing him off to Mitch, but not before she had given Blaze a good hug and scratch behind his ears.

"Jesus, dude, I don't think I've ever seen you look at a girl like the way you're looking at Whitley. And I know for a fact that it has nothing to do with what I drove up on." Reed punched me lightly on my left arm.

I smiled, but I couldn't pull my eyes off of her. She had made her way into the stables, and I was guessing she wanted to see the other horses. Once she rounded the corner and was out of my sight, I turned to look at Reed.

"*Fuck*. I've never in my life felt like this, Reed. I mean…" I let out a small laugh and shook my head.

Reed smiled and slapped my back. "Well, damn, it's about fucking time, dude, about fucking time."

I knew the grin on my face was goofy as hell. I wanted to shout how much I loved her from the top of the world.

"I love her, Reed."

He snapped his head and looked at me. "What? Layton, y'all hardly know each other. I mean, I get that you're probably having mind-blowing sex, which, by the way, is great for you but sucks for me since I can't even remember the last fucking time I had sex—"

"Reed."

"Oh, right. But love, Layton? Are you sure?"

I glanced back at the stables and watched as Whitley walked toward us with a huge smile on her face.

"I've never been more sure of anything in my entire life."

"Then, I'm happy for you, Layton. I just want you to be happy." Reed pushed off my truck and kicked the dirt.

I smiled as she got closer to us.

"Oh my God, you have a beautiful buckskin filly in there that Mitch said was a gift for someone."

I smiled and nodded. "Surprise."

Whitley looked at me funny and tilted her head.

This past week, she had told me that she always wanted a buckskin, so she could name it Tinker Bell and give it the barn name of Tink.

"Layton…you didn't…" She had a shocked look on her face.

I let out a laugh and nodded. "What can I say? Blaze seemed to be in love with that filly. I couldn't very well part them, now, could I?"

Whitley threw her hands up to her mouth.

"She's yours, baby."

Whitley ran, jumped into my arms as she wrapped her legs around me, and kissed the shit out of me. She pulled back and put her lips up to my ear. "I'm not letting you give me a horse as a gift."

I smiled at her. "I won the bet. I get to do whatever I want."

She chuckled as I slowly let her slide down my body.

She crinkled her nose up at me and giggled. "Can I name her Tinker Bell?"

I threw my head back and laughed.

Reed said, "Tinker Bell? Holy shit, that poor horse."

I nodded and pulled her to me again. I leaned down and gently kissed her. "Are you mad at me?" I asked.

She shook her head and gave me a look that just about knocked me down to the ground. "I love you, cowboy," she whispered.

"I love you too, Whit." I looked over at Reed. "Pontoon party?" I asked.

Reed smiled. "Ah, hell yeah!"

Whitley started laughing as Reed walked up to her, grabbed her, and spun her around. He put her down, and she looked over at me.

"Hell yes! Turns out CG stands for country girl! Get your party on, Whit. We're gonna show you how the country folk do it!" Then, Reed yelled over at Mitch, "Mitch! Pontoon party!"

Mitch smiled and gave a thumbs-up.

Whitley started laughing harder, and then she looked at me, confused.

"You in the mood for a party?" I asked her with a wink.

She slowly nodded as she walked up to me. I grabbed her and pulled her up against me.

"What should I wear for this…pontoon party?"

I moved my lips over toward her ear. "I don't care what you wear…as long as I can get it off of you fast."

She snapped her eyes up to mine, and the look she was giving me caused my heart to skip a beat. I grinned as she raised her eyebrows up at me.

"A pontoon party is a party we have down by the lake on my property. The lake covers about twenty-five acres. Mike put a pontoon on it a few years back. We just hang by the lake all day, swimming, drinking, and pontoonin'."

"Sounds like bathing suit attire!" she said with an evil smile. "Can I invite Courtney?"

"Of course you can!" I gave her a quick kiss, opened the passenger door for her, and helped her into the truck.

I turned around and called back to Reed. "Five?"

"Five, it is. I'll call the normal gang!" Reed yelled back as he took out his cell phone.

By the time I got Whitley back to her car, I wanted to rip off her damn clothes and finish what we'd started earlier.

She walked up to her car and threw her bag into the backseat before shutting the door and turning to face me. "Is it weird I'm going to miss you?" She looked down at the ground.

I used my finger and moved her chin up until her eyes captured mine. "Why would that be weird?"

She shrugged her shoulders. "It's just...I don't know. I promised myself I wouldn't fall in love again, that I wouldn't need someone, but...all I want to do is be with you. I don't want to leave your side, and that...that scares me."

I leaned down and gently kissed her soft lips. "Whitley, please don't be scared. I promise you, I'll never hurt you. Ever. I'm going to miss you, too, so please hurry. And pack a bag to stay with me for a few days," I said with a smile.

I watched as her cheeks filled with that beautiful rose color.

She barely whispered, "Okay."

I opened her door and smiled as she got it. I leaned in to kiss her good-bye once more before watching her pull down the road. My heart was pounding in my chest as I thought about what she'd just said. I was just as scared by the intense feelings I was having for her.

"I promise not to hurt you. I pray to God you make that same promise to me," I said as I watched her car pull out of sight.

I practically ran out of the house when I saw Courtney's truck pulling in. I walked out onto my front porch and watched them both jump out and grab bags out of the backseat.

My heart was pounding.

"Motherfucker. What in the *hell* is she wearing?" Reed said.

I turned and looked at him. "Which one?"

Reed shook his head. "Courtney! Could her shorts be any shorter? And those fucking cowboy boots with those shorts? What in the hell?"

I glanced back at both girls. They both had on jean shorts, T-shirts, and cowboy boots. They were both carrying bags, and when I looked at Whitley, she had the sweetest look on her face.

"Her shorts aren't that short." I looked Whitley up and down.

Courtney leaned over and said something to Whitley that caused her to blush.

"Motherfucker," I whispered.

"Yep…that's what I said." Reed turned and walked back into my house.

Kevin, Richard, and Mitch were already in the house, taking all the food I had and loading it up into my truck.

"Hey," I said.

Whitley made her way up the porch steps. "Hey, yourself."

I looked over at Courtney and smiled. She smiled back and shook her head.

I held up my hands. "You look like you want to give me the third degree."

She laughed. "Nope, I just wanted you to know I have not seen this girl this happy in a long time." She started walking by me and stopped. "You're either really fucking good in bed, or you used your Southern charm to bewitch her."

I stood there, just looking at her. "Can I say both?"

She looked me up and down and then turned to Whitley. "I'm going with the well-endowed junk and a Southern charmer." She spun around and walked into my house.

I slowly turned back to Whitley, who was laughing.

"Holy shit. Is she always so…open?"

She nodded. "Yep! That's Court. She doesn't sugarcoat shit."

I grabbed her and pulled her into my arms. She was biting on her lower lip, and I used my finger to pull it out from her teeth. I leaned down and gently started to suck and bite on her lip. She let out the sweetest, softest moan, and it moved through my body like a warm sensation.

I barely moved my lips from hers. "Whitley, I want you, baby."

"Layton…" She pushed her hips into my dick.

"Um…Layton, we got everything packed up. Dude, don't forget to open the gate for people to come in," Kevin said from behind me.

"Okay, Whit and I will take the ranch truck. Y'all can head on down."

Whitley smiled as she shook her head. "Layton, I can't leave Courtney alone with all your friends. She'll be pissed at me."

Just then, Courtney came out. "Hey, Whit. I'm driving down with these guys, okay?"

Whitley peeked around me to look at her best friend. "Court, are you sure?"

"Jesus, Whitley, I think I'll be fine. If one of them makes a move, I'll junk-punch their asses. Don't be too long!"

I took Whitley's hand and pulled her into the house. The moment we were inside, she dropped her bag and jumped into my arms. I pushed her against the wall and moved my hand up her shirt.

"Fuck, Whitley, I want you so damn bad that I can hardly stand it."

She threw her head back against the wall. "Yes, I missed you, Layton."

I put her down and was just about to unbutton her shorts when my fucking doorbell rang. I closed my eyes, and then I looked at her. I could see the disappointment in her eyes, but she was also giggling.

I walked over to the door and opened it up. I shook my head as I saw the guy who delivers my hay standing at my door.

"Mr. Morris, I just need you to sign for your delivery."

"Yep, sure thing."

"Your gate is open, sir. Were you aware of this?" he asked.

"Yep. Having a party." I signed the form and handed it back to him.

"Same location, sir?" he asked.

I saw him look behind me and smile. I turned around to see Whitley there. I glanced back at the delivery guy and took a step to my left to block his view of her.

"Yeah, same place. Thank you." *Fucker.*

I shut the door and turned around to see Whitley smiling at me. She slowly hooked her fingers in her shorts and began to slide them down. When she stepped out of them, I walked up, grabbed her, and picked her up.

As I brought her into my bedroom, I said, "I love how you drive me so crazy, Miss Reynolds."

She yelled as I threw her down onto the bed.

➤➤➤➤➤➤➤➤➤➤❌❮❮❮❮❮❮❮❮❮❮❮❮

Before I knew it, she was whispering my name into my ear as we both came together.

I couldn't get enough of her, and it was beginning to scare me. I'd never felt this way about anyone.

"I don't want to, but I think we better head down to the lake," I said as I moved my fingertips up and down her side.

"Courtney is probably ready to beat my ass!" She jumped up and started to get dressed.

I smiled, thinking about how I was about to make a clear statement to every one of my friends.

I was in love, and Whitley Reynolds was officially off the market.

SEVENTEEN

-》》》》》》》》》》><<<<<<<<<<<<<-

Whitley

By the time Layton and I finally got down to the lake on his property, there must have been at least fifty people there.

"Holy shit! Where did all these people come from?" I looked around at all the parked trucks.

Layton let out a laugh and grabbed my hand. I glanced over at him, and he had the goofiest smile on his face. I couldn't help but smile back.

"You ready?" he asked with a wink.

"Yep!" I gave him a wink back.

He jumped out of his truck and ran over to help me out. I was never going to get used to his Southern charm and manners. I glanced around, looking for Courtney. She was so outgoing that I wasn't worried about her feeling left out.

I looked around to see where the music was coming from. *Gesh, it almost sounds like a DJ is here.* I turned and saw about five huge speakers.

"Wow! Do y'all have parties here often? That is a major setup you guys have there."

Layton laughed and threw his arm around my shoulders, pulling me closer to him. "Mike used to be known for his parties. He would go all out. We called them pontoon parties. We haven't had one in a long time."

"How come?" I asked.

"I haven't had a reason to party…until now." He stopped me and pulled me closer to him, and then he gave me the most passionate kiss ever.

I let out a small moan, and I couldn't believe that my body was aching for him again. "Layton," I whispered.

"Layton!"

I turned and saw about three girls walking up to us. They all had huge smiles on their faces, and one girl with short blonde hair walked right up to me and hugged me.

She leaned down by my ear and whispered, "I don't know what you did, but thank you for bringing my cousin back." She pulled away and gave me the sweetest smile.

I grinned back and felt my face blushing.

Each girl took a turn giving Layton a hug and a kiss, and then they turned their attention to me, each thanking me. We stood there for a few minutes, talking. I found out they were all sisters and Layton's cousins. Each was married and had at least one child. I absolutely loved talking to them and had not laughed that hard in so long.

We made our way over to a fire pit with a huge grill next to it. Kevin was manning the grill, wearing an apron that said, *Kiss the Cook*. I saw hot dogs, hamburgers, and sausages. A nearby table had buns and all the fixings.

"Hey, Kevin," I said with a chuckle.

"Hey, Whit! Glad you made it to your party!" he said with a wink.

I let out a giggle and shook my head. "How in the world did y'all plan this so fast?"

Kevin laughed. "Oh, baby girl, we are pros at throwing together a party. Mike and I used to be known for our parties. As soon as Reed called and said Layton wanted to have a pontoon party, that was all I needed to hear to spring into action."

I smiled as I glanced over toward Layton. He was talking to a few guys I'd never seen before. At least ten kids, all under the age of six, were running around. One little girl ran by, and I swore she was the spitting image of Layton. I laughed as I watched them play.

I turned back to Kevin and gave him a slight smile. "Um…Kevin, what did you mean when you said this was my party?"

Kevin's smile faded for a quick second. He looked around for Layton. He grinned when he saw him. Layton turned toward me, and his smile about knocked my socks off.

"Whitley, Layton lost a part of himself when Mike died. Then, that bitch of a girlfriend walked out on him the night after Mike died. We were all worried about Layton. For a while there, he didn't even seem like he wanted to live. We tried like hell to throw a party. Layton and Mike loved having parties. We've all seen a change in Layton since the very first day you showed up."

I looked down to the ground, and I could feel my face getting hotter.

"Whitley, he's having this party to show everyone that he's okay. He's letting us know that he found you. I also think that bastard is trying to tell all these horny country boys that you're his."

I laughed as I peeked up at Layton. He was taking a drink of his beer and looking right at me. My heart stopped, and my knees felt like they were going to buckle out from under me.

"Whitley?"

I didn't even take my eyes off of Layton's. "Yes, Kevin?"

"Please don't hurt him."

My head snapped over, and I looked into Kevin's eyes. If I didn't know better, I would swear he had tears in them.

"I would never hurt him—*ever*."

"It's just…I've never seen him this happy before. It's like he's walking on cloud nine, and I don't wanna see him get hurt again."

I tried my best to smile at Kevin. "I feel the same way, Kevin. I've never in my life felt like this about anyone. Honestly, it scares the shit out of me!" I said with a giggle.

Keith Urban's "Big Promises" started to play, and I glanced over as Layton was walking toward me.

"Dance with me?" he asked with that drop-dead gorgeous smile of his.

I nodded as he pulled me closer to him. He led me over to an open area where a few other people were two-stepping. We took off dancing, and he started laughing.

"What's so funny?" I asked as I hit his shoulder.

"Damn, CG…you're my dream girl," he said with the biggest smile I'd seen on his face yet.

I tilted my head and giggled. "How's that?"

"You know your shit about horses, you can two-step better than half the girls here in Llano, and you are the most beautiful thing I've ever laid my eyes on."

I laughed as I put my face into his chest.

The song ended, and he spun me around a few times before I came face-to-face with Olivia.

"I heard a pontoon party was going on," Olivia said as she looked me up and down.

There was no way I could plan this girl's engagement party anymore. She was staring at me like she wanted me to disappear. I glanced over her shoulder to see Justin standing there, staring at Layton.

"What are you doing here, Olivia?" Layton asked as he grabbed my hand and pulled me closer to him.

It was almost like he was protecting me from the bitch.

The way she was looking him up and down made me sick to my stomach. Then, she licked her lips and glanced at me.

Bitch.

"I thought your pontoon parties were open to everyone, Layton. I'm just happy you finally decided to have one. Save me a dance." She winked.

Then, she turned and grabbed Justin's hand, and they walked over to a bunch of people talking near Reed and Richard.

Ugh, I'd like to slap the shit out of her.

"Don't let her being here ruin anything, baby," Layton whispered in my ear.

I looked up and saw Courtney talking to Mitch. She was laughing, and I saw that twinkle in her eyes as she looked Mitch up and down. I couldn't

blame her. He was good-looking, not as good-looking as Reed by any means, but Mitch was still cute.

"Layton, Mitch isn't with anyone, is he?" I asked as I glanced back at him.

He looked over toward where Court and Mitch were talking. He shook his head and smiled. "Nope. He was engaged to be married about four years ago, but he broke it off. I don't think he's really dated much since then."

"Huh...well, Courtney sure seems to be interested," I said with a laugh.

"Reed's gonna be pissed," Layton said.

"Does he like Courtney?"

Layton shrugged his shoulders. "He says he doesn't, but I have a feeling he does. What about Courtney?"

"I was pretty sure she liked him, but with the way she's looking at Mitch, I'm not so sure now. It's like she wants to devour him."

Layton pressed himself into me and whispered in my ear, "Is it crazy that my body is craving you again?"

The passion in his eyes caused me to suck in a breath of air. He leaned down and started to kiss me so sweetly that I almost wanted to cry.

"Jesus, Layton. My God, show some restraint. Whitley, honey, you're not making a very good impression on Layton's friends," Olivia said as she walked up and put her hand on his arm.

Oh no, she didn't.

"Excuse me?" I pulled away from Layton.

Layton stood there with his mouth hanging open.

"Well, I mean, I get that you two are...together...but honestly, Layton, you're making Whitley seem like a tramp."

"Olivia!" Layton said as his head snapped back over toward me.

What. A. Bitch.

I let out a laugh and took a deep breath. "I think my virtue is really none of your business, Olivia, but thank you so much for your concern."

I'd noticed when Courtney had walked up, but she'd turned around and walked away. A few seconds later, The Pussycat Doll's "Buttons" started playing. I smiled because I had a feeling Courtney was behind it. I walked up to Layton and grabbed his hands.

"Dance with me?" I asked in the sexiest voice I could muster.

He raised his eyebrows and smiled as he nodded. He pulled me into him, and I instantly felt how much my sexy voice had worked on him. I started grinding and dancing as close to him as I could. Layton leaned down and kissed my lips as he moved his hands up and down my body.

My whole body felt like it was on fire. When he pulled his lips away, I turned around, and he pulled me into him. I'd never danced so provocatively in my life, and it was turning me on more than I wanted.

Layton's hands traveled up and down my body, and I was practically shaking with desire. I glanced up and saw Courtney dancing with Mitch. I smiled, and before I knew it, Layton had turned me back around, and he was kissing me again.

He pulled away barely, his lips still touching mine. "You drive me crazy, Whitley."

I smiled as I grabbed his ass and brought him closer to me. I started moving my hips with his. "I don't know what it is, but I can't get close enough to you."

He gave me the gentlest kiss as the song ended, and "Why Wait" by Rascal Flatts started. He spun me around, and we took off two-stepping.

I've never been so happy in my entire life. I never want this moment to end. Ever.

➤➤➤➤➤➤➤➤➤➤➤❯❮⫷⫷⫷⫷⫷⫷⫷⫷⫷⫷⫷

I glanced over toward Courtney as we sat on the back of the pontoon boat with our feet in the cool water.

"Court, I have never had this much fun in my life. I mean, I almost feel like I'm dreaming, like the rug is going to be pulled out from underneath me, and I'm going to fall flat on my ass. I'm not supposed to be this happy."

Courtney snapped her head in my direction and threw her hands on her hips. "What? How can you say that, Whit? You deserve it more than any person I know. You are allowed to be happy, Whitley. I see the way that boy looks at you. I've never seen anyone look at another person with so much love. It's pretty damn clear that he was making a point with this party."

I smiled as I felt the heat move into my cheeks. I nudged Courtney's shoulder and smiled at her. "So, what's going on with Mitch?" I moved my eyebrows up and down.

Her smile faded for a moment as she looked back to the shore at Reed. He had been talking to some girl all afternoon.

"He's nice, really nice, but..." She glanced down and started kicking her feet in the water.

"But he's not Reed?"

She peeked up at me and frowned. "I hate him, Whit. I really hate him. He's stubborn, he knows he's good-looking, and he fucking plays around with goddamn plants! Ugh, just talking about him gets me all upset."

I laughed as I shook my head. "But?"

She threw her head back and let out a sigh. She looked around before speaking. "But I'm so attracted to him that I can't even think straight. God!

I've been fucking dreaming about his ass. I can't get him out of my head, Whit. I don't like him! I can't like him, but my God, he's so damn good-looking, and his body is out of this world. And his lips—I just want to taste them. Oh God, what am I saying?" Courtney buried her face into her hands.

"Court, honey, if you have feelings for Reed, don't fight it. God, I can't imagine if I had kept denying my feelings for Layton. I feel like he is the best thing that has ever happened to me."

Courtney glanced up, and her smile faded.

I looked over toward where she was staring. Layton was dancing with Olivia. My heart stopped. Florida Georgia Line's "Never Let Her Go" was playing.

"Not the best song for him to be dancing with her to," Courtney said as she turned back to me.

I couldn't pull my eyes away from them. He wasn't dancing very close to her, but a few people were watching them.

"Whit, he's had a lot to drink. Maybe he just isn't thinking straight."

I slowly looked at Courtney and then turned around and called out to Kevin. "Kevin, can you please take me back to shore?"

Kevin's smile faded when he turned toward where Layton and Olivia were dancing. He looked back at me and shook his head. "Wait, Whitley, I'm sure that means nothing. I know Olivia has been bugging him all day about dancing. It means nothing."

I felt the tears burning, but I tried to hold them back. "Please…just take me back," I whispered.

As we pulled up to the shore, "Done" by The Band Perry started playing. I couldn't help but let out a gruff laugh.

Kevin grabbed my arm before I jumped off the boat. "Whitley…"

I looked him in the eye and smiled slightly. "And here, you were afraid I'd be the one who would hurt him." I turned and jumped off the pontoon, and then I started to make my way toward the road.

Courtney came running up and grabbed my arm. "Whit, stop! He's not even dancing with her anymore or talking to her. I think Kevin was right. Layton was just trying to be nice. Please don't do this, Whitley. Don't walk away from him without giving him a chance to explain."

"I need to be alone. Please just give me a minute or two. Please, Court."

She gave me a weak smile and nodded. I looked over her shoulder and saw Layton walking toward me. I quickly spun around and walked away.

Please stop him from following me, Courtney. If you're really my best friend, you will stop him.

I was too afraid to look back, and by the time I reached the giant oak I'd had my sights on, I was crying.

Fuck! Why was he dancing with her? How could I be so stupid?

"Whitley," I heard Layton say from behind me.

I quickly wiped the tears away from my eyes. The last thing I wanted was for him to see me crying.

I knew this was too good to be true. I wasn't meant to find happiness.

"Whit, it kills me to know you are crying because of me, baby."

The tenderness in his voice was my undoing. I started crying harder. All I wanted was for him to take me in his arms and tell me he loved me and that Olivia meant nothing to him.

The moment I felt his hands on me, I swore I felt the love flow through my body. I turned to look at him. When I saw a tear rolling down his face, I let out a gasp.

"I'm so sorry, baby. She kept asking me to dance with her, and I finally just broke down to shut her up. I wasn't even thinking how it would look to you, and I wasn't even paying attention to the song. I swear to God, Whitley, when I look at her, I don't have any feelings at all for her. Baby, when I saw the look in your eyes before you walked away…I wanted to fall to the ground, just knowing it was me who put that hurt there. I love you, Whitley. Please believe me. I'd never do anything to hurt you. God, I promise you, I'll never hurt you."

The next thing I knew, I was in his arms, and he was holding me so tightly while I just cried. I wasn't even sure I was crying about him dancing with Olivia anymore.

He was moving his hand up and down my back. "Shh…baby, it's all right."

I pulled back and stared into his beautiful blue eyes. I took a deep breath and knew what I had to do. I had to be completely honest with him.

"He beat me so badly that last night that I ended up in the hospital."

I saw the look in his eyes turn from hurt to anger. He swallowed and was about to say something.

I shook my head. "Let me just get this out."

He nodded and grabbed my hands as we sat down on the ground.

"I met Roger in high school, and I fell fast and hard for him. He was the guy who all the girls wanted. Everyone said we were the perfect couple, that we were made for each other. He ended up getting an opportunity to work for his father in New York City. It was a no-brainer for me to just follow him there. I applied to a school in New York to pursue my dreams of getting into event planning." I smiled and shook my head, thinking back to those first few months in New York.

"I think I always knew he was cheating on me early on after we moved to New York. One day, I found a note in his pants from someone at the office. I didn't even confront him about it. I just pretended it wasn't meant for him. Then…the first time he, um…"

Layton held my hands tighter, and I saw tears building in his eyes. My heart was pounding. All I wanted to do was get lost in Layton's love and never think about Roger again. But I had to do this.

I cleared my throat. "The first time he hit me was over a stupid disagreement before a dinner party. He slapped me so hard that I was sure my eye was going to come out of my socket. The moment he did it, he apologized and said he didn't know what had come over him. He blamed it on being so stressed out from his job and from trying to keep his father happy. He even cried. I actually ended up feeling bad for him…if you can believe that," I said with a gruff laugh.

"Motherfucker." Layton looked away.

I took a deep breath. "A few months went by, and things seemed to be back to normal. Then, he saw me talking to a guy outside our building. He was a neighbor, and I had just come back from a run, so he started telling me about a marathon. As soon as Roger and I walked into our apartment, he grabbed me by the arm, spun me around, and got right in my face. He kept yelling at me for flirting with the guy. I pulled my arm away and told him he was being an asshole and to stop being so damn jealous."

I felt my body start shaking as I could still hear Roger's voice and feel his breath on my skin. When I closed my eyes, I was brought back to that night.

"He got right in my face and started calling me a whore. He said I was never to call him names again. I told him to fuck off, and he…"

I could feel tears rolling down my cheeks. As I felt Layton wipe them away, I opened my eyes and looked into his loving ones.

"Baby, I'm so sorry he hurt you."

I smiled and took a deep breath. "He pushed me so hard that I flew backward and hit my head on the coffee table. I ended up missing three days of classes that week because I had a killer headache. When the beatings became a regular occurrence, I slowly started to pull away from my family and friends. If I wore a skirt that was too short, he would hit me. If I talked to another man or even looked at one, he would hit me. I kept telling myself that if he did it again, I would leave. But he broke me into a million pieces—not just by hitting me but also with his words. I felt like I deserved the punishments, and I often wondered if maybe I was provoking him, and I didn't realize it."

"God, Whitley, no! Of course you didn't."

"I see that now, but back then, I couldn't see it. When I looked in the mirror, I only saw the person he wanted me to see—someone who was weak and not able to survive without him."

"Jesus, Whitley. I don't even know what to say."

"That last night, we were at a company party. Roger was flirting with this girl, Lucy, all night. It turned my stomach at how openly he touched

her and whispered in her ear. I got pissed and purposely danced with a coworker of his, Nick, who was up for the same promotion as Roger. I was thanking him for the dance, and I placed my hand on his arm. The moment I did it, I realized my mistake. I certainly paid for it when we got home. It was the worst beating of them all. I just knew that, this time, he was going to end up killing me because he was so angry. I woke up in the hospital, and…"

I started to cry a little harder as I thought about that night. I quickly wiped away my tears and smiled at Layton as I took a few deep breaths.

"When I woke up and realized I was okay, I decided that was enough. I was done. I would never again let him hurt me, physically or mentally. I remembered the man at the racetrack talking about the little town of Llano. I asked Court to move to Texas with me, and we started making plans for me to check myself out of the hospital and leave New York. I was so scared, Layton. You'll never know how scared I was when I left, thinking he was going to walk into the apartment and see me packing up."

Layton shook his head and looked into my eyes. "Where was he?"

"He had gone out of town for business. I knew that was my only chance to leave. So…I did. I left, and I never looked back."

Layton moved closer to me. "Did you tell your parents?"

I smiled slightly. "I did. My father was so angry. I had to practically beg him not to drive to New York to beat Roger's ass. He did tell me he better never see Roger again, or he would kill him."

Layton placed his hands on the sides of my face, and the butterflies in my stomach took off with his touch.

"Whitley, I would do anything to take all that pain and hurt away. You're the bravest person I've ever met. You amaze me, baby."

I got up on my knees and wrapped my arms around him. He pulled back and cupped my face with his hands again as he used his thumbs to wipe away my tears.

"As God as my witness, I promise you, no one will ever hurt you again, baby. I'll kill them before I let them hurt you."

I slammed my lips against his and kissed him with everything I had. The moan from his lips moved through me like a warm blanket covering my body. I'd never felt so loved and so safe in my entire life.

In Layton's arms, I knew I would always be safe.

I just wished I could shake the feeling that something terrible was about to happen.

EIGHTEEN

-》》》》》》》》》》》《《《《《《《《《《《《《-

LAYTON

I was so angry, and all I wanted to do was beat someone's ass. It had about killed me to listen to Whitley tell me how that asshole had beaten her. The whole time, I'd made plans to track his ass down and give him a taste of his own medicine.

By the time we had returned to the party, Whitley seemed to be back to her normal self. She was laughing and talking to Courtney and Mitch about something.

When I felt a hand on my arm, I looked to see Olivia standing there. I rolled my eyes, and I looked back toward Whitley.

"Layton, please, can we go somewhere and talk? I just want a few minutes of your time. Please."

I never took my eyes off of Whitley.

I love her. I love her more than the air I breathe.

Whitley glanced up, and her eyes captured mine. The way she stood there, looking so beautiful, actually caused my legs to shake.

"Sorry, Liv, don't think so," I said.

I started to walk up to Whitley as I watched Richard make his way over to her. He stepped in front of her, and I saw her smile and shake her head. I stopped right behind him.

"So, you won't dance with me, Whitley? What? Are you, like, with Layton now?"

I put my hand on his shoulder and moved him out of the way as I looked Whitley in the eyes. The way they sparkled caused my stomach to do all kinds of weird shit.

Blake Shelton's "Honey Bee" started playing, and I smiled bigger, causing her to laugh.

"Richard, Miss Reynolds is officially off the market." I held out my hand, and she placed her hand in mine. "Dance with me?"

She glanced at Richard, and her smile faded just a little. "Excuse me, Richard. My boyfriend is asking me to dance with him."

I laughed as I brought her lips to mine. We didn't even talk during the song. I just spun her around as she kept laughing and throwing her head

back. When the song ended, I dipped her, and she busted out in the biggest grin I'd ever seen.

"Will you accompany me to a fancy dinner in Austin on Monday night?"

She giggled and nodded as she bit down on her lip.

I brought her up and tilted her chin up toward me. I put my lips next to her ear. "I'm ready to leave."

Pulling back from me, she licked her lips and gave me the sweetest smile as she nodded.

"Let me go tell Reed and Kevin that we're leaving."

I finally found Reed, Kevin, and Mitch all in the old deer cabin.

"What in the hell are y'all doing in here?" I looked at the three of them.

Kevin shook his head. "Reed here is drunker than a motherfucker, and Mitch isn't too far behind. They're arguing over Courtney."

I looked between both of them. "What in the hell are you arguing about?"

Mitch looked over at Reed. "This fucker. I mentioned I was going to ask Courtney out, and he starts bad-mouthing her."

Reed started laughing. "Dude, first off, I don't think she is the type of girl who only dates one guy at a time. I mean, her job is to read fucking sex novels. She probably knows more about getting a guy off than you could ever dream. I'm just saying, she seems...very experienced, if you know what I mean."

"Reed, knock it the fuck off. You don't know the first thing about Courtney, so you need to shut your mouth," I said as I looked over at Kevin, who seemed to be trying to get Reed's attention and mine.

"You know, you're right, Layton. I don't have a clue about her fucking sex life, but you can't tell me she doesn't read those fucking sex books and then goes and finds a man to get off with it. She's a bitch with a rich city-girl attitude."

"Um, Reed...shut up," Kevin said.

Reed kept running at the mouth. "Dude, if you really want to ask her out, go for it, but I wouldn't touch her with a ten-foot pole. That's all I'm saying."

Mitch looked behind Reed and closed his eyes.

"I mean, maybe you want a girl like that—"

I reached over and punched Reed in the arm. "Reed, shut the fuck up."

"What? I call the whores as I see them."

I heard a gasp, and Reed realized why we had all tried to get him to shut up. He slowly turned around and saw Courtney standing there. She looked like she was about to start crying, but she squared off her shoulders and cleared her throat.

"Um…Mitch, I was just coming to let you know I was heading back with Layton and Whitley. I'm, uh…I'm really tired and just wanted to say thank you for giving me the number to that painter. I, um…I guess I'll see y'all around." Her voice cracked as she spoke.

She turned to leave, and Reed closed his eyes.

"Ah, fuck," he whispered.

He took off after her, and I followed behind him. Courtney was walking away as fast as she could when he grabbed her arm. She spun around and had tears streaming down her face.

"Courtney, wait…I didn't mean to say all that shit. It's just…it's just…" Reed was shaking his head like he was trying to clear his thoughts.

"Don't you ever speak to me again, Reed. You made yourself pretty damn clear about what you thought of me. I wouldn't want you to have to associate with a whore like me."

She turned and started to make her way toward Whitley. Whitley was standing off to the side, and the moment she saw Courtney, she walked up to her and took her in her arms. They turned and started making their way back to my truck.

I walked up to Reed and gave him a push. "What in the fuck was that all about, you asshole? I've never in my life heard you talk about a girl like that."

He started shaking his head. "I don't know what happened. Fuck! I heard Mitch telling Kevin how much he liked Courtney and how he was going to ask her out…and I don't know, Layton. Something fucking snapped. I got jealous, and the last thing I wanted was for her to go out with him."

"So, what? You thought you would bad-mouth her and turn him off of her? Did you ever think of just telling Mitch you liked her, too?"

He just stared at me. "I guess so. I mean, shit…I don't know."

"You're an asshole, Reed Moore. Do you know that? I hope you saw the hurt in her eyes. I hope it's burned into your memory." I turned toward my truck and started to walk off.

Stupid motherfucker. I have no idea how he's going to dig his way out of this hole, and I don't want to be a part of any of it.

➤➤➤➤➤➤➤➤➤➤➤❳❬❬❬❬❬❬❬❬❬❬❬❬❬-

Whitley walked into my bedroom and let out a sigh. "Can Courtney stay here tonight? I just don't think she should drive home. She'd had a few beers at the party, and I'm pretty sure she just drank half a bottle of wine while we listened to Christina Aguilera's 'I Hate Boys' over and over again."

"Sure, baby. As long as I have you next to me tonight, I don't mind at all. She can sleep in any one of the guest bedrooms." I got up, and I placed a kiss on her forehead before we headed out to the living room.

I watched as Whitley tried to wake up Courtney, who was passed out on my sofa. She turned to me and shrugged her shoulders. I walked over, reached down, and picked up Courtney. I carried her upstairs to one of the guest bedrooms.

By the time Whit and I got back to my room, I flopped onto my bed. "Jesus, I'm exhausted."

Whitley laughed and lay down next to me. "Can we just snuggle, Layton? I don't think I even have the energy to kiss you right now!"

I rolled over and kissed her lightly on the lips before I got up and started to take off my clothes. I watched as she looked my body up and down. As exhausted as I was—and my dick was—I was still hoping she would follow me into the shower.

After walking into the bathroom, I reached in and turned on the shower. I stepped inside and closed my eyes as I let the hot water run over my body. When I felt the warmth of her touch on my arm, I couldn't help but smile. I turned around and saw the most beautiful woman standing in front of me. I picked her up as she wrapped her legs around my body. I leaned her against the wall and kissed her as she let out a small moan.

"God, Whit." I moved her body over me.

The moment my dick sank into her warm body, I felt like I was going to come.

"Oh, Layton, faster," she whispered.

I gave her exactly what she wanted. When she started to call out in pleasure, I captured her cries with my mouth. Nothing felt better than coming and feeling myself pour into her body. I couldn't get enough of her.

As I slowly let her down, I grabbed a washcloth and washed her whole body. She took the washcloth from my hand and washed my body in return.

By the time we both crawled into bed, I was exhausted, and so was Whitley. She moved and threw her leg over my legs as she put her head on my chest. It wasn't long before I heard her breathing slow down.

I closed my eyes and thanked God for this beautiful gift wrapped in my arms. As I listened to her breathing, I thought about tomorrow and how I couldn't wait to introduce her to Jen and Kate. I knew they would love Whitley just as much as I did.

As I drifted off into sleep, I started to dream. All I could see was the sun setting, and someone walking toward me in a beautiful white dress. Just as she got close enough for me to see who she was, her face was blurred, and I heard Mike's voice.

Go to her, Layton. She needs your help. She needs you to save her.

I woke up with a jerk and felt sweat dripping off my body.

What in the fuck? What was he talking about? Who needed my help? Was he saying someone needed to be saved?

I looked down at Whitley. She was sleeping so peacefully. I knew Mike couldn't have been talking about Whitley. She would always be safe in my arms. She'd never have to worry about that asshole again.

I gently kissed her forehead. "You're safe now, baby. I'll always keep you safe."

NINETEEN

Whitley

I made myself a cup of hot tea and sat on Layton's back porch, which was probably bigger than my living room. The cool breeze on my face actually made me chilly.

I closed my eyes and thought about last night when I'd heard Layton whispering about keeping me safe. My heart swelled up with so much love that I could hardly stand it. I'd wanted to let him know so badly that I had been awake, but at the same time, I had been so damn sore. I didn't think we could possibly have any more sex.

I looked up to see Courtney walking up from the barn. I'd been wondering where she had gone off to this morning.

She smiled at me as she got closer. Her eyes looked so empty and sad. I was so pissed-off at Reed for the things he'd said about her, but Layton had said Reed was so jealous from the idea of Mitch asking Courtney out that he'd just snapped and started talking shit about her, hoping to throw Mitch off. It didn't matter. The things he'd said were terrible and mean-spirited. I'd never seen Court cry as much as she had last night. I hadn't really realized how much she liked Reed.

"Hey, sleepyhead," Courtney said with a fake-ass smile.

"Hey, yourself. Where were you?" I gave her a wink and a grin.

Her smile grew just a little bigger. "Mitch saw me out walking this morning and invited me to ride along with him as he checked on the fence in some pasture or something." She shrugged.

She sat down next to me, and I bumped my shoulder against hers.

"Oh yeah? How did this ride go?" I wiggled my eyebrows up and down.

Courtney turned away and looked back toward the barn. I watched as the blush swept over her cheeks when Mitch walked out of the barn and waved to her. I looked between the both of them.

"Holy shit, Court. Did something happen between the two of you?"

Courtney snapped her head over and just glared at me. "What do you mean, Whit? Like, did I have sex with him? Contrary to what Reed might think, I'm not actually a whore."

My mouth dropped open, and I sat up a little. "Holy shit, Court. I wasn't thinking that you'd slept with him. I was thinking more along the lines of maybe kissing him!"

She looked back toward Mitch as he jumped into his truck and took off down the road, pulling a trailer with two round bales of hay on it.

She smiled as she let out a giggle. "Oh. My. God." She looked back at me and shook her head. "I've never in my life been kissed so passionately. It was like he couldn't get enough of me. God, Whit…I swear if he had told me to strip down and let him make love to me out in the open, I would have done it!"

I let out a laugh. "You've either just read a really good book, or you've gone too long without sex."

She laughed. "I think it's a little bit of both. But honestly, he's such a gentleman. He never brought up what that fucker, Reed, had said last night. Mitch asked me about my job, how long I've been in love with reading, and how much I knew about horses. It was all about me. I didn't have to hear about how he was master of the plant world and the king of two-stepping. He truly wanted to get to know me. It was amazing. He even told me he would read a book if I gave him one."

I crinkled up my nose and giggled. "Mitch? Mitch said he would read a book that *you* gave him? Does he know what type of books you read?"

She threw her head back and laughed. "Yes! I was thinking of giving him *Knight and Play!*"

I just looked at her, and then we both busted out laughing. I looked up to see Layton walking toward us. He was covered in dust and looked sexy as hell.

"Holy shit. Damn…that boy is fine, Whit."

I smiled as I took a sip of tea and watched Layton moving closer. The way he was walking about had me ready to tell Courtney it was time for her to leave.

"How lucky am I? Two beautiful women are sitting on my porch," Layton said with a wink.

I let out a giggle. I looked over at Court and winked before turning back to Layton. "So, this dinner on Monday night? Fancy?" I asked as I set my cup down.

Layton walked up, leaned down in front of me, and kissed me so sweetly that I almost let out a soft moan.

When he pulled back, he frowned. "It is fancy. It's a dinner for an investment bank in Austin. I sit on the board of directors, and they're hosting it."

For one brief moment, a surge of panic rushed through my body as I thought of Roger.

Jesus, Whitley, calm the hell down. Roger is not going to be at an investment party in Austin, for cripe's sake.

"Baby, are you okay? You turned white as a ghost." Layton placed his hand on the side of my face.

My stomach dropped, and it felt like it was twisting and turning.

The things his touch does to me—will it always be like this?

I smiled as I looked into his eyes. "Yes, I guess I just realized I better get into town to go shopping for a fancy dress!"

Courtney laughed as she grabbed my hand and pulled me up. Layton stood and kissed me on the forehead, and then he smiled at me even bigger.

"Please, Whit, I have a closet full of dresses. Excuse us, Layton, but I'm going to have to take her away from you. We have prepping to do."

Layton's face dropped for a quick second before he leaned over and whispered into my ear, "I'll be over around seven? Dinner?"

I smiled as I nodded, and then I let Courtney lead me back into the house. I turned back one more time and gave him the sexiest smile I could. He winked as he gave me the sexiest damn smile ever in return.

"Jesus, Courtney, you're pulling my arm out of the socket. What the hell?"

She stopped and looked at me as she dropped my arm. "Didn't you see the fucker walking up from the barn? No way do I want to be within ten feet of him."

"Reed?" I asked.

She tilted her head and put her hands on her hips. "Yes, Reed. Do you know any other fuckers who would be walking up from the barn?"

"Well…" I laughed.

"Oh God, Whit. Just go pack up your shit. We're going home to play dress-up!" She turned and walked toward the stairs and up to the room where she'd stayed last night.

By the time I was packed and ready to go, Courtney was already in her truck and giving me a hurry-the-fuck-up look.

I ran up to the truck, and as I jumped in, I saw Courtney glaring at someone. I glanced in the direction and saw Reed walking toward us. He looked like he was trying to get Courtney's attention.

I looked back at Courtney. "He looks like he wants to talk to you, Court."

She watched him as he walked around the front of her truck to the driver's side. He stopped and knocked on the window. Courtney was staring straight ahead as she gripped the steering wheel tighter. She slowly looked over at Reed. The next thing I knew, she slammed her foot on the gas, and we spun out and took off down the driveway.

"Oh my God! Courtney! You could have hurt him by doing that. What in the hell were you thinking?" I spun around and saw Reed standing there, watching the truck speed away.

"Is his ass still standing?"

I turned and looked at her with my mouth hanging open. "Um…yes, thank God."

Courtney started shaking her head as she laughed. "Shit. I was really hoping he was standing closer, so I could have run over at least one foot."

What? This girl has lost her damn mind!

"Courtney! What in the world is wrong with you?"

She turned and gave me an evil grin. "Come on, let's go find you the perfect dress to wear for Monday night. No more talk of the plant-loving, dickhead asswipe."

I shook my head and turned to look out the front window. I smiled, thinking about the most amazing few days I'd spent with Layton.

I can't believe how much has changed in my life in just a few short weeks. I closed my eyes and tried to picture myself in his arms. He made me feel so safe, so loved.

An image of Roger entered my mind, and my eyes snapped open. I instantly had a sick feeling in my stomach.

Thank God he has no idea where I am.

TWENTY

-》》》》》》》》》》》《《《《《《《《《《《《-

LAYTON

I pulled up outside of Whitley's house and put my truck in park.

Shit! I really hate these benefit dinners. Mike was always better at this stuff than I was. The last benefit I attended, I talked more to all the wives and girlfriends than anyone else. I would much rather castrate a bull than spend a few hours with these city folks.

I took a look at myself in the rearview mirror. I was freshly shaven, and my blue eyes seemed to have life back in them. My messy brown hair was still messy, which caused me to smirk.

No way am I changing for anyone. They can either take me or leave me.

I let out a long sigh as I opened the door of the truck and got out. My black tux felt awkward, and the fucking shoes were going to kill my feet by the end of the night.

As I walked up to the front door of Whitley and Courtney's house, my heart started beating faster.

Why in the hell am I nervous? I spent the last few days with this incredible girl, so why in the fuck am I so jumpy?

Before I could even knock, the door flew open, and Courtney was standing there with a shit-eating grin on her face. I couldn't help but laugh as I thought back to yesterday when Reed had told me how Courtney had nearly killed him when she pulled out of the driveway.

"Layton," she said with a wink.

I smiled and returned her wink with one of my own. "Courtney, I heard you almost ran over Reed yesterday. I assured him it must have just been an accident."

Her smile grew bigger, and she let out a small giggle. "Of course, it was an accident." She stepped to the side to let me in. "Whitley should be down in a minute. She looks beautiful."

I smiled, just thinking about Whitley. *She always looks beautiful.*

"Does she ever not look beautiful?" I asked with a wink.

Courtney's smile faded, and she walked right up to me. "Nice. Very sweet with all the Southern bullshit and all, but listen, and listen good, bud. That's my best friend up there. She's been through hell and back one too many times. You so much as make a tear fall from one of her eyes again,

and I'll hunt you down and make sure you're never able to use that dick of yours *ever* again."

My smile faded, and my mouth dropped open. I went to say something, but Courtney put her finger up.

"I'm not done talking."

I took a step back and actually began to feel sorry for Reed because he'd pissed off this girl.

"I haven't seen Whit this happy in—well, shit, I don't know if I've ever seen her this happy. Either you're really good in bed, or you've truly shown her how much you care about her. I'm hoping it's both, but ya know, I'll be happy with the latter. Treat her right, Layton. She deserves it. She deserves to be loved and looked after, to be spoiled and treated like a princess, to feel safe. Please just don't ever treat her any less than what she deserves."

I forced my tears back from seeing the tears building in Courtney's eyes. I had to take a moment before I could even respond to her.

"Courtney, first off, you scare the shit out of me."

She smiled and winked at me.

"Second, I've never in my life felt this way about anyone. It's like Whitley has filled something that's been missing for so long. I feel so renewed and alive. I can hardly breathe when she's in the same room as me. I can't keep my hands off her because I have this overwhelming need to have her as close to me as possible. The moment I first laid eyes on her, I knew what was missing in my life—true, honest-to-God love. From the very first day when her eyes looked into mine, I knew that I loved her. I'll never hurt her, and I will *never* let anyone else hurt her again. I'd lay down my own life to protect her."

She took a step closer to me as a smile spread across her face, causing me to smile in return.

"Oh, Layton Morris, I'm not that easily swept off my feet, but that…that just put me totally in your corner."

I laughed. "Thank you. I think?"

"Oh, trust me, you always want the best friend in your corner." She turned and started to head into the kitchen.

I followed behind her and leaned against the counter.

She looked over her shoulder. "Speaking of best friends, I hope what Reed said about me didn't—"

I held up my hand. Now, it was my turn to stop her from talking. "Court, listen, he was drunk. He was jealous, and he didn't mean a damn word he said."

Her eyebrows lifted, and she tilted her head. "What do you mean he was jealous? Of what?"

I took a deep breath. I was pretty sure I was fixin' to break some man code, but it would be worth it. It killed me to think that Courtney would believe anyone thought of her in any negative way.

"Listen, what I'm about to tell you, I'm sure, breaks some kind of man code, so this stays between you and me. Is that a deal?"

She slowly sat down on one of the kitchen bar stools. "Okay. Deal."

I looked around, and leaning down closer to her, I whispered, "I'm pretty sure Reed likes you…like, as in, likes you a lot."

She moved in closer and whispered, "What makes you think that?"

"Well, he kind of got drunk last night and told me he…told me he…"

"Told you he, what?" Courtney shouted.

"Shh! Damn, Court."

"Oh shit! Sorry, go on. Please go on," she said, going back into our whispered conversation.

I sucked in a deep breath and let it out. "I'm pretty sure I'm also breaking a best-friend code here, so you better take this shit to your grave."

She sat up a little and used her index finger to cross her heart. "I promise. I won't even tell Whit."

Before I knew it, I was spitting out what Reed had spilled to me last night in his drunken fest. "Last night, he told me that he thinks he loves you."

She pulled back with a shocked look on her face. "What?"

I made a face and nodded. "Yep. I've never, in all the years I've known Reed, ever heard him say he thought he loved a girl."

Courtney looked down to the floor and started to shake her head. "But…he said all those things, and every time I see him, he's always such a jerk to me. I mean, he is always picking a fight with me."

I used my finger and gently lifted her chin up to me. "Courtney, men are…well, hell, I don't really know how we are. But I can tell you, I've never seen Reed's eyes so full of hurt and regret like I did when you walked in and overheard him. You have to know that he was just talking bullshit because Mitch had just said he was planning on asking you out. I don't think Reed really knows what to do with these feelings toward you, and he just panicked and handled it all wrong."

My heart broke as I saw a tear slowly slide down Courtney's face. She wiped it away and stood up.

She took a deep breath and gave me a weak smile. "Well, to be honest, I'm glad I walked in and heard him say those things. It just opened my eyes to the type of person he is. I actually enjoyed my time with Mitch the other morning, and if I hadn't heard Reed running off at the mouth, I would have just been sitting around, waiting for him and waiting to be hurt by him. Instead, I decided to give things with Mitch a try, and…" Her voice cracked a bit, and she forced a bigger smile. "And he is a complete gentleman.

We're going out to dinner tonight. Mitch will treat me with the respect I deserve. Reed Moore is the furthest thing from my mind."

My heart dropped a bit because her mouth was saying one thing, but her eyes were saying something totally different.

"Listen, Courtney. Reed is my best friend, and Mitch is a friend as well. I don't want to see either of them hurt. Just be sure you're not running into Mitch's arms to avoid your feelings for Reed. Reed is probably one of the nicest guys I know. He would never purposely hurt you, and I know he would love you one hundred and ten percent. Mitch just might not be the safer choice, sweetheart. He seems like it now, but—"

She was just about to say something when we heard Whitley coming down the stairs. I could hear her shoes on the hardwood floor.

"Hey," her sweet voice said from behind me.

I slowly turned around, and all the air in my lungs was immediately gone.

Her brown hair was pulled up and piled into loose curls on top of her head. My eyes moved down to her neck where she was wearing a small delicate necklace. My dick instantly got hard from thinking about kissing her exposed neck. I looked down at her beautiful red chiffon evening gown, fitting her curves perfectly. I couldn't believe how beautiful she looked.

I went to open my mouth, but I had to shut it again. Courtney let out a giggle, and Whitley smiled.

"Do you like it?" she asked with the cutest damn smile on her face.

"Um," was all I could get out.

"It's Court's dress. It's a mermaid gown with a sweetheart neckline. I've always wanted to wear it!" she said with a nervous laugh.

"Whitley, you look…" I had to clear my throat before I continued. "My God, you look stunning, sweetheart." I looked down into her eyes.

The blush spreading across her face made my dick even harder.

Fuck dinner. I just want to take her home and make love to her all night.

She slowly made her way over to me and used her finger to gesture for me to move closer to her. As I moved my ear closer to her mouth, I felt her hot, sweet breath.

"I can't wait for you to take me out of this dress. I have a surprise for you underneath it."

I pulled my head back and looked at her. I couldn't even think straight. "Ah…excuse me for one moment, ladies." I stepped around Whitley and Courtney and made my way out the front door.

I took a few deep breaths to calm down my racing heart. "Damn the things that girl does to me."

I pulled out my phone and made my first of two phone calls.

TWENTY-ONE

Whitley

I stood there and watched as Layton made his way out onto the front porch.

"Jesus, Whit! What in the hell did you say to that poor boy?" Courtney said with a laugh.

I shrugged my shoulders. "I just told him that I had a surprise underneath the dress, and I couldn't wait for him to take it off and see it." I turned and looked back at Court.

Courtney started laughing. "Way to give the poor guy a hard-on right at the very beginning of the night!"

I covered my mouth up with my hands and started shaking my head. I felt my face turning hotter. "My God, Courtney, this is all your fault!"

Courtney's face dropped, and she just looked at me with a stunned expression. "What? What's all my fault? That you finally discovered your own sexuality? That you're actually able to wear a sexy dress and have a man appreciate it? He couldn't pull his eyes away from you, girl!"

"You turned me into a horny bitch, Court! It's that damn book's fault...and that stupid vibrator you gave me. Do you know I had a dream about Layton last night, and I had to take that damn thing out? I closed my eyes and thought about him the whole time while I used a stupid vibrator to have an orgasm!"

The smile spreading across Courtney's face instantly told me that Layton was behind me. I glanced over my shoulder and saw him standing there with his mouth hanging open.

"Ah...I think I need to take a cold shower before we leave."

Oh. My. God. Where is the hole for me to crawl into?

Courtney walked right up to me and smiled. "Oh, the power of a good erotica book!"

She walked up to Layton, laughing, as she closed his mouth with her finger.

I tried to smile. "Layton, I didn't know you were standing there."

He walked up to me and took me into his arms. He kissed me so passionately it almost felt like all the air left my body. He slowly pulled his lips away from mine. The smile crossing his lips caused me to giggle.

"Will you do me a favor?"

"Anything," I whispered.

"Go back upstairs and get that vibrator."

I let out a chuckle and held up my clutch. "I don't think it will fit in here."

He smiled. "Put it in something else."

Oh my God. I can't believe I'm going to even entertain this idea!

"Mr. Morris, are you planning on being naughty later?"

He closed his eyes and then slowly opened them, capturing my eyes with his. I sucked in a breath at the smoldering look in his eyes.

I stepped back and made my way upstairs to get the Lelo vibrator, my heart pounding the whole way.

By the time I got into Layton's truck, my heart was slamming in my chest.

I can't believe I went back upstairs to get a vibrator, for Christ's sake! I'm never reading another one of Courtney's books again.

Layton got in, shut the door, and gave me a panty-melting smile.

Jesus…he is so damn good-looking. I need someone to pinch me 'cause I have to be dreaming.

"I can't believe I did that!" I felt the blush on my cheeks.

Layton placed the back of his hand on my cheek and slowly moved it down. "My God, you're so beautiful. I can hardly believe you're here with me."

Oh. My. God. I can barely breathe, and my stomach is in knots.

"I was just thinking the same thing about you!" I said with a giggle. "Hey, why did you go outside earlier?"

Layton shook his head and laughed. "Jesus, Whit, it's bad enough, just seeing you in that sexier-than-hell dress, but when you tell me you can't wait for me to take it off and see what's underneath…there's no way in hell I am going to be able to wait to get you back home. I called and booked a hotel room in Austin."

My mouth dropped open before I let out a laugh. "Layton, do you know how happy you make me?"

He leaned over and kissed the tip of my nose. "I hope to always make you happy, baby. Come on, let's go get our groove on."

"I can't get my groove on in this dress!"

"Fine, let's go mingle around in a room full of tight-ass investors and maybe take a spin around the dance floor a time or two."

I smiled and laughed. "Sounds like the fun will be after dinner—at the hotel," I said with a wink.

-⟫⟫⟫⟫⟫⟫⟫⟫⟩⟨⟪⟪⟪⟪⟪⟪⟪⟪⟪-

My feet were killing me, and I was pretty sure I was getting dirty looks from almost every woman in the room. It seemed like we had been here for hours already. Layton and I had danced a few times, and it reminded me of the dinners I had gone to for my father's practice—*or Roger's investment dinners.*

I was standing there, talking to a Melinda Ross, hearing all about her fiancé and how he had been cheated out of a promotion because the boss's son got it instead. I tried to seem interested, but I just wasn't. I kept looking over at Layton, who was deep in conversation with the only man in the room wearing cowboy boots.

I couldn't help but giggle. *My cowboy.*

Every now and then I would say, "Oh, really?" Or I'd nod my head like I was listening. Finally, Melinda must have followed my eyes to see whom I was staring at.

"Is he yours?"

I snapped my head back to see she was practically panting while looking at Layton. I turned back just in time to see him looking at me. I smiled, and he winked.

"Yes, he is," I said as I gave him a little wave.

"Lucky girl. He's drop-dead gorgeous. What investment firm does he work for?"

I let out a chuckle. "He sits on the board for Smithson Advisory here in Austin, but his real job is far less glamorous. He's a cattle rancher in Llano, Texas, and he also dabbles in racehorses."

"He's on the board for Smithson? How old is he?"

I felt a sense of pride just bubbling up inside me. "Twenty-five, almost twenty-six."

"Holy shit." She looked back over at Layton.

Layton shook the hand of the older gentleman before he started to make his way over to me. Right as he reached for my hand, an announcement was made, saying that dinner was ready and asking for everyone to be seated.

I quickly introduced Melinda to Layton. "Layton, this is Melinda Ross. Melinda, Layton Morris."

I watched as the red moved across her cheeks when Layton took her hand.

"It's a pleasure, ma'am."

"For the love of God, I'm only twenty-three. Please don't call me ma'am," she said with a fake laugh.

"Yes, ma'am," Layton said.

The moment he placed his hand on the small of my back, guiding me over to the table, my heart started pounding, and I swore I was suddenly aroused. I was so fucking horny that I couldn't even think straight. All

evening, I kept thinking about Layton asking me to bring the vibrator. I was even beginning to have fantasies of him using it on me.

Shit! Shit! Shit! Whitley, get a damn grip, girl. This is insane.

Layton pulled out my chair for me, but before I could sit down, he brought me in closer to him.

He whispered in my ear, "You look so beautiful. Every man in this room can't take his eyes off of you."

I was ready to apologize for what I was wearing, but then he brought his lips closer this time. The feel of his hot breath on my bare neck was driving me insane.

"I just want to make love to you right this very second. I think we need to skip out after dinner and make our way to The Intercontinental."

I let out a giggle. "The Intercontinental? What's that?"

"The Intercontinental Stephen F. Austin hotel. It's only one of the most luxurious hotels in Austin."

"Layton, I don't ever have to stay anywhere fancy. As long as I'm with you, we could sleep in the truck for all I care."

He let out a laugh and kissed me quickly on the lips before taking my hand as I sat down in the chair. As he pushed my chair in and then sat down next to me, I noticed Melinda sitting a few seats down from us.

"Whitley, I want to introduce you to my fiancé," she said with a smile.

As I looked over at the young man taking a seat, his eyes met mine.

I let out a gasp as Nick smiled.

"Oh my God. Whitley! What an unbelievably nice surprise to see you here."

My head instantly started spinning. Clearly confused, Melinda looked back and forth between Nick and me.

Layton leaned over. "Whit, do you know him?"

I couldn't talk. My heart was pounding. I immediately started looking around the room for Roger.

If Nick is here, does that mean Roger is here, too?

Melinda grinned. "So, Whitley, how in the world do you know my Nick?"

I reached for Layton's hand and squeezed it. "I, um…I…" I glanced around the room again and then down the table, scanning all the faces. I didn't know anyone else besides Nick.

"Baby, are you okay?" Layton asked as I squeezed his hand again.

Nick laughed. "Melinda, I know Whitley from New York. She used to date Roger."

I noticed Layton sit up straighter as he grabbed my hand tighter.

Melinda looked at me and smiled slightly. "You poor thing. He is such an asshole."

"Melinda!" Nick said.

"What? He is." Melinda practically drank down a whole glass of wine. She looked back at me and frowned before giving me a small smile.

"No, she's right. He is an asshole," I said as my voice cracked.

"Well, it's a good thing he isn't here, huh?" Melinda said with a wink. She must have noticed how nervous I was.

I slowly felt my body relaxing just a bit.

Oh my God! I told Melinda Layton's last name and where he lives. If she tells Nick, and he tells Roger—

"Would you like to leave, baby?" Layton asked.

I shook my head, my eyes never leaving Melinda's. "Actually, if you'll excuse me, I need to use the restroom." I stood up.

The men at the table, including Layton, stood also.

Melinda jumped up, startling Nick. "I'll join you. Nick, please, would you order me another glass of wine?"

Nick smiled. "Sure, sweetheart."

I leaned down and whispered in Layton's ear, "I'm fine. Just give me a few minutes."

He gave me a weak smile and nodded.

When I walked into the restroom, I almost had a full-blown panic attack. I felt a hand on my shoulder, and I turned around to see Melinda standing there.

"Whitley."

The look in her eyes told me she knew why I was so upset.

"You've slept with him, haven't you?" I asked.

She slowly looked away, and when she turned back, I saw tears rolling down her face.

"He totally swept me off my feet. Nick hadn't told anyone at his job about me or that we were engaged until a few months ago when he brought me to an office retreat. I was out, walking alone, and I ran into Roger. He seemed upset, and I asked if he was okay. He told me he was upset because his girlfriend had run out on him with no good-bye or anything. I felt so bad for him, out alone in the woods, just walking. We talked for almost an hour. Before I knew it, I was up against a tree while he was fucking the shit out of me."

My hand came up over my mouth. "Oh my God! What about Nick?"

She shook her head. "After it was over, I was sitting on the ground, crying. I mean, at the time, it was the hottest thing I'd ever done. I felt so alive, but as soon as he pulled out, he told me how I had been one of the best fucks he'd ever had…and then what I had just done hit me."

Oh my God. This is not happening right now. I left this behind!

"I tried to tell Nick all weekend what had happened. Then, they announced that Roger was being promoted, of course, and Nick was

devastated. I couldn't tell him, Whitley! I couldn't break his heart more. I've been trying ever since then to tell him."

"Have you? I mean, have you been with him since that one time?"

Her head snapped up, and the tears came faster. "No! Oh my God, no! I ran into him once, and he tried like hell. I was walking down a hall, and he came up behind me, grabbed my arm, and took me into a meeting room. He pushed me down on a table and started putting his hand up my skirt and into my panties. I was so shocked at first that I didn't know what to do. I told him to stop, and I said that what had happened before was a mistake. He laughed as he ripped off my panties and put them up to his nose. I wanted to throw up. He told me if I wanted Nick to keep his job, then I would do what he asked me to do."

"Oh God." I felt like I was going to be sick.

What kind of a monster was I with?

"I pushed him away from me and called him a prick. That's when he…he…"

"He what, Melinda? What did he do?"

"He slapped me so hard across the face that I was stunned for a few seconds. He smiled and put my panties in his pocket, and he said he was keeping them as a souvenir. It turned my stomach, and I got so angry. I reached for my purse and pulled out a small hand revolver that my daddy makes me keep at the house. The only reason I had it in my purse was because I was taking it to my dad's to trade out for a different pistol he wanted me to have at home. It wasn't even loaded, but I pointed it at him and told him if he ever touched me again or ever threatened Nick's job, I would kill him."

"Jesus, Melinda." I grabbed her shaking hands.

She let out a laugh. "I know! But it worked. He's never even glanced my way since then, and Nick said he has been really nice at the office as well. Now, I'm thinking I should just forget the whole thing ever happened and not even tell Nick. What if I lose him over some stupid, impulsive mistake?"

I pulled her into my arms and held her while she cried.

After a few minutes, there was a knock on the ladies' room door. I heard Layton ask if everything was okay. I walked up to the door and opened it to see him standing there with such a worried look on his face.

"Yeah, baby, I'm so sorry. We will be right out." I reached up and kissed him.

I walked back toward Melinda as she was trying to fix her makeup.

"You have to tell him, Melinda. You have to, or the guilt will eat you alive."

She took a deep breath and let it out. "I know I do. I was actually planning on telling him during this trip. I think tonight might be the night."

I smiled before we both turned and made our way back out to the dinner. Before we made it around the corner, I took her by the arm.

"Melinda, Roger can never know you saw me tonight. Please, make sure you let Nick know not to say anything. Please."

She smiled and nodded. We quickly exchanged numbers and made our way back to the table.

For the next hour, I watched as Melinda drank glass after glass of wine. My heart broke for her, but at the same time, I prayed she would remember to tell Nick what I asked of her.

I glanced down at my cell phone. It was almost midnight, and I was exhausted. Melinda was well on her way to being drunk as was Nick and a few other people.

Layton walked up to me and pulled me into his arms. "I'm ready to leave," he whispered into my ear.

I smiled as I pushed myself into him. "Me, too."

⟶≫≫≫≫≫≫≫≫≫≪≪≪≪≪≪≪≪≪⟵

By the time we got up to the hotel room, I was feeling a bit more relaxed. The suite was beautiful, and when we'd first walked in, I couldn't believe my eyes. Red roses were everywhere. Rose petals covered the bed, and a trail went into the bathroom. I smiled at the thought that Layton had done all of this for me. I removed Roger, Nick, and Melinda completely from my mind, and I appreciated the fact that Layton hadn't asked me a single question about any of it.

I felt his hand on my back as he slowly unzipped my evening gown. He placed gentle kisses all across my back from one shoulder over to the other as I let out a small moan.

"I love you, Whitley," he whispered.

"Oh God, Layton, I love you, too," I practically purred as my desire for him grew stronger and stronger.

Once the zipper was completely down, I let go of the dress that I had been holding on to across my chest. When it pooled at my feet, I heard Layton suck in a breath of air.

I smiled, knowing that if he loved what he saw from behind, he would love the front even more. It just happened to be luck that I had a red lace strapless garter slip that I'd never even worn before. I hadn't needed to wear thigh-high stockings since my dress went to the floor, but I had them on anyway. The matching red lace thong made me feel even sexier.

"Mother of God…Whitley. Turn around, baby."

I glanced back over my shoulder at him, only to see his eyes moving up and down my body. I could feel the wetness between my legs soaking my thong, and I'd never been so turned-on in my life.

I slowly turned around and stood in front of him.

His eyes moved greedily over my body as he licked his lips. "You take my breath away, Whitley."

I felt myself squeezing my legs together. If I didn't know any better, I would say I was about to have an orgasm just from the way he was looking at me.

I was just about to say something when he dropped to his knees and started to unhook the garter. Picking up my leg, he kissed the inside of my thigh, and I felt my whole body quiver. As he slowly rolled the stocking down my leg, I could feel the heat from his hands on my skin.

Oh. God. I. Want. Him. I want to lose myself in him.

"Layton…" I moaned.

He repeated it all over again with my other leg, and I jumped when I felt his hands moving up my legs.

"I love what my touch does to your body, Whitley." He looked up at me and smiled. "Do you want me, baby?"

I bit down on my lower lip until I realized how hard I was biting it. "Oh God, yes."

"I want you so much, Whit. I can't stand it. I want to be inside you so badly."

"*Yes.* Now, Layton, please. I just want to lose myself in you now!"

The next thing I knew, I was lying on the bed, and Layton was entering my body. I couldn't even remember him undressing.

He moved so slow and sweet as he made love to me. It was like he knew what I needed. He covered me with kisses and kept repeating how much he loved me and how he couldn't believe this wasn't a dream.

I was lost in his lovemaking. I was completely and utterly lost in the love he was spilling into my body.

-»»»»»»»»»»«««««««««««-

I opened my eyes and looked around the room. My whole body felt so relaxed. I felt the weight of Layton's arm around me with the heat of his body up against mine. I could feel his hard-on pressed up against my ass, and I smiled, wondering what it would be like to try something different.

Can I? How bad would it hurt? What would Layton think if I told him I wanted to try anal sex? Would he think any less of me?

I reached down and felt myself.

Shit! I'm soaking wet. What in the hell is wrong with me? Oh God…the vibrator.

I'd seen Layton set it down on the bedside table. I gently lifted his arm off of me as I reached for the black drawstring bag. I opened it up and saw the vibrator and the small bottle of lube that Courtney had put in there when she had first given it to me.

I bit down on my lip and looked over at Layton. I'd never in my life done anything like this. Just the thought of it though was turning me on even more.

I took both items out of the bag and gently moved next to Layton. He moaned just a little. I chewed on my bottom lip for a little bit more before I got up the nerve.

"Layton?" I whispered.

"Hmm…"

"Layton, I'd like to try something. If you're up for it?"

He put his arm across my stomach and moaned again. "Anything you want, baby."

"I'd, um…I'd like to use the vibrator to maybe…you know…try something different."

He smiled but didn't open his eyes. "Can I watch you use it? I've always wanted to watch a girl use a vibrator on herself."

I smiled and shook my head. "I can do that for you, but I kind of want you to play with me, using the vibrator a little differently. I want you to play with it in my, um…you know…the back door." I cringed and held my breath.

His eyes snapped open, and he looked at me. "What?" He sat up straight.

I buried my face under my arms. "Oh God! I can't even believe I said that. Never mind! Just forget I said a thing."

Layton gently pulled my arms down and looked into my eyes with the sexiest smile I'd ever seen.

"Whitley, that was one of the hottest things anyone has ever said to me."

I shook my head as he put his hand on the side of my face. He slowly leaned down and bit on my lower lip. He moved his hand down my neck, over my breasts, and then between my legs. I opened my legs to him and moaned as he placed two fingers inside me.

He put his head down into my neck and moaned. "Ah…Jesus, Whitley, you're so wet."

"Layton…" I could hardly talk. I pushed my hips into his hand.

He looked up at me and then down at my lips. I licked them right before he slammed his lips onto mine. He kissed me so passionately that it almost seemed like he couldn't get enough of me. He moved his fingers in and out of me faster, and I felt that familiar build-up as his thumb kept rubbing against my clit.

When he pulled his hand away, I wanted to cry out.

He winked at me and smiled. "I've never done anything like this before, Whit," he whispered.

"Neither have I. I'm so excited at the idea of you touching me there, but I'm so scared at the same time."

"Please tell me if anything hurts, okay? Promise me, Whit," he whispered as he kissed along my neck.

I began panting. Just the thought of what he was going to do to me had the desire building even more.

"I promise, Layton. I promise you."

"Roll over and get up onto your hands and knees, baby."

My heart started pounding harder as I did what he'd said. I was breathing so heavily that the sound of it was turning me on even more.

I watched as he reached for the vibrator and the lube. I jumped when I felt his fingers slowly enter me. He moved them in and out until he stopped and moved his finger back to my ass. The moment he touched me there, I gasped.

"Oh God…" The feeling of him touching me there was more than I could take.

"Fuck, Whitley." He leaned down and kissed my back as he moved his hand around to the front of me and began playing with my clit.

I dropped to my elbows and wanted nothing more than for him to touch my ass again. I began pushing my ass back toward him.

"Layton…touch me…please."

"Whitley, I'm not going to last two minutes."

I turned and looked back at him with a smile. He sat up and never took his eyes from mine as he lubricated the vibrator. My breathing started picking up again.

I turned back around and closed my eyes. Then, I felt him slowly entering me, moving in and out, as his finger played with the outside of my ass.

"Oh God! Oh my God."

I could feel the orgasm coming on already, and all he was doing was touching the outside of my ass.

"Layton, oh God."

I felt his finger slowly enter my ass again as he started moving faster. Having sex from behind like this made his dick feel so damn big, and he was going so much deeper this way.

"Faster, Layton."

I felt his finger moving in and out, and the feeling was amazing.

I want more. I need more.

"More, Layton."

I pushed my ass back into him, and he moaned.

"Whit…I'm trying to hold on here, but fuck…"

"More, Layton…please…more."

He must have either placed more fingers in or the vibrator because it began stinging. I let out a whimper, and he stopped.

"Whitley, do you want me to stop, baby? I don't want this to hurt you."

Oh my God…it feels so damn good.

"No, don't stop, Layton!"

"Whitley…motherfucker…you look so damn good like this, baby."

I put my head down and pushed back into him again. He slammed so hard and deep inside me, and I felt it building. I felt him moving the vibrator in and out of my ass. It burned so bad, but it felt so good at the same time. Then, I felt the vibrator turn on, and I about lost it.

"Layton!" I called out. "Oh God…I'm going to come!"

I yelled out as the orgasm took over my body, and Layton began going faster.

"Oh God…yes! Oh God, yes!" I couldn't even form any other words. This was probably the longest, most intense orgasm of my life.

"Oh, baby…I can feel the vibrator…*fuck*…I'm going to come, Whit."

I could feel him getting harder, and I swore I felt every ounce of him pouring into me. My orgasm was still going so strong that I could hardly stand it. I needed it to stop.

I was slowly coming down from my orgasm when I felt Layton pull out the vibrator. I let out a gasp. The next thing I knew, Layton collapsed next to me as we both desperately tried to get our breaths back.

Layton started to talk in between breaths, "Hottest. Fucking. Moment. Of. My. Life!"

I let out a giggle and rolled over onto my side. I watched as he tried to get his breathing back under control. My heart filled with so much love for him as I lay there and watched his chest moving up and down.

Is it even possible? We just met, and I feel like I've known him for so long. I don't want him to ever leave my side.

Ever.

"Layton?" I ran my fingers up and down his chest and stomach.

He looked over and gave me that smile that just melted my heart.

"Yeah, baby?"

"I love you. I've never in my life felt this way or this comfortable with anyone. I'm almost scared because I love you so much, and we haven't known each other very long."

He rolled over and took me into his arms. He pulled me on top of him as he moved onto his back.

"Do you know what I dream about?"

I shook my head.

"I dream about you and me always—ever since the first time I saw you. I dream about riding along the fence lines with you, standing in the kitchen and making breakfast with you, you helping me birth a calf or run a horse. I dream about the look on your face when I ask you to marry me and the moment you become my wife. I dream about your stomach all swollen with our child. I've never in my life felt like this, Whitley. You are my entire life, and yes…that scares the hell out of me, but it also makes me so damn happy."

I smiled as I felt tears rolling down my face. I could hardly talk. "Oh, Layton," I whispered. I gently placed my lips onto his.

As I pulled back from his lips, he wiped the tears from my eyes.

"Thank you. Thank you for loving me, Layton."

Layton placed his hands on my face and gently began kissing me. He rolled me onto my back as he continued to shower my body with sweet kisses.

He pulled the covers up and over our bodies as we settled in next to each other.

I began to drift off into sleep, but not before I barely heard Layton whisper, "I'm madly in love with you, and I want to marry you, Whitley."

My heart started pounding as I listened to him fall asleep.

I closed my eyes and felt tears running down my face.

This has to be the most magical moment of my life.

"Yes," I whispered.

TWENTY-TWO

-≫≫≫≫≫≫≫≫≫≫≫≪≪≪≪≪≪≪≪≪≪≪≪≪-

LAYTON

It was the middle of October, and two months had passed since the night Whitley and I shared in Austin. I couldn't believe how close we'd grown. She was always at my house, and when she wasn't, I felt completely and utterly lost without her.

I smiled, thinking about this morning. Neither one of us had wanted to get up and leave each other.

I stood outside the jewelry store, just staring into the window. I couldn't tell if my body was shaking from the idea of what I was about to do or from the cold that had moved through, making it chillier than normal. I was glad Whitley had talked me into bringing a light jacket even though I'd insisted it wasn't that cold out.

I smiled to myself, thinking about how excited Whitley was to go to the high school football game tonight. I knew she was happy about spending time with Kate and even more excited that Kate was going to stay the night with us tonight. During their little conversation at dinner the other night with Jen, all I'd heard were words like *princess, tea party, dress-up,* and something about Uncle Layton being the king.

I glanced up and saw the saleslady grinning at me. She waved her hand for me to come in, so I smiled and took a deep breath.

This is it. I'm really going to do this.

As I stepped in, I noticed two other ladies. They all made a beeline right toward me.

Ah hell. Maybe this is a mistake, coming to a jewelry store right here in town.

I recognized one of the girls right away. Anna Macbeth was her name, and Reed had had the biggest crush on her in high school.

"Well, if it isn't Layton Morris. My God, I haven't seen you in years!" she said with a huge smile.

I noticed how the other two ladies backed off immediately once they realized Anna knew me.

I smiled as I reached my hand out to shake her extended hand.

"Anna, isn't it?" I asked with a smile.

I was pretty sure I'd heard one of the other girls say, "Oh God," when I'd smiled. I glanced over, and her face instantly turned red. I gave her a wink, which only caused her to giggle.

Anna snapped her head back and looked at the girl. "Sweetie, don't you have some things to do in the back or something?"

The girl who giggled shot Anna a dirty look and nodded before turning and walking into the back. The other girl turned, grabbed some window cleaner, and began cleaning the glass on the display cases.

Anna turned back toward me and winked. "So, Layton, what brings you into my grandfather's jewelry store?"

I let out a laugh. "Oh shit! I forgot your grandfather is Jim. I thought you moved to Dallas for college, and last I heard, you were fixin' to marry some oil tycoon up there."

Her smile faded just a bit before she grinned from ear to ear again. "I missed the country life along with my parents and my younger sister as well. It's her senior year in high school, and I wanted to be here for her. Plus…the oil tycoon turned out to be a cheating bastard."

"Damn, I'm sorry to hear that. How long have you been back in town?" I asked.

"About three weeks. Today is my third day back on the job here. Almost feels like high school again," she said with a wink.

"Does Reed know you're back?" I asked with a chuckle.

She tilted her head and gave me a shit-eating grin. "Reed Moore? Is he living in Llano still?"

I nodded. "Yeah, he works for the Texas Parks and Wildlife, and he helps me out on the ranch a lot as well. Trying to talk him into going in as business partners."

She nodded and seemed to be making a mental note. "Well, when you see him, tell him to stop by. I'd, um…I'd love to catch up with him."

I agreed and made a mental note myself to call Reed the moment I stepped outside this store. He had been drinking himself drunk almost every night for the last few months—ever since Courtney had started dating Mitch.

Maybe Anna is the distraction Reed needs to move on from Courtney.

"So, what brings you in, Layton?"

I felt my whole body start shaking again. "I, um…well…um…I'm actually looking for…well, I'm looking for a ring."

She let out a small giggle. "What kind of ring?"

I looked around and then back out toward the windows. When I looked back at Anna, her smile caused me to chuckle.

"A, um…well…an engagement ring."

"Oh, Layton! Are you and Olivia getting married?" she asked as she jumped up and down.

Wait—what?

"No! God, no! Damn, you have been gone a while."

She stopped smiling and came to a complete standstill. She took a deep breath and slowly let it out. "Um…I didn't know if I should bring this up or not, but I'm really sorry to hear about your brother. He was a really great guy."

I gave her a weak smile. "Thank you, Anna. Yeah, he was. Back to the ring. It's for my girlfriend, Whitley."

"Oh my God! Whitley Reynolds? The girl from New York?"

"Yeah. How do you know her?" I asked.

"She came in here the other day, looking for a little silver locket. She said she was buying it for a special little girl. We got to talking, and she told me how she moved here from New York. She mentioned that she'd fallen head over heels for a cowboy here, but I never dreamed that cowboy was you, Layton! Congratulations. My God, that girl is beautiful."

I couldn't help but grin from ear to ear, just hearing someone talk about Whit. "Yeah, she is beautiful, inside and out. Kate's birthday is this weekend, so I'm guessing she was buying her a gift."

"I bet that's what it was. She didn't mention whom it was for, just a special little girl. So, back to this ring! You're going to pop the big question, huh? Did you have a certain shape in mind? Were you wanting a loose diamond, and maybe design your own setting? Platinum, white, or yellow gold? What were you thinking?"

I just stood there, staring at her. "I'm thinking I was nervous as hell before I walked in here, and now, I'm just plain scared to death."

She threw her head back and laughed. "I'm so sorry. I guess, sometimes, I get a bit carried away. Let's start with the basics, shall we? First off, is this the first time you've looked for a ring?"

I nodded.

"Okay. Next question. Do you know what size you want? What shape of diamond?"

"I don't want anything huge…but nothing small. She's mentioned liking a princess cut and an oval shape before."

"Perfect! Now, metal?"

"White gold or platinum for sure. I've never seen her in yellow gold."

"Got it. Let's walk over here. I have a few rings I'd like to show you."

As I followed her, I glanced up and out the window and saw Whitley walking toward the jewelry store.

Holy fuck! What in the hell is she doing? Is she coming into the store?

"Holy shit! Anna! It's Whitley!" I shouted.

Anna jumped. "What? Oh my God. Um…hide!"

I just looked at her. "Where?"

She grabbed me by the shirt, practically dragged me down the counter, and then yanked me behind it. She pushed me down right as I heard the door to the store open.

"Whitley! Oh my gosh, what brings you back so soon?" Anna said in an overly chipper voice.

I could just see Whit's face now, wondering what in the fuck was wrong with Anna. I couldn't help it, but I let out a chuckle—which was followed by a grunt when Anna kicked me with her fucking high-heel shoe.

"Hi, Anna. It's so nice to see you again. Well, I got a picture that I wanted to see about putting into that locket I bought the other day. It's for my boyfriend's niece. It's her birthday this weekend."

I could practically hear the smile in her voice. I grinned, thinking about Kate's face when she opened the gift.

"I see. Okay, well, I'd be more than happy to do that for you. Do you have the picture with you?"

"Yep, I sure do. I just printed it off and decided to take a walk up here. I just don't think I could work with something so small. I wasn't sure if you guys would do that or not."

Anna giggled. "*You guys*—yep, you are so from the North."

Both girls laughed. Then, I heard Anna gasp.

"Oh, Whitley, this is a great picture of you and Layton!"

I closed my eyes and shook my head. *Fuck! She's not supposed to know about me!*

Now, it was my turn. I hit Anna on the leg, and she let out a yelp.

"Are you okay, Anna? What happened?"

Anna leaned down and rubbed her leg before she gave me another kick. "Oh, nothing. Lack of bananas or something. Pain in my leg…among other things."

I thumbed her leg, and she kicked me again—this time, harder.

"Oh, well, is this something I should just drop off and come back by later to get?" Whitley asked.

"No! Oh no, I can do this right now. Won't take me any time."

I leaned my head back and cursed to myself. Just then, the girl who had been cleaning the glass walked behind the counter. She quickly looked down at me and then back up at Whitley.

"Um…would you like to see the garden I've been working on out front? I remember you were asking about what type of flowers you could plant since you weren't familiar with the Texas weather," she said to Whitley.

Just then, the other girl came walking out from back and stopped dead in her tracks when she saw me sitting on the floor. I put my finger up to my lips for her to be quiet, and she was just about to say something when the other girl grabbed her by the arm and started off toward the back again.

"Sorry, sweetheart. Just forgot I've got to talk to Jane about something. Maybe another time on those flowers."

I slowly let out the breath I had been holding in.

"Okay…sounds good," Whitley called out.

"There ya go! Easy-peasy!" Anna said.

"Holy cow, that was fast. Thank you so much! What do I owe you?"

Anna laughed. "Nothing! It's on the house."

"Thank you so much. That's so sweet of you. I really appreciate your help."

"Sure, no problem," Anna said.

"So, you know Layton?" Whitley asked.

Fuck. I knew she would catch that.

"Uh…yeah, we went to high school together. So, y'all are dating, huh?"

"Oh, really?"

"Yep, I'm going to safely guess from that picture that you've stolen his heart."

I heard Whitley giggle, and my whole body was covered in goose bumps just from that sound.

"I hope so. He's certainly stolen mine. Well, I guess I should be…oh my God!"

I perked my head up and wondered why she had just let out a gasp.

"What? What is it?" Anna said with a panicked voice.

"That ring! Oh my God…it looks just like my grandmother's ring," Whitley said with so much excitement in her voice.

I noticed Anna did a little hop as she quickly looked down at me and then back up at Whitley.

Okay…is this really happening? Is Whitley going to pick out her own engagement ring and not even know it?

I couldn't help but smile.

This is perfect. Everything happens for a reason.

There was a reason she'd walked into this store while I was here.

I poked Anna in the leg, and she kicked me again. I was going to walk out of here, broken and bruised.

"Which one, Whitley? I'll show you it!" Anna said with a little too much excitement in her voice.

I rolled my eyes and shook my head. *Way to play it cool, Anna.*

"Oh no, I couldn't ask you to waste your time doing that."

"Please…I have nothing important to do. Is this the one?"

"Yep, that's it," Whitley said with a giggle.

I looked up and watched as Anna unlocked the cabinet. She reached in and pulled out a ring.

"Whitley, you have very good taste. This is a Tacori platinum ring. It's from their Heirloom collection. Rather fitting since you said it reminded you of your grandmother's ring, wouldn't you say?"

Whitley started laughing. "Yes, that is funny. Oh my God. It's breathtaking. I can't believe how much it looks like her ring. It's almost unreal."

"The princess cut center diamond is one-point-two-five carats. The channel set diamonds and crescent diamond details keep it contemporary, yet it has that heirloom look to it. Total carats of the engagement ring, minus the center stone, are about one-point-one-seven carats."

Anna gave me another kick.

What the fuck? I didn't even move!

"It's perfect. I can't believe how perfect it is," Whitley said.

I could practically hear the smile in her voice.

Is it really going to be this easy?

"It is, isn't it?" Anna said as she reached her hand down and gave me a thumbs-up.

"How much is it?"

"Ah…"

I almost wanted to laugh. This was the first time I'd ever seen Anna stunned into silence.

"Oh, ya know…it's up there."

Whitley laughed. "I bet. What is it, like ten thousand?"

Anna glanced quickly down at me, and I nodded my head. It wasn't like Whitley would never find out how much it cost.

She quickly looked back up at Whitley. "Well…um…with that center diamond, the ring is nineteen thousand dollars."

"Holy fuck!" Whitley yelled out. "Oh my God, Anna. I'm so sorry. I didn't mean to yell that out."

Anna laughed. "Here, let me see your left hand. Let's try it on."

Oh yeah…I'm going to owe Anna big time.

"Well, now, it's my turn…holy fuck! That fits you like it was made for you, Whitley. How does that feel on your finger?"

Shit…I'd give anything to be able to see Whit's face right now.

"Wow…I've never tried on a ring that fit perfectly the first time. Okay, well, here ya go. I don't want to break it or anything." Whitley laughed. "Maybe someday, right?"

I watched as Anna put it back into the cabinet. All the while, she was kicking my leg in her excitement.

Shit, I'm not going to be able to stand. My leg is going numb.

"Thank you so much, Anna. I better run. I'm meeting with a potential client. She wants to throw her daughter a sweet-sixteen party."

"Whitley, this was fun! Thanks for adding a little bit of excitement into my morning."

Whitley laughed. "Anytime! Nothing like trying on a nineteen-thousand-dollar engagement ring for fun, right? Bye, Anna. Have a wonderful day."

"Bye, Whitley. Good luck at your meeting. I hope you get the, uh…party."

Whitley laughed. "Thanks, Anna. I'll tell Layton I ran into you."

"Sounds good! See ya around."

I heard the door open and then close.

"Don't get up yet. Wait until she walks away."

"Okay," I said. My stomach was flipping around and around.

Another thirty seconds or so passed by before Anna turned and looked down at me.

"You lucky son of a bitch! She just picked out her dream engagement ring." Anna jumped up and down.

I got up and rubbed the ache out of my leg from where Anna had kept kicking me. "Well, if my damn leg wasn't hurting so much, I'd be jumping up and down right along with you."

Anna looked down at my leg and then back up at me as she frowned. "Cowboy up. Look at this ring, Layton. I have to say, she has exquisite taste!"

As Anna took the ring out of the cabinet, I walked around to the other side of the counter. One look at the ring, and I knew, without a doubt, I was doing the right thing. Everything in my body screamed that this was it and that Whitley was the one I wanted to spend the rest of my life with.

I looked at Anna and smiled. "I'll take it."

"Smart man. I knew I always liked you for a reason. Do you know how you're going to ask her or when?"

I shook my head as I followed her over to the register. "I have no clue, but next week is her birthday. I was thinking of asking her on her birthday."

After Anna rang up the ring, she put it into a box and wrapped it all up. She kept telling me to make sure I made it romantic. My heart started pounding.

Shit! Mike was always the romantic one, not me. What in the hell am I going to do to make it romantic?

"Layton? Layton! Snap out of it. I'm talking to you."

I looked back at Anna, who was standing there with her hands on her hips.

"Did you even hear a word I just said?"

I shook my head. "I can't do it."

"What? What in the hell do you mean you can't do it? You sure as shit can and will do it. Don't you dare walk around, carrying that ring in your

pocket for two years, because you're too damn afraid to take a chance, Layton Morris."

I just stared at her. "What if she says no?"

She raised one eyebrow at me, and for one brief moment, I felt like I was about to be sent to the corner for time-out.

"Please. No woman in her right mind would ever say no to you. Layton, you're one of the sweetest, most caring guys I know. Trust me, she's not going to say no. Promise me that you will at least attempt to make it romantic for her."

I let out a laugh because Mike of all people had asked Jen to marry him in his truck. He had been so nervous that he'd just blurted it out. I smiled, just thinking about Mike and what he would say to me right now.

I winked at Anna as I took the small ring box and put it into my jacket pocket. "I promise, Anna. I'll make it a night she'll never forget." I smiled at her, and I turned to leave.

I quickly opened the door and walked outside, looking around to make sure Whitley wasn't nearby. I had no idea where she could have met this client of hers. I put my hand in my pocket and held on to the ring box as I jogged the two blocks to my truck.

When I got to my truck, I jumped inside, pulled out my cell phone, and hit Reed's number.

"What's up, dude?" Reed asked, breathing heavily.

"Hey, what's up? What in the hell are you doing?" I asked.

"Do you really want to know?" Reed laughed.

"Well, I don't know, Reed. I'm assuming you're at work, so fuck, I don't know."

Reed let out a laugh as I heard him talking to someone. It sounded like a girl.

"Dude, do you want to, um…call me back? Are you busy?" I asked as I looked at my watch.

"Nah…I'm finished. I just got laid at work. That was a first," Reed said.

My mouth dropped open. "*What?* What in the hell, Reed? With who?"

"Some cute little secretary that just started," Reed said.

"Ah hell, Reed. Really? So, are you going to just fuck girls until you forget about Courtney?"

"To hell with Courtney. I told you, I don't give a shit about whom she's dating or what she's doing. Shit, Layton…this damn blonde has been flirting with me for two fucking days, so I gave in. Don't act like you've never fucked a girl just to do it."

I let out a sigh and shook my head. "Anyway, guess who I just ran into?" I said, hoping to change the subject.

"I don't know, Layton. Who?"

"Anna MacBeth," I said with a smile.

"No shit. Is she in town visiting or something?" Reed asked.

"Better. She moved back to town and is working at her grandfather's jewelry store—Jim's. I just left there, and she told me to tell you to give her a holler."

Reed let out a laugh. "First off, what in the hell were you doing in Jim's? And second, I thought she was getting married."

"Nope. Turns out the guy was a cheat, and she missed Llano, so she moved back. And I bought Whitley an engagement ring."

"Wait—what? Dude…no fucking way! Are you for real? You're going to ask Whit to marry you? When?"

I laughed as I started up my truck. "I think on her birthday next week."

"Jesus, Layton. That is huge. Congratulations, man. I mean, I knew the two of you were pretty damn serious, but…dude, marriage? Are you sure?"

"I've never been so sure of anything in my life. Anyway, I think you need to pay a little visit to Jim's. Anna really perked up when I mentioned your name."

"Really? Awesome. I think I might head on out and make my way into town for lunch. I'll ask her if she wants to go to the game with me tonight."

I shook my head. "You fuck a girl at work and then go to lunch to make plans to take another girl out tonight? Real nice."

"Fuck off, asshole. You're just jealous. Hey, I've got to run. I have a meeting to get to. I'll see y'all tonight at the football game, right?"

"Yeah, we'll see ya there, and, Reed…trust me, dude, I'm not jealous."

Reed let out a gruff laugh. "Yeah, I know you aren't, you lucky bastard. Later."

I hung up the phone and put my truck in drive. I was about to pull out and head home to put Whitley's ring in my safe. There was no way I was going to walk around with it. Right before I pulled out, someone knocked on my window. I turned to see a young guy standing there, staring at me.

I rolled the window down and smiled. "Can I help you?"

The way he was looking at me was almost like he wanted to rip my eyes out before he slowly let a smile play across his face. His green eyes were filled with contempt, and I was almost wishing I had just driven off. I looked him up and down. He was dressed in dress pants and a button-down shirt with a light jacket. His brown hair was perfectly in place, but he looked completely out of place.

"Thanks so much, dude. I'm actually looking for a hotel. My cousin is getting married right outside of town, and I lost the paper she'd sent me with the hotel names on it. I just flew into Austin and drove straight out here. My cell coverage is hit or miss here in the middle of nowhere."

I let out a laugh. *Yep, city folk.*

"Where you flying in from?" I asked as I threw my truck back into park.

"Denver, Colorado." He extended his hand and smiled. "The name is Pete, Pete Miller."

I reached for his hand and gave it a good shake. "Well, Pete, welcome to Llano, Texas. Layton Morris. There's a Days Inn on Bessemer Avenue and a Best Western on West Young Street."

I quickly glanced down at his rented convertible. I wasn't surprised to see he had the top down.

"I guess, being from Colorado, this type of weather feels good for you." I gestured toward the car.

He looked back at the car and then turned back to me and smiled. "Yeah. Well, I'm also picking up my fiancée. She was staying here for a bit, but it's time for her to come back home now. I've missed her…if you know what I mean," he said with a wink.

I let out a laugh. "Oh hell yeah, I'm ready to see my girl tonight as well, if you know what I mean," I said, giving him a wink back.

His smile faded for a quick second before he replaced it with another look, one I wasn't too sure how to read.

"Thanks for the warm welcome. I look forward to getting to know this little town."

"How long are you in town for?"

"Oh…not long. Long enough to get back what was mine and head out on the road."

I nodded. I didn't like this guy at all. Something about him was throwing up warning flags in my head.

"Okay, well, enjoy your stay, Pete."

"I will. Trust me," he said with a shit-eating grin on his face.

I watched as he turned and got into his rental car. He punched something into his phone and took off.

As I watched his car drive off, something came over me—anger. Something about that guy didn't sit right with me, and I was hoping that was the first and last time I ever ran into him.

TWENTY-THREE

-»»»»»»»»»«««««««««-
Whitley

As we walked into the stadium, Kate was begging Layton to let her sit on his shoulders. I couldn't help but smile at how she totally had him wrapped around her little finger. Jen, Kate's mother, had told me since Mike had passed away that Layton had pretty much stepped in as the father figure for Kate. It showed. There wasn't a thing he wouldn't do for Kate to make her happy.

I let myself wander into a daydream as we stood there, waiting to pay to get in. I imagined Layton at the ranch on top of the hill at sunset. He was swinging our little girl around and around in circles as she laughed and cried out for him to go faster.

I felt someone tug on my shirt. "Whitley, why are you closing your eyes? Are you tired?"

I looked down at Kate and laughed. "I guess I was lost in a daydream, sweetheart."

I glanced up at Layton and winked. He'd been acting so strange ever since he came to pick me up. He had been nothing but a nervous Nellie.

As he smiled back at me, he leaned down and put his lips right up to my ear. "What were you daydreaming about?"

His hot breath instantly turned me on, and I felt the blush moving up my cheeks.

I was just about to answer him when Kate started laughing.

"You were sleeping while you were standing up, Whitley? Uncle Layton, she must be really tired to sleep and dream while standing up, huh?"

Reaching down, Layton picked up Kate and swung her up and over his head until she was sitting on his shoulders.

"Yay! I can see everything now!" Kate called out.

He pulled me closer to him and gently kissed my lips. He smiled as he pulled slightly back. "Maybe we should get her home and to bed right away."

I giggled and shook my head. "I think I'll be okay for now. But we might have to leave early."

Layton laughed and grabbed my hand as we paid and made our way into the stadium.

"My God, it's been forever since I was at a high school football game," I said as we headed toward the stands.

"It's gonna be fun. The Yellow Jackets are gonna kick some ass tonight," Layton said with a laugh.

"Uncle Layton, you said a bad word. You owe me an ice cream!"

Layton laughed. "I'm sorry, sweetheart. I'll get you an ice cream. I got a little carried away 'cause I love football, and I love Llano high school football even more."

Layton reached up and took Kate off his shoulders. As he set her down, she looked between the two of us.

"Do you love Whitley?" Kate asked as she giggled.

Layton snapped his head up, looked at me, and gave me the most panty-melting smile ever.

"Yeah, baby girl, I love Whitley more than anything. She's my honeybee."

Kate jumped up and down and clapped her hands. "Oh, like Mommy's song she plays all the time."

I laughed. I leaned over and kissed Layton.

Kate pushed us apart. "Now, me! I want kisses, Uncle Layton! You love me, too, right?"

Layton leaned down and scooped up Kate. He started giving her small little kisses all over her face as she laughed.

"You're my number-one girl, Kate. Don't you ever forget that. Now, come on, let's go find Reed and Anna," Layton said as we headed to the bleachers.

"I still can't believe Reed and Anna are here together! I just saw her today at the jewelry shop."

"Whatcha doing at the jewelry store, Whitley?" Kate asked as Layton put her back down.

"Well, you see, I know a little girl whose birthday is tomorrow. I had to pick up her present."

Kate started jumping up and down, and then she saw Reed. She took off running, calling out his name. He jumped up from his seat and bent down to catch her in his arms as she slammed into him.

Layton shook his head. "Poor Anna. Kate has a massive crush on Reed, and I'm sure she's not going to like the idea of Anna being on a date with him."

I laughed as I got a glimpse of Courtney and Mitch walking toward us. I waved as she smiled and made her way over to me.

"I'm going to say hi to Court. I'll be right there."

Layton stopped and talked to Mitch for a few seconds before he invited Mitch and Courtney to sit over by us. I thought for sure Mitch was going to say no, so I was shocked to see him turn and follow Layton.

Mitch and Reed shook hands, and then Mitch hugged Anna. They all sat down with Mitch sitting on the other side of Layton.

Courtney had watched the whole thing play out. She slowly turned to me and gave me a weak smile. "Looks like we're sitting with y'all. Um, who's the girl with Reed?"

"That's Anna. They all went to high school together. I guess she just moved back to Llano from Dallas. Layton said Reed had a massive crush on her and was devastated when she left for college."

"Did they date in high school?" Courtney asked as she turned back to look at Reed and Anna.

"I'm not really sure. It doesn't sound like it though. I got the impression that they both maybe liked each other in school."

"Huh." Courtney started looking around. "I've had the strangest feeling that someone's been watching me all day."

"Oh my God! Me, too, Court. I can't shake it. Then, to top that off, Layton's been acting all weird since he picked me up, like he's freaked out about something."

"Pesh, that's normal for Layton."

I hit Courtney in the arm and laughed. "So, how are things with Mitch? Have you…"

Courtney's face instantly turned bright red.

"Oh. My. God. You've slept with him? When, you bitch? I can't believe you haven't told me!"

Courtney laughed. "My God, Whitley. Announce it to the whole damn town. I would have told you, but you're never home anymore. It just happened last night."

"Wow. Y'all held out a long time. Was it worth the wait?"

Courtney turned back to look at Mitch before looking back at me. She didn't even need to answer my question. The smile on her face said it all.

"Holy hell, Whit. He's amazing. I mean…the things he does with his lips."

I held my hand up in Courtney's face. "Ugh! Stop! Oh my God, Court. I won't ever be able to look at him again."

"Really? Like I didn't feel that way when you told me about the little fun you and Layton had with the vibrator at your back-door party."

Just then, someone cleared their throat, and Courtney and I both looked down at a mom sitting there with her two young daughters.

"Really? Can you take this conversation somewhere else?" she asked as she pointed to her girls.

"I'm *so* sorry. Please excuse us." I grabbed Courtney and started making my way up the bleachers toward Layton and Mitch.

I turned and gave Court a dirty look. "Jesus, Courtney! You talk about me being loud."

Courtney started laughing.

Before we sat down, I leaned toward her ear and said, "I want to hear all about last night though."

She pulled back and smiled as she nodded. Her smile faded as she looked over at Reed and Anna. I turned to see the two of them snuggled together, and Anna was whispering something into Reed's ear. My heart instantly dropped.

Is Courtney still hung up on Reed? Shit, I hope not since she just slept with Mitch.

As Courtney and I went to sit down between Mitch and Layton, Reed looked up and smiled at Courtney.

He leaned forward and said, "Courtney, this is Anna MacBeth, a friend of ours from high school. She just moved back to town. Anna, this is Courtney Will, Whitley's best friend, and Mitch's, um…"

Courtney forced a smile. "Mitch's girlfriend." She glared at Reed before turning toward Anna and smiling. "Hey, Anna. It's a pleasure to meet you."

"Hi, Courtney. How are you liking Llano?" Anna asked as she grabbed Reed's hand.

I looked back at Courtney, who was now looking down at their hands. *Ah shit, this is not looking good.*

"I love it. Some things I could do without though," Court said as she looked directly at Reed.

Reed snapped his head up and looked at Courtney. He laughed and then turned to Anna and said something to her, causing her to laugh.

I leaned over and hit Layton in the leg. He yelled out.

"Shit, I'm sorry, Layton! Is your leg sore?" I asked.

He was rubbing his leg. He glanced over toward Anna and then back at me. "Yeah…I must have hit it on something."

I leaned up and whispered in his ear, "I think we might have a problem."

He looked at me with a questioning look. "What?"

"I think Anna might have picked up on the tension between Reed and Court. And, um…Court seems to be slightly jealous even though her and Mitch just slept together last night."

Layton pulled his head back and looked at me. "No shit!" he said with a smile on his face.

"Uncle Layton is swearing, and Whitley is telling secrets! I get more ice cream!" Kate called out.

Everyone started laughing.

I couldn't help but notice Anna glaring at Courtney.

Yep, she certainly noticed something between Reed and Court.

Just then, I felt the hairs on my back stand up. I looked around.

"You okay, babe?" Layton asked.

"Yeah, I've just had the strangest feeling that someone has been watching me all day. It's nothing. I'm being paranoid over nothing."

We spent the rest of the game laughing, drinking, and buying Kate more ice cream than she needed. I couldn't believe how much Layton and Reed got into the football game. Reed's younger brother played on the team, and Anna's sister was a cheerleader.

"I wouldn't be surprised if little Anna down there was a cheerleader herself. She looks like the type."

I looked at Courtney and rolled me eyes.

As the night went on, Reed and Anna were hanging on each other more and more. At one point, I swore Reed has his hand up her shirt.

I glanced at them, and they were kissing each other as Anna was sitting in Reed's lap. When she pulled away, she moved her ass and lifted her eyebrows.

"Oh, please." Court rolled her eyes. "I think I'm going to puke. What a slut. I mean, Kate is sitting right next to them. Show a bit of restraint, for fuck's sake."

Layton hit Reed on the shoulder and pointed to Kate. Anna got up and moved to sit next to Reed.

"I need a beer or ten." Courtney got up and made her way down the bleachers.

Reed jumped up and asked, "Does anyone want anything?"

"Ice cream!" Kate yelled.

"No more ice cream, Kate. I think we're going to be heading out of here shortly," Layton said as he hugged Kate and looked up at Reed.

Reed made his way down the bleachers and went in the same direction as Court. I glanced over toward Anna, but she was busy talking to Kate.

About fifteen minutes later, Courtney came walking back up the bleachers. I could tell she was upset, and it almost looked like she was about to cry.

When she sat down, I asked, "Hey, are you okay?"

"I hate him so much," she whispered.

I didn't even need to ask whom she meant. Reed came walking up and looked directly at Courtney before turning and smiling at Anna. He handed her a Frito pie and a beer.

"Layton, I think I'm ready to leave," I said.

He jumped up and grabbed Kate's hand. Clearly, he had been ready to leave for some time now.

"Say good-bye to Reed, Kate. We're leaving now," Layton said as he reached and shook Reed's hand. "I'll call you tomorrow. I'm gonna need help with the cattle if you're free."

Reed nodded. "Yeah. You know I'm always ready when you are."

Kate gave Reed a long hug good-bye before taking Layton's hand.

I reached down to hug Courtney good-bye. "Will you be at home this weekend?" I asked with a wink.

She shook her head. "I'll probably see you out at the ranch. I don't want to be alone this weekend with this weird feeling I'm having."

I gave her a weak smile. A part of me thought she just didn't want to be alone, thinking about Reed with Anna.

"Okay. See ya tomorrow, Lollipop."

-》》》》》》》》》》》《《《《《《《《《《《《《-

I stood in the kitchen, making pancakes, as Kate went on and on about how she was going to marry Reed when she grew up. She even had their kids' names picked out.

"Don't you think Reed might be a little bit too…oh, I don't know…old for you, Kate? I mean I know you just turned six and all." I asked with a wink.

She shrugged her shoulders. "Well, until something better comes along, I'm going to marry him."

I let out a laugh as I flipped her pancake. I glanced up to see a grumpy Layton walking into the kitchen.

"Hey, Uncle Layton! Whitley is making us pancakes for breakfast."

Layton attempted to smile at Kate before looking up at me. I knew he was pissed at me. I could see it in his eyes. Kate had begged to sleep with us in Layton's bed last night, and I'd given in and said she could. I knew Layton was disappointed.

"Happy birthday, munchkin," Layton grumbled.

"Are you a grumpy bug today, Uncle Layton?" Kate asked.

"Yes. Yes, I am, Kate. I'm grumpy because I got no sleep last night. You kept kicking me in your sleep while pulling off my covers and laughing all night."

I frowned as I glanced down at Kate whose little smile had faded.

Damn it, Layton. You hurt her feelings.

"But I thought—" Kate started to say.

"You know the rules, Kate. You're not allowed to sleep in any other bed besides your own. Now, your mother is going to be pissed at me because Whitley here gave in to you last night and let you sleep with us."

My mouth dropped open, and Kate's little head just hung down.

"Why didn't you tell me her mother had a rule about that, Layton?"

He spun around and looked at me. "I told you no, Whitley. I told you she couldn't sleep with us, and you still said she could. I didn't realize I had to give a full blown-out reason."

I started to butter Kate's pancake. I looked at her and smiled.

When I set it in front of her, she shook her head. "I'm not hungry anymore."

"Eat your pancake, Kate. You know your mom likes you to eat breakfast. Whitley, can I talk to you outside?"

I leaned down and smiled at Kate. "I didn't know your mom had a rule, Kate. If you know that you're breaking a rule and I don't…you can't just go along with it, okay? That's still breaking the rule."

Kate nodded and gave me a weak smile. She reached for the syrup as I stood and followed Layton outside. I was ready for him to lay into me.

Here, I thought he was grumpy from not getting sex last night.

As I shut the door behind me, I braced myself for his onslaught.

I turned around, and he grabbed me and pulled me to him.

He put his hand behind my neck and barely brushed his lips against mine as he said, "God, I'm so sorry I snapped at you just now. I'm so sorry, baby."

The feel of his tongue moving against my lips made me moan. I wanted him so badly.

I instantly relaxed and whispered, "Layton…"

He reached down and picked me up as I wrapped my legs around him. I instantly felt how much he wanted me, and I was aching to have him inside me.

"When is Jen picking up Kate?" I pushed myself into him.

He moved his lips down and kissed along my neck. "Any. Moment," he said between kisses.

"Thank God. I mean, I love Kate and all—"

Layton slammed his lips against mine as he moved his hand up my shirt and then along the top of my pants. "I want you, Whit, so damn bad."

"Yes. Touch me, please, before I go insane."

Just as I felt his hand about to go down my pants, I heard a female voice.

"Um…excuse me for interrupting."

Layton pulled his lips from mine and put his head against my forehead.

"What do you want, Olivia?" Layton closed his eyes and slowly moved his hand out of my pants.

"My event planner. I realize it's a Saturday, but if she wants to plan my wedding and reception, we should probably talk about it. It seems like every time I see her though, she has her damn legs wrapped around you like a horny-ass teenager."

I leaned my head against the house and sighed. I was so tired of this girl. I'd had enough. I leaned in and kissed Layton on the lips before motioning for him to put me down.

I walked up to the edge of the stairs and looked down at Olivia. "Listen, Olivia, I worked your engagement party. I never said I was going to help you plan your wedding."

She let out a laugh. "Well, I would think if you're trying to start a business, you wouldn't want to turn down any jobs."

I wasn't going to do this. *I am so done with letting people walk all over me.*

"I'm sorry, Olivia. This is one job I'm going to turn down. I don't think it's very appropriate for me to be the event planner for your wedding and reception."

Her smile dropped, and she snapped her head over toward Layton. I looked over my shoulder at him. He was smiling as he gave me a wink. I knew he was happy that I was telling her no.

"What do you mean, it's not appropriate? Why the hell not?"

"Well, for starters, I'm dating your ex. And to be honest, the first wedding I'm going to plan is gonna be my own wedding."

Olivia's hands flew up to her mouth as she started to shake her head. "Oh my God. You're pregnant?"

"What?" Layton and I both said at the same time.

Just then, Jen opened the back door. "Oh my God, you're pregnant, Whitley?"

Kate came running out, singing, "Whitley's got a baby in her tummy!"

I started shaking my head as Layton reached down and grabbed Kate. I turned to see Mitch and Courtney walking up with one pissed-off Reed following behind them.

The moment Kate saw Reed, she jumped down from Layton and started to run toward him. "Guess what? There is a baby growing inside Whitley's tummy!"

Reed and Courtney quickly looked up at me, and both said, "What?"

"Wait—what? How? I mean…when?" Layton asked from behind me.

Oh shit, my head is spinning.

"You bitch! You're pregnant, and you didn't tell me?" Courtney pushed her way past Olivia, who was now staring at Layton.

"I'm shocked that you would knock up this poor girl, Layton." Olivia slowly shook her head.

"What?" I spun around and looked at Olivia and then Layton.

Layton just stared at me as I tried to push Courtney away from me.

She was leaning down, talking to my stomach, "You're going to be the best dressed baby in Llano!"

Layton took a step toward me and smiled.

Ah shit…does he think I'm pregnant?

The smile on his face made me weak in the knees.

Would he be happy if I were pregnant? Oh. My. God.

Everyone was talking all at once. Courtney was still talking to my stomach, and Mitch started saying something about teaching the baby how to rope as he smiled down at Courtney. Olivia was trying to tell Layton what a huge mistake this pregnancy was, and Reed was trying to grab Kate, who was running around, screaming that I had a baby growing in my stomach.

The only two people not talking were Jen and Layton. Jen was standing there, smiling at me.

No, wait. Oh my God, this has to stop!

"STOP!" I screamed. "Everyone, just shut up!"

Instantly, everyone stopped talking, including Kate.

"Oh…Whitley said shut up, mama," Kate said.

Courtney was now on her knees with her hands on my stomach. I pushed her away and took a few steps back.

"For Christ's sake, stand the hell up, Court. You look like an idiot!" I said, shaking my head.

Courtney jumped up and started smiling.

"I'm not, let me repeat this, I'm not pregnant." I looked around.

Jen's, Layton's, and Court's smiles all disappeared. Olivia smiled and seemed to be relieved.

I took a few steps closer to Olivia. "I really don't appreciate you assuming that I'm pregnant because I want to plan my own wedding first, Olivia. I'm sorry, but I'm just not interested in planning your wedding. Period. You're going to have to find another event planner or wedding planner for that. And when Layton and I decide to have children, it sure as hell will not be any of your business, so don't ever say what you just said again. Do I make myself clear?"

"But—"

"No, I'm done with this conversation with you."

Olivia put her hands on her hips and gave me a drop-dead look. "Fine. I was just trying to do you a favor by having you plan what is sure to be the year's most talked about wedding in Llano. But if you don't want to—"

"I don't want to," I said with a smirk.

Olivia gave me the dirtiest look I thought she could muster. "Layton, it was good seeing you." She looked around at everyone else and shook her head. "Have a good day, everyone."

I watched as she walked toward her BMW. I rolled my eyes and turned back to look at everyone staring at me.

Kate walked up to me and pulled on my shirt. "So, you don't have a baby growing in your tummy?"

I bent down and took her hands in mine. "No, sweetheart, at least not yet, but I hope to someday soon."

I looked up at a smiling Layton. The butterflies in my stomach were going crazy. I almost fell back on my ass just from the smile on his face. I was going to have to talk to him about his reaction to all of this.

"So, are we still going out for my birthday tonight?" she asked me with the cutest smile.

"Of course, we are! This is your day."

Jen walked up and took Kate's hand. "Speaking of your day, birthday girl, come on. We have to go shopping for a new birthday dress for tonight."

Kate jumped up and down and ran to give Reed a hug good-bye. Then, she hugged Layton, smiled at Mitch, and said good-bye to Courtney before running back to Jen.

After they left, I started laughing. "You're going to have to keep a close eye on her, Layton. That girl likes to flirt."

Everyone started laughing.

I looked at Courtney.

Her smile faded for a quick second before she took a deep breath and smiled. "So, Mitch and I are taking a drive toward Fredericksburg. He wants to take me to Enchanted Rock."

"Oh, I want to go there!" I glanced back at Layton, who was looking at Reed.

"Reed, I didn't think you would be here so early this morning," Layton said with a wink.

Reed quickly looked at Courtney, who had walked up and put her arm around Mitch. The hurt on his face about gutted me.

"Well, Anna spent the night last night, and she had to be up early to get ready for work this morning. Since I was up, I thought I'd head on over."

Oh, Reed, why would you say that?

I took a peek at Courtney. I could tell she was trying to hide her disappointment in finding out that Anna had spent the night with Reed.

Layton, Reed, and Mitch started talking about the cattle, so I took Court by the arm and led her into the house.

Once we were inside, I poured her a cup of coffee and handed it to her. I was just about to ask her about last night when she let out a laugh.

"I can't believe she spent the night with him! What a total slut. I mean, they haven't seen each other in how many years? And he has the nerve to call me names!"

Ah hell. She is totally not over her feelings for Reed.

"Court—"

The sound of the back door opening and Layton and Reed arguing stopped me from saying anything else.

"Reed, you don't know what in the hell you're talking about," Layton said as he grabbed a coffee cup out of the cabinet.

"I disagree with you, Layton. I do know what I'm talking about. You're making a mistake by not getting rid of it."

Courtney rolled her eyes, and Reed saw her.

Reed walked up to Courtney and leaned down. "You have something to say there, Miss High and Mighty?"

Courtney sat up straight and smiled. "Yes. Yes, I do, King of all Assholes."

"Let's hear it."

Courtney stood up and put her game face on.

"Uh, Court, how about you and I head on up to, um…the guest room?" I glanced at Layton, who was shaking his head. I shrugged my shoulders. "What? I'm not good at spur-of-the-moment things."

Courtney walked up and started poking Reed in the chest. "You and your I-know-everything bullshit. You don't know shit, Reed Moore. You run off at the mouth and then turn around and sleep with exactly what you were accusing me of."

"Oh shit," Layton and I both said at the same time.

"*What?* What in the fuck are you even talking about? I'm talking to Layton about some damn plants his cows are eating. What in the hell are you going off on?"

Then, it hit Reed what Court was talking about. He took a step back and looked at Courtney. "Are you fucking kidding me? Are you talking about Anna staying with me last night? Last I checked, Courtney, what I did was none of your business."

Courtney laughed and shook her head a few times. "Why can you call me a whore, but then you turn around and fuck a girl you haven't even seen since high school? Who's the whore now?"

"I tried to apologize to you a million times, Courtney, but you never let me. I was drunk and also…"

Courtney's head tilted, and her eyebrows went up. "You were also, what? Come on, Reed. You're always so quick to run off at the damn mouth. What were you? You certainly weren't having any trouble calling me names. So, what was it, Reed? Drunk and what?"

Reed just stared at Courtney. His fists balled up as he started to back away from her. "Nothing. I already said I was sorry for the things I said!" he shouted.

Courtney jumped from the sound of him yelling.

"And what in the hell do you care what I do with Anna or any other girl for that matter? You're one to talk. You're sleeping with Mitch, and you seem to be pretty damn happy with him, so I think you can just mind your own business. I'll fuck whoever I want to fuck."

Courtney's eyes started to fill with tears as Reed turned and walked toward the back door.

He looked back at Courtney as he opened the door. "I was drunk and also jealous. It killed me, seeing you and Mitch together, and the only reason I fucked Anna was so I could forget about you. Are you happy now, Courtney?" Reed spun around, walked out the door, and slammed it shut behind him.

Layton walked out of the kitchen as I ran up to Courtney. She practically collapsed into my arms, crying.

"Court, why? Why are you with Mitch if you have feelings for Reed?" I asked as we both slowly sat down on the kitchen chairs.

Courtney was sobbing hysterically now. I got up and went into the half bathroom to grab some tissues as Courtney settled herself down.

"Court, talk to me."

She looked up at me and tried to smile. "I can't…a guy like Reed Moore will only end up hurting me. You heard what he just said."

My mouth dropped open. "What? Why in the world do you say that?"

"Because it's true, Whit. He's all talk, and he's such an asshole. He's rude, he's a know-it-all, and he always argues with me."

I shook my head. "Okay, first off, I've never seen Reed be rude to anyone…well, anyone besides you. I think the two of you bring out the worst in each other because you're both fighting this attraction that you clearly have for one another. Neither one of y'all have ever been in a serious long-term relationship. Do you think that scares you maybe?"

"No! I want to be with someone, Whitley. I want what I've read about in all those damn books."

"That's the problem, honey. You're comparing Reed to all your book boyfriends. You never even gave him a chance. What makes Mitch different from Reed?"

Courtney smiled. "Mitch is…just Mitch."

"Um…that's not really an answer."

"He's safe, and he's polite. He always tells me how much he cares about me and how beautiful I am. He makes me feel special."

"Reed's not safe?"

"Fuck no, Reed's not safe. I mean, come on, Whitley, you heard what he just said. He slept with Anna to forget me? Who does that? Asshole men who don't care if they hurt you or not."

"I don't think he's like that, Court. I mean, he just admitted he has feelings for you."

Courtney laughed. "He also admitted to sleeping with Anna to forget about me. If I'm that easy to forget, what does that tell you about him?" She stood and tried to dry her eyes. "It doesn't matter anyway. He just tries

to make me upset every time he sees me. He is always saying something to make me mad."

I thought about last night at the game when Courtney had come back upset. "What did he say last night when y'all were both getting drinks?"

Courtney stopped and looked at me. "What?"

"Last night at the football game, when you came back, you were clearly hurt, and Reed was following you. He seemed to be upset also. What did y'all say to each other?"

Courtney just stood there, staring at me.

"Court? Hello? What in the hell is wrong with you?"

She shook her head. "Nothing. It doesn't matter. It was a mistake."

I looked at her with the same look my mother used to give me when she had pumped me for information. "Courtney…"

"Um…well, he, um…he pulled me to the side and told me I looked really good. When I told him to let me go, he, um…he—"

"For Christ's sake, Courtney, spit it the hell out!"

She took a deep breath and slowly let it out. "He asked me if I was sure."

"Sure about what?"

"Mitch. He asked me if I was sure of my feelings for Mitch. He was standing so close to me, and all I could smell was his cologne. And his eyes—they were looking right into mine. My head was spinning, and I was so confused as to why he was asking me that."

"What did you say?"

Her eyes filled with tears. "I told him yes, that I'd never been so sure of something in my entire life."

"Oh, Courtney. Don't you see what he was doing? He wouldn't have been with Anna last night if you had just told him the truth. Courtney, you have to be honest with your feelings—not only for Reed but also think about Mitch."

Courtney's head snapped up as she looked me in the eyes. "I care about Mitch—a lot."

"Do you love him?"

Her eyes started to tear up again. "I think I'm falling in love with him. Yes."

"Do you love Reed?"

She shook her head and looked away from me.

"Court, do you love Reed also?"

She looked up at me as a tear rolled down her cheek. "Yes," she whispered.

"Courtney…oh no." I sat there in the kitchen, holding my best friend in my arms, as she cried hysterically.

"Court, you have to listen to your heart, not your head. Who does your heart tell you to follow?"

Courtney stood up and wiped the tears from her eyes. She took a calming deep breath and smiled. "Thank you, Whitley, for letting me get all that off my chest. I need to go find Mitch. I'm sure he's ready to head out. Have fun today with Layton and tonight with Jen and Kate. Give her a big birthday kiss from me." She smiled as she gave me a hug, and then she turned to leave.

"Court?"

She stopped and glanced back at me. "Yeah?"

"Please follow your heart, babe."

She gave me a weak smile and walked out the door.

I sat there for a few minutes before I felt Layton's hands on my shoulders. The moment he touched me, I felt a sense of peace.

I stood and turned to him. "Will you make love to me?"

He smiled as he reached down and picked me up. The whole way to his bedroom, he just kept telling me how much he loved me.

As he laid me down on the bed, I smiled at him. "I still have the vibrator in my overnight bag, you know."

The smile that spread across his face caused me to instantly blush.

"Ah, hell yeah, let's make up for last night!"

I laughed as I watched him practically rip off his clothes. My heart was filled with so much love for him.

I thought of Courtney and said a quick prayer that she would follow her heart and not her head.

Layton started to take off my jeans oh-so slowly.

Oh God…the feel of his hands on me is pure heaven.

"I'm going to make the sweetest, most passionate love to you, Whitley."

Oh my, I can't breathe.

"Yes," was all I could manage to get out of my mouth as I felt his lips all over my body.

I grabbed the sheets with my hands as I felt his hot breath against my clit. It didn't take long before I was screaming out his name with one of the most intense orgasms ever.

God, the way he makes me feel when he does that…

As I slowly came back down, I had the feeling we were being watched. It quickly disappeared when I felt Layton slowly enter my body.

I closed my eyes and got lost in Layton's lovemaking.

"I love you, Whitley. I want to be with you forever."

I felt a tear roll down my face as I pulled him closer to me. I needed to feel him closer…deeper inside me.

"I'll love you always, Layton."

TWENTY-FOUR

-»»»»»»»««««««««««-

LAYTON

As Whitley and I lay in bed, I had the strangest feeling we were being watched.

Fuck, I really need to get that alarm system fixed. I'm all paranoid now.

"Baby, are you and Courtney using the alarm system I had put in at your house?"

"Mmm…"

I smiled as I felt her warm body up against mine.

"Was that a yes?"

"Mmhmm."

I let out a small laugh. I had been thinking all night about how I was going to ask her to marry me, and I finally figured it out.

Whitley might be from New York, but she is a simple country girl at heart.

I needed to keep it simple. My heart started pounding. Four more days, and I was going to ask her to be my wife.

"Layton?"

"Yeah, baby?"

"Can I ask you something?" Whitley rolled over to look at me.

"Always."

"Earlier today, when everyone started freaking out because they thought I was pregnant, you seemed…well, you almost seemed like you were disappointed when I said I wasn't. I mean, I might have been reading it all wrong, and that's okay if I was. It's just that it kind of confused me, and I—"

I put my finger up to her lips to quiet her. "Whitley, I'm not going to lie to you. For a brief few moments, I was thrilled with the idea of you carrying our child."

She slowly let a smile play across her face.

"But I want to do things right. I want to get married and spend time with you. I want to spoil you and make love to you anytime I want. I don't think we can really do that with a little one. I want to discover everything about you. Then, I'd like to have a baby…or two."

She giggled as she wiped away her tears. "I want the same thing, Layton. I've never been so happy in my entire life."

I gently kissed her as I reached over and grabbed the little black bag with her vibrator. I took it out of the bag and turned it on. She smiled against my lips and turned her head away from me.

"Don't turn away from me, Whitley."

When she turned back and looked at me, I almost had to suck in a breath of air.

My God, her eyes are beautiful and filled with nothing but love and passion.

"Layton…"

"I love it when you say my name. It sounds so beautiful coming from your lips."

I turned on the vibrator and put it up against one of her nipples. It instantly got hard as she let out a small moan. I took the other nipple into my mouth and sucked and lightly bit on it.

"Oh God, Layton!"

I moved the vibrator down to her stomach. I wanted to watch her use it on herself, but I wasn't sure how she would react to that request.

"Take the vibrator, Whitley."

Her eyes snapped over to mine. I saw fear and lust mixed together.

She slowly moved her hands down and took it from me. I put two fingers inside her and then pulled them out. I put her wetness onto the vibrator. I pulled my eyes from hers and watched as she started to put the vibrator inside her before she stopped.

I glanced back up at her, only to see her smiling.

"If I have to do this, you have to play with yourself."

I grabbed my dick and started moving my hand up and down. I watched her as she just stared at me while I stroked myself. When she bit down on her lip, I let out a small moan.

"Whit…"

She moved her eyes back up to mine. She turned up the vibrator, threw her head back, and let out a moan. I moved my eyes down her beautiful body and watched as she worked the vibrator in and out.

So fucking hot.

"Jesus, Whitley. You drive me insane. Go faster, baby."

As I watched her, I could feel myself getting closer and closer. I did everything I could to hold myself off.

Think puppies…babies—

No, not babies.

She was letting out more and more moans. When she reached down and grabbed my dick, I almost came on the spot.

"Layton. Oh God, it feels like I'm going to come. Oh God…"

The next thing I knew, she was calling out in pleasure. I pushed her hand off my dick, grabbed the vibrator, and pulled it out of her as she was still coming. I turned her over onto her knees and hands and slammed my

dick into her as deep and hard as I could. I reached my hand around the front of her, and I started to play with her already sensitive nub.

"Oh God...Layton. Harder. It. Feels. So. Good."

I moved faster and harder as I rubbed against her clit.

"Oh God! God, yes...yes...Layton."

She just kept calling out my name over and over again as I felt her getting tighter and tighter around my dick.

Just when I didn't think I could hold off any longer, she pulled away from me slightly and then pushed back against me.

"Ah...Whitley! I'm going to come, baby."

I grabbed her hips and pumped as hard and fast as I could. I could feel every ounce of me pouring into her as she repeated that she loved me.

As I came to a stop, she collapsed onto the bed, and I followed, lying on top of her.

Trying to catch my breath, I whispered into her ear, "Every time gets hotter and hotter with you, Whit."

She let out a giggle. "I don't know how it keeps getting better."

She started to roll over, and I moved to the side of her.

"Wow. That was intense and felt so good. Thank you. I hope that made up for last night," she said with a wink and the cutest damn smile I'd ever seen.

"How is it you can look so damn sweet and innocent right after having some of the hottest, mind-blowing sex of my life?"

She shrugged her shoulders as I kissed the tip of her nose.

"I guess I need to go do some work before we have to get ready for tonight," I said as I kissed her neck.

Whitley sat up in the bed and yelled out, "Oh shit! Shit! Shit! Shit!"

I put my hand on her back. "What's wrong, babe?"

She glanced back down to me and slowly shook her head. "I left the necklace at home last night. I forgot to grab it."

"It's okay, babe. We'll just run back to your house and get it."

"No, that's going out of the way. The restaurant is in Marble Falls, Layton. I'll just get dressed and run home and get it. I have to pick up a few extra changes of clothes anyway. I mean, that's if you still want me to stay through my birthday," she said with a wink.

"Of course I do, Whit, but I hate the idea of you driving all the way back to your house. We can just leave early."

She jumped up and pulled on her black lace thong and Victoria's Secret sweats. "Honestly, it's okay, babe. I have to grab a few other things. I promise, I won't be long. Let me run now, so I have time to come back and get ready."

"Okay. You want me to go with you?" I called out.

She stood in the bathroom, throwing her beautiful long brown hair into a ponytail. "Nope. Take care of what you're supposed to be taking care of with Reed. I'll be back soon."

After walking back toward me, she leaned down and kissed me so softly and passionately that I almost wanted to rip off her clothes and make love to her again.

She pulled away and smiled. "I'm pretty sure you're thinking you want to make love again."

I smiled at her and laughed. "Yep, that's exactly what I was thinking."

She stood up and took a few steps away. "Well, Mr. Morris…that was not making love. That was fucking."

I felt my dick jump at just her mentioning the word. She arched her eyebrows at me and laughed.

"Did you enjoy that, Miss Reynolds?"

"Yes, I did very much indeed, but I'm thinking I'd love some sweet, soft, romantic lovemaking this evening."

I smiled as I stood and let the sheet fall away from me. I watched while she looked greedily up and down my body as she chewed on her lower lip.

"Your wish is my command, baby." I cupped her face with my hands and kissed her softly on the lips.

"You're killing me, Layton. Killing. Me."

I stepped back and watched as she made her way out of the bedroom. She looked once over her shoulder to give me a wink.

"I love you!" I shouted after her.

"I love you more, baby!" she said as she rounded the corner.

After she was gone, I made my way to the shower with a smile on my face, thinking about next week.

What will her reaction be when I ask her to marry me? Will she cry?

Shit, I hope she doesn't laugh. Shit! Shit! Shit!

Is it possible for me to miss her already? She's only been gone two minutes.

I looked down at my growing dick. "Down, boy…she's not even here. Christ."

I turned the shower on full blast and moved it over to cold. I stood under the water, thinking about Whitley.

I've never in my life loved someone as much as I love her. I would lay down my life for her.

At that moment, I had the strangest feeling come over me, and I remembered my dream when Mike had told me that someone needed my help.

I stepped out of the shower, dried off, and then got dressed. The whole time I was trying to shake the bad feeling I had.

As I made my way down to the barn, I kept hearing the same thing over and over in my head.

Go to her. She needs your help. She needs you to save her.

I walked into the barn and was startled to see Courtney sitting in there, reading.

"Hey, Court. I thought you and Mitch were heading to Enchanted Rock."

She smiled and shook her head. "I guess something happened with a cow or a calf or something. I think Reed sent you a message on your phone. They headed to the north pasture to go take care of it. So, I thought I'd get caught up on some reading, but I just can't seem to concentrate. I've had the strangest feeling all day."

I stopped saddling up Hope, my new paint horse, and turned to look at Courtney. "What do you mean?"

She shrugged her shoulders. "It just feels like I'm being watched. I've felt like this for the last few days. I don't know. Maybe I'm just worried because everything seems to be falling into place, especially for Whitley. It's like I'm waiting for the floor to fall out from under her feet. Ya know what I mean?"

Just then, Mitch and Reed came riding back in. Reed jumped off his horse and walked straight up to me.

"Dude, there was someone on the ranch."

"What?"

"Mitch and I were in the north pasture, trying to get some barbed wire off a calf when I glanced up and saw a car driving on the ranch. Mitch and I got on the horses and headed over, but by the time we got there, the car was gone. A hole was cut in the fence line, and we could tell the car had driven in and out, maybe once or twice."

My heart started pounding. I looked at Courtney, who was now standing up.

"*Whitley*. Did she tell you that she thought she was being watched, too?" she asked.

I nodded and turned back toward Reed. "What kind of car was it?"

"Oh, um…shit, I don't know. A sports car, wouldn't you say, Mitch?"

Mitch nodded and then said, "Maybe a convertible because it almost looked like the top was down."

"Motherfucker." It all hit me at once. "Pete Miller."

"Who's that?" Courtney asked.

I looked up at Reed and Mitch and then over at Courtney. "I met him after I bought Whitley's engagement ring and—"

Mitch and Courtney said at the same time, "What?"

"Oh my God, Layton! You're going to ask Whit to marry you? When?" Courtney began jumping up and down.

I smiled. "On her birthday. I have the whole thing planned out."

Courtney put her hand up to her mouth, and I saw tears building in her eyes.

Mitch walked up and shook my hand. "Congratulations."

"Damn, dude, I still can't believe you're getting married." Reed gave me a quick hug.

Courtney snapped her head and looked at Reed. "You knew about this? Why did you…" Then, she stopped talking as she quickly looked back at me. "That's great, Layton! She's going to be so surprised."

"Thanks, y'all, but listen, back to what I was saying. This guy knocked on my window. He said he was in town for his cousin's wedding and needed to find a hotel 'cause he lost the paper with the name of the hotel he was supposed to stay at. He was driving a convertible, and something about him just didn't sit right with me. I asked him how long he was in town for, and he said only long enough to get back what was his. I thought it was strange because he mentioned being in town for his cousin's wedding."

Reed's face turned white as a ghost. "I ran into that guy. After the football game last night, he walked up to me and asked me if I knew Whitley and Courtney. He said he needed an event planner for his sister's wedding, and someone had given him Whit's name. I'd never seen him before, so I asked him why he would ask me. He said he saw me, um…he saw me talking to Courtney, and he thought he had recognized her as Whitley's friend. Now, looking back, the whole thing doesn't make any sense, but then, I'd had a few beers in me, too."

Courtney started shaking her head. "Oh God, Reed…did you tell him anything?"

"No, of course not. I told him I didn't have your business card, so I didn't know your numbers offhand. Then, I went to get my truck. Anna stayed behind and talked to him, and—oh fuck."

Reed reached into his back pocket and pulled out his cell phone. "Anna, hey, it's Reed. That guy you were talking to last night when I went and got my truck…yeah, the guy who got into the convertible. What did you say to him? Did you tell him anything about Whitley or Courtney?"

Reed's mouth dropped open, and he looked over toward Courtney. "Fuck! No…no, it's okay, Anna. Listen, I can't explain right now. I'll talk to you later."

He hung up and looked at me. "She told him where Whitley lived."

"What the fuck? How in the hell does she even know where we live? And why would she tell him that? She doesn't even know him! Who does that?" Courtney shouted as she pulled out her cell phone.

"Whitley must have told her when she was in the jewelry store," I said as I started pacing.

"She didn't tell him Whitley's address. She just said she told him Whitley lived down from the coffee house in a place she was restoring."

I looked at Courtney.

"She's not answering, Layton."

"Courtney, do you have a picture of Roger?"

Courtney started shaking her head and then began crying. "No! No, Layton. He can't possibly know where she is. How would he know?"

"At the benefit dinner a few months back, a guy was there who Whitley knew. He works with Roger."

Courtney slowly started to fall to the ground, but Reed quickly ran and grabbed her. Mitch was next to Courtney and took her from Reed's arms as Reed shot him a dirty look.

"Courtney, I need to see a picture of him."

She quickly wiped away the tears and started looking on her phone. "I think I have a picture of us from last Christmas on my phone. Here! Here it is." She handed the phone to Reed, who looked at it, and then handed it to me.

"That's the same guy I talked to, Layton," Reed said.

My heart slammed in my chest as I dropped the phone to the ground. I ran out of the barn and toward my truck.

Go to her. She needs you.

TWENTY-FIVE

-➤➤➤➤➤➤➤➤➤➤➤➤❮❮❮❮❮❮❮❮❮❮❮❮❮-

Whitley

After I packed up a few things I would need for the next week, I grabbed the box that had Kate's necklace in it and threw that in the bag as well. I jumped into the shower for a quick rinse-off, and then I started getting dressed when I heard a noise downstairs. I glanced over and looked at the alarm.

Shit! I forgot to set it.

I pulled my hair up into a ponytail and threw on a Texas A&M T-shirt that belonged to Layton. It was almost a dress on me, so it covered up the pink lace thong I had on.

I sat there for a few seconds and just listened. It was silent. I shook my head and put my hand on my stomach.

Gah! This feeling of being watched is driving me insane and making me paranoid.

I turned back around and walked into my bathroom to grab the new perfume Layton had bought me. I loved it and wanted to make sure I wore it for my birthday. Layton kept telling me he was taking me somewhere special.

Maybe I should pack a dress as well. He hasn't mentioned if it's someplace fancy or not.

As I turned to head back out into the bedroom, I stopped dead in my tracks. I slowly brought my hands up to my mouth and whispered, "Oh my God."

Roger was sitting on my bed, looking at me. I dropped the bottle of perfume and jumped when it hit the hardwood floor and broke into a million pieces.

Roger slowly shook his head. "Look at what you've gone and done, Squeak. You've broken it, just like you've broken my heart so many times."

"How?" I couldn't even talk.

"How did I know where to find you? It wasn't really that hard, Squeak. Once Nick said he had seen you at a benefit dinner in Austin, I started putting two and two together. Then, when Nick told me about how you and Melinda spent some time in the restroom together, it didn't take much to convince Melinda to give me a little bit of information."

I felt like I was going to throw up. "You bastard! You better not have laid a finger on her."

Roger threw his head back and laughed. "Worried about your new little friend, are you? Don't worry. I didn't have to. You see, I happened to have set up my phone when we had our little fuckfest under the tree. One look at it, and she gave me your new boyfriend's name. Then, I remembered how you used to always talk about some little fucking town in Texas. So, you see, Squeak, it wasn't hard to find you at all."

I tried to talk, but my mouth was completely dry. I managed to finally get some words out. "Layton is going to be here any minute, and I suggest you not be here when he gets here."

Roger's smile quickly dropped, and his eyes filled with anger.

Oh God. Please, God, no…not again.

He stood and started to walk toward me. I went to take a step back, but I stepped on a piece of glass and cried out. He grabbed my arm, pulled me over toward the bed, and threw me down onto it.

Please, no. Layton, I need you!

I put my hands up and instantly started crying. "Wait! Roger, please don't do this."

"Don't do what, Squeak? Don't touch you? It seems to me that you like to be touched nowadays. You've even gotten into kinky sex now, haven't you?"

I started to shake my head. "What are you talking about? Roger, please don't do this. We're not meant for each other. I don't love you. I love Layton. I've moved on, and so can you. We aren't good together. We never were."

He jumped on the bed, put his hands on both sides of my face, and got inches away from me. "Don't. Say. That! Ever! He can't fucking give you what I can. He can't possibly love you as much as I do. I was your first, Whitley. I'll always be in your heart. You think 'cause he uses some goddamn sex toy and fucks you hard from behind that he can make you happy?"

My heart slammed into my chest. I couldn't breathe.

Oh. My. God. Roger was in Layton's house. He watched us having sex.

I barely whispered, "What?"

Roger gave me an evil smile that caused me to start crying even harder.

"Oh yeah, baby. I stood there and watched the whole show—him kissing your pussy and you screaming out in pleasure. You know, Whit, I never pegged you for one who would like oral sex. I have to tell you though, Squeak. As fucking pissed-off as I was, watching another man fuck you, I got pretty turned-on from seeing him touch you and hearing you call out in pleasure. How about you show me some of the new things you've learned?"

"I can't believe you watched us! Fuck off, you fucking lunatic!" I screamed out as I started trying to push Roger off of me.

He grabbed my hands and put them above my head. I kicked and screamed, trying everything I could to get him off of me.

"Stay the fuck still." He hit me across the face as hard as he could.

I instantly tasted blood and stopped moving. He slowly traced my jaw line and moved it down my body. He began running his finger along the edge of my lace panties, and it felt like he was choking me.

"Please don't do this, Roger. Please," I cried out.

He grabbed my face and looked me in the eyes as he smiled. "You're mine, Whitley. You always have been, and you always will be."

I quickly turned my head and saw an empty bottle of wine sitting on my table. Roger bent down and started kissing me on my neck. I pulled my one hand free, grabbed the bottle, and hit him as hard as I could on the side of his head. I used every ounce of energy to push him off of me. He was cursing me up and down as I started to run out of the bedroom.

I heard him jump off of the bed as he called out, "Whitley, stop! Now!"

I was just about to run down the steps when I heard a gunshot. I instantly stopped.

"Don't. Do. This," Roger said from behind me.

I slowly turned around to see him pointing a gun at me.

No…this isn't happening. Oh God, no. He's going to kill me if I don't do what he wants.

I started to step backward, and I ran into the table at the top of the stairs. "Roger, please. For the love of God, what has gotten into you? Are you going to shoot me if I don't have sex with you?"

He threw his head back and laughed. "Oh, trust me, Squeak, you're gonna fuck me, and you're going to love every minute of it. You just need to be reminded of what we shared, that's all."

My heart was beating so fast. *Layton, I need you.*

"What we shared? Are you kidding me, Roger? You beat me. You beat me so badly that I ended up in the hospital. You couldn't possibly love me. Who hits someone they love?" I screamed out as tears streamed down my face.

His smile faded, and his eyes began to fill with tears. "Baby, I don't mean to hurt you. I love you so much, Whit. I'm so afraid you're going to leave me. Hell, you did leave me, and it about destroyed my world. And now, you're fucking some damn rich cowboy. Baby, I can make you feel like he makes you feel. I can love you better. Let me show you how good I can make you feel. Whit, let me put my lips on you and make you scream out in pleasure like he did."

Oh God…please, God. Please help me.

My whole body was shaking as I watched him walking closer with the gun pointed right at me.

"Roger…" I couldn't even say anything else through my sobs.

"Baby, just let me help you remember what we had."

I looked around, frantically trying to find something to use to protect myself.

The candlestick!

An iron candlestick that Courtney had bought a few months ago was sitting on the table I was leaning against. I closed my eyes as Roger drew closer and closer to me.

"Please don't do this…*please*," I whispered.

He walked up to me and leaned down to kiss me. "Let me show you, baby."

I bit down on my lip, knowing that it turned Roger on more than anything.

He smiled his crooked half-smile at me and whispered, "That's right, baby."

As his lips met mine, I felt like I was going to be sick. I moved my hand up his chest, around his neck, and into his hair, and then I pulled on it slightly. He let out a low moan into my mouth, and it was everything I could do not to start gagging. I reached with my right hand and felt for the candlestick. I could feel his erection pushing into my stomach as he leaned in closer to me.

He slowly pulled away from my lips. "Tell me you missed me and that you want me, Whitley. Tell me now."

I slowly smiled as I took the candlestick in my hand. "Roger…you have no idea…how much I have *not* missed you."

His smile faded, and I used all my power to swing the candlestick around and hit him in the head. He instantly fell to the ground as I screamed and made my way down the two flights of stairs.

Jesus, Whitley, don't fucking fall!

I had almost made it to the bottom of the stairs when the front door busted open, and Layton came in. The moment I saw him, I started crying hysterically and ran into his arms.

"Jesus, Whitley, are you all right? What the fuck is going on?"

I held on to him, sobbing. "We. Have. To. Go! Now!" I managed to get out in between sobs.

He pulled away and looked into my eyes. Then, his eyes moved to my mouth, and I saw the anger in them.

"Where is he?"

I started hysterically shaking my head. "No! We have to leave—now! We have to call the police now, Layton." I pulled on his arm to get him to leave with me. "Layton…please…my God, please, we have to leave!"

"I called the police, baby. They'll be here any second. Where is he, Whitley? Tell me now."

I tried so hard to stop crying. I glanced up the stairs and pulled on Layton's arm. Layton followed my eyes and yanked his arm away before he started running upstairs.

"Layton, no! He has a gun! Please don't go up there!"

I looked around for my purse and ran to it. I grabbed my cell phone and hit nine-one-one. When the operator answered, I was running up the stairs and heard a loud crash.

"Oh my God! He's in my house with a gun...please...please, hurry."

Then, I saw Layton and Roger at the top of the stairs. Layton went to go after Roger, and before I could even yell out, Roger pointed the gun and shot at Layton.

"No!" I screamed.

Layton flew forward and knocked the gun out of Roger's hand. Before I even knew what was happening, Roger was on the ground, and Layton was beating the shit out of him.

"You will never hurt her again for as long as I live, you fucking piece of shit." Layton kept hitting Roger over and over again.

I ran up, grabbed Layton, and tried pulling him off of Roger.

"Layton! Please stop! Please, Layton!"

Just then, two men came around me and pulled Layton off of Roger.

"No, stop! Don't...it's Roger! He had a gun, and he shot at—" I stopped talking when I saw the front of Layton's white shirt covered in blood. I threw my hands up to my mouth. "Oh God...oh God...he shot you, Layton. My God, he shot you!"

The officer let go of Layton as I ran up to him and took him in my arms. Everything started moving in slow motion. I saw the officers pick up Roger and push him against a wall as they put handcuffs on him. Then, I felt Layton's legs go out from under him, and we both fell to the floor.

I turned back to the police officers and screamed, "Help him! He's been shot, and he's not breathing right!"

I heard an officer on his radio, asking for EMS.

I looked down at Layton as he looked up at me. He tried smiling but started coughing. Blood was everywhere.

"Please don't...don't leave me, Layton. I love you. I need you, baby." I could hardly talk from crying so hard. "You can't leave me. You promised to take care of me forever. You can't break your promise to me. Kate needs you, too, Layton."

He tried to talk.

"No...no, baby, don't talk." I cried and shook my head. "Just stay with me, Layton."

"I...promise...he...won't...hurt...you."

I put my lips to his and started frantically kissing him over and over again.

"Stop talking. Please. Layton...please."

I looked up to see Reed dropping to his knees.

"Reed! *Please* do something!" I cried out.

I looked back down, and Layton was smiling up at me.

"I love you, Whitley." Then, he closed his eyes.

"No! No! No! Don't do this to me!" I screamed out as I grabbed on to Layton's shirt and cried. "You can't leave me, Layton! Please..."

The next thing I knew, Courtney and Mitch were pulling me away from Layton as the EMS workers surrounded him. I couldn't see him anymore.

Oh God...I can't see him. What are they doing to him?

"Stop! Don't take me away from him. He needs me, Courtney. Please let me go back to him. *He needs me! I can't leave him! I promised.*"

As I watched them performing CPR on Layton, I looked into Reed's eyes that were filled with tears.

No. No...please don't leave me. Mike...please don't take him from me.

The room slowly started getting darker as I felt my legs giving out on me.

I heard someone say, "I got a pulse again, but it's weak."

Then, Courtney yelled out my name as I drifted off into darkness and silence.

TWENTY-SIX

-➤➤➤➤➤➤➤➤➤➤➤➤❮❮❮❮❮❮❮❮❮❮❮❮❮-

Whitley

I sat in the chair, staring out the window, watching the raindrops slide down the glass. My head was pounding, and I was beginning to feel weak.

Courtney walked up to me and put her hand on my shoulder. "Whit, please come with me to the hotel. You can take a hot shower, change your clothes, and maybe even get a few hours of sleep."

"You need to get something to eat, Whitley," Reed said from across the room.

I turned and looked at them. I tried my best to give them a smile, but I barely had the energy to move.

"You know, when the nurse comes back in here, she's gonna be pissed. Only two people are allowed in the ICU rooms," I said as I winked at Reed.

Reed gave me a weak smile as he glanced up and looked at Courtney. Neither one of them had fought once in the last four days. I knew they were holding back for my sake.

"Courtney, you should go to the hotel. You look tired," I said.

She shook her head and looked over toward Reed. "Um...Mitch is on his way into Austin now. I'll probably head to the hotel when he gets here and sees Layton."

I glanced over to the man I was so desperately in love with. He was lying in a hospital bed, hooked up to a number of machines.

Wake up, Layton. Please wake up.

I felt tears rolling down my face. I turned and looked back out the window. Every time I looked at him, I started crying.

Courtney began running her hand down my hair. "Can we at least take you out to eat for your birthday?"

I pulled me knees up to my chest, buried my face, and cried. Layton had told me he had something special planned for my birthday. The thought of it made me sick to my stomach.

What if I never find out what his plans were? What if he wakes up and hates me for being the cause of all of this?

What if he doesn't wake up?

I cried harder.

"Whitley, stop this right now. This was not your fault, and you have to stop beating yourself up over it. You're going to have to leave at some point," Courtney said.

I snapped my head up and looked at my best friend, who had stood by my side for everything.

"I. Can't. Leave. I've already told you, Court. I won't leave him. I'll never leave him alone. I can't leave him alone. Everyone always leaves him. What if he wakes up, and no one is here?" I said.

Reed stood up and walked over toward me. He bent down and looked into my swollen red eyes. "Whitley, I'll stay with him. We won't let him be alone...ever. I promise you."

I shook my head back and forth. "No! Reed, you know how he is with promises. I promised him I'd never leave him. I'm not leaving until he wakes up. So, would you both please just stop asking me to leave? I'm not going to leave him!" I practically shouted.

Reed looked up and over at Courtney as she nodded.

As he stood up, he kissed me on the forehead and wiped away my tears. "Okay, Whitley. No more asking you to leave. How about some food? Can you eat some food for me, sweetheart?" Reed asked.

I glanced over toward Courtney and noticed how she was looking at Reed with so much love in her eyes.

I was so hungry. I couldn't even remember the last time I had eaten. I nodded and gave him a weak smile. "I could really go for some Chick-fil-A," I said.

He smiled and nodded. "Sandwich or nuggets?"

"She likes the nuggets...but get her enough sauce to dip her french fries into also."

We all snapped our heads over toward the bed. Layton's eyes immediately caught mine. I threw my hands up to my mouth and started crying as I jumped up and ran over to him.

"Layton! Thank you, God. Thank you so much." I began kissing him softly all over his face. I picked up his hand and began kissing it.

"Are you okay, baby?" He lifted his hand and rubbed the side of my mouth where it had been cut.

I grabbed his hand and held it against my face as I nodded. "I'm fine. No, I'm perfect now that you're awake and looking into my eyes again. I've never been better. I love you so much, Layton. Please don't ever leave me."

He smiled that smile of his that made me weak in my knees—the smile he had given me when I first met him on the side of the road.

Then, his smile faded. "Where is he?"

I knew he was talking about Roger. "I don't want to talk about him. I just want to sit here and thank God for bringing you back to me. Are you in pain?"

I turned and looked at Courtney. "Maybe we should let them know that he's awake."

She nodded and made her way out to find a nurse.

Reed walked up and smiled. "Jesus, dude. You scared the shit out of us. What in the hell were you doing, playing hero, when that asshole had a gun?"

"Is that why I hurt so fucking bad?" Layton tried to laugh but stopped himself.

"Yeah. He shot you in the stomach, but you're one lucky son of a bitch. It missed everything it needed to miss."

Layton winked at me. "Good. I need to be ready for Wednesday."

I tried to smile, but I felt a tear roll down my face. "Layton, it is Wednesday."

His smile faded, and he closed his eyes. When he opened them, he had tears in his eyes. I leaned up and began kissing him on the lips. He reached his hand up, grabbed on to the back of my neck, and held me tighter to him. I wasn't sure how long we were kissing before Reed cleared his throat. I pulled slightly away and smiled when I saw Layton smiling.

"Happy birthday, baby. I'm so sorry. I promise, I'll make it up to you."

"Layton, I don't care about my birthday. The only thing I care about is you."

"Excuse me, but I'm going to have to get in there."

I looked up and saw the sweet older nurse who had been on duty since six this morning.

"Well, Mr. Morris, I'm sure you're probably hurting."

"Yes, ma'am. A lot in my stomach."

She smiled the sweetest smile. "Well, let's take care of that, shall we?"

Layton smiled and glanced over at me.

"Ma'am?" he asked.

"Please, call me Katie," she said with a wink.

Layton smiled. "That's my niece's name, but we call her Kate."

"It's a good, strong name," she said with a smile. "What can I do for you, Mr. Morris?"

"Please, it's Layton. Can you please tell this beautiful woman behind you to go home, take a shower, and get something to eat?"

She threw her head back slightly. "Your friends have been trying for four days to get her to leave your side, but she wouldn't."

I smiled as I looked over at Courtney and Reed.

After a few minutes, the doctor came walking in. He told Layton everything about his gunshot wound, what they had done to fix it, and what he thought the recovery was going to be like.

I had to sit down. My head was spinning. It wouldn't be long before the police came in to talk to Layton. They'd stopped by every day since the shooting, waiting for him to wake up, so they could take his statement.

"So, how long will I need to stay here?" Layton asked.

"Well, depending on how well you do, I'd like to get you up and moving around as soon as possible. I'm hoping to have you home soon, son."

The doctor and Layton spoke a few minutes longer. Once the nurse and doctor left the room, I felt everything hit me all at once. I went to stand up and started to lose my balance. Reed ran over and grabbed me before I fell.

"That's it. I'm taking you to the hotel, Whitley," Reed said as he helped me sit back down in the chair.

I looked up at Layton, and his expression about killed me. His eyes were filled with worry.

Courtney walked up and leaned down. She whispered in my ear, "You're causing him to worry about you, Whit. Please go with Reed. I'll wait here until you come back."

I nodded and reached for Reed's hand.

I walked over and bent down to kiss Layton. "I love you so much. I'll be back soon, I promise you."

Layton let out a small laugh. "Baby, go get some food, and please get a few hours of sleep. I know you're not leaving me. I'll be here, promise," he said with a wink.

I gave him one more quick kiss good-bye before walking out with Reed. As we walked by the nurses' station, I saw the police officers.

"Oh wait, Reed—"

Reed grabbed me tighter and kept walking. "He's fine, Whit. Courtney is there. Come on, let's go to Chick-fil-A. I'm starving."

I watched them walk into Layton's room with the nurse. As the elevator doors closed, I let out the breath I had been holding, and I walked right into Reed's arms and cried.

"I don't think I could listen to him talk about what happened. Oh God, Reed. He almost died. What if he hadn't gotten there when he did, and Roger—"

Reed began stroking my hair as he said, "Shh…Whitley, it's over. Sweetheart, it's all over now. You never have to worry about him again. Layton made sure of that."

◆≫≫≫≫≫≫≫≫≫≫≫≪≪≪≪≪≪≪≪≪≪≪≪◆

I sat down on the hotel bed and looked around. For one brief moment, I panicked. I jumped up, ran to the bedroom door, and pulled it open. Reed was sitting on the sofa, watching TV.

He got up and ran over toward me. "What's wrong?"

"Um...nothing. For a second, I just thought I was alone, and I don't want to be alone."

Reed smiled and sat back down on the sofa. "I'm not going to leave you, Whit. I promise."

"Reed?"

"Yeah?"

"Would it be inappropriate if I sat on the sofa with you and slept? I just don't want to be in a bed all alone, and..." I felt my throat tighten up as I tried to hold back my tears.

Reed smiled as he moved over and grabbed the blanket sitting at the end of the sofa. "Come on, baby girl. I made my own promise to Layton to always protect you when he wasn't around. He'd kick my ass if he knew you were scared, and I let it go."

I giggled as I sat down and curled up next to Reed. I started to think of Courtney and how she was in love with Reed but wouldn't admit it.

"Can I ask you a question, Reed? And you can tell me to mind my own business."

He let out a small laugh. "Go for it."

"How do you feel about Courtney? I mean, what are your feelings for her?"

I felt him take a deep breath and slowly let it out.

"I've never in my life met a girl like her. She's so confident in herself, yet she seems unsure of herself sometimes, too. She's so damn beautiful, inside and out, but she makes me madder than hell. She's stubborn, and she's a smart-ass. But I lie in bed every night and wonder how I could have let her slip away from me. I hate that my pride kept me away from her. It kept me from just telling her that I..." His voice trailed off.

I looked up at him. "That you, what?"

"That I love her. I think I've loved her since the moment I laid eyes on her. It's just that I've made so many mistakes in my life, Whitley. I'm no angel, and I just feel like I'm not good enough for her. She could do so much better than me."

I pulled back and sat up. I crossed my legs and just stared at him. "Reed, first off, no one is perfect, and we've all made mistakes. I can tell you that Courtney is no angel herself, but she has a good heart, and she tries her damnedest to be a good person. I know you're the same way. I've never met anyone who would do anything for his friends with no questions asked, like you do. Reed, if I asked you right now to give me the shirt off your back, I know you'd say okay and not think twice about it. Don't let

your past stand in the way of your future. What's in the past is meant to stay in the past. Trust me…I know."

He smiled and pushed my shoulder back. "Layton is one lucky son of a bitch. I'm so glad y'all found each other. But I think it's too late for Courtney and me. Too much has been said between us. Besides, she's with Mitch, and she seems to be…very happy with him."

He frowned, and I swore I saw tears in his eyes.

"Reed, don't give up. Trust me, I know Courtney cares about you…a lot."

Reed's eyes lit up, and he smiled. "Yeah?"

I smiled as I nodded. "I'm probably breaking some kind of sisterhood code by telling you this, so you have to swear this stays between us."

Reed sat up straight and nodded as he used his index finger to cross his heart. "I promise. My lips are sealed."

I took a deep breath and let it out. "Courtney is confused, really confused."

He tilted his head and scrunched up his nose. "Okay…about what?"

I rolled my eyes. *Men—everything has to be explained in full detail.*

"She's confused because she has feelings for both you and Mitch. She loves you, Reed…but she's also slowly falling in love with Mitch, and that confuses her. Mitch is her safe choice."

Reed's face fell. His eyes filled with sadness, and a part of me was wondering if I should have just kept my mouth shut.

"Her safe choice? She thinks I'm going to hurt her? How?"

I took another breath. I wished to God I had just fallen asleep and not started this conversation. "I'm not really sure, but I think she thinks you're a player. Something happened to Court in high school, and she changed. She began not trusting any guy. I mean, none. I never could get her to tell me what happened. She's so scared of being hurt that she'll never give her heart fully to anyone. But with you…I think she would hand you her heart in a second, and that scares the shit out of her."

Reed looked away for a few seconds. "What do I do? She's with Mitch, and he's a friend. I won't do that to him. And then, there's Anna."

"Do you have strong feelings for her?" I asked.

"I did, once. She's probably the only other girl besides Courtney who I've felt like I wanted to really be with. I was crushed when she left for college, but—"

"But, what?"

"What I feel for Courtney is so different than anything I've ever felt before for anyone, even Anna. Half the time, when I'm with Anna…I'm thinking of Courtney. I mean, I know we've only been out a few times, but that night she stayed with me…I kept thinking…ah shit, I'm such a fucking dick." He shook his head and let out a sigh.

I put my hand on his shoulder. "Did you sleep with her, thinking it would hurt Courtney if she found out?"

He shook he head. "No. I mean, in a way, I was hoping it would make her jealous. I wanted to be with Anna…I really did. At least I used to dream of being with her, but the whole time…I couldn't stop thinking of Courtney. I'd close my eyes and…" His voice trailed off. "That's not fair to Anna. I know that. The last thing I want to do is hurt her."

I snuggled back up next to him as he leaned back onto the sofa.

"I'm so confused, Whitley, because I don't want to give up something with Anna to chase someone who won't ever want me in her life…or give me a chance to be in her life."

I nodded. "I understand, Reed, but if you truly love Courtney, don't give up."

Reed let out a long sigh. "Get some sleep, Whit. I'll set my alarm in case I fall asleep, so we can head back up to the hospital in a few hours."

I slowly felt my body relaxing for the first time in four days. "Mmm, okay."

As I drifted off to sleep, I saw Layton's face. I could almost feel his love wrapping around my body, keeping me warm and safe.

TWENTY-SEVEN
LAYTON

As I rode up toward the house in the ranch truck, I saw Whitley standing out front, talking to someone. It had been two months since the whole Roger incident, and even though he was in jail, my heart still stopped anytime I saw Whitley talking to a stranger. I knew the moment she saw me, she was going to be pissed that I had taken off.

All this sitting around is killing me. I'm bored out of my fucking mind and ready to do manual work, something with my hands.

As I drove by, making my way down toward the barn, Whitley glanced over and waved. I knew she would ask a ton of questions. I'd told Mitch to tell her I was going to mend a fence even though I knew that would piss her off. I couldn't tell her what I had really done.

As I was walking toward the house, Whitley came around the side of the house, laughing at something the guy had said to her. I instantly didn't like him. I didn't like the way he was looking at her.

Jesus. Calm the hell down, Layton. She's a beautiful woman, and men are going to look. Get over it.

She walked up to me, and the smile she gave me caused my heart to skip a beat. I smiled back as I leaned down and kissed her gently on the lips.

"Hey, baby." I looked up and reached my hand out to the stranger standing in front of me. "Layton Morris."

"Mr. Morris, my name is Robert Mitchel. I represent a law firm in New York and Chicago."

Oh great. Watch that motherfucker Roger try to sue me for beating the shit out of him.

"I guess I can see the whole lawyer thing now with the briefcase and all. Listen, if this is about Roger and—"

Whitley put her hand on my arm. "It's not about Roger. Mr. Mitchel is being very secretive, but I can tell you it's not about Roger at all."

"Is there somewhere we can go to sit down, Mr. Morris?"

"Am I being sued?"

Mr. Mitchel let out a laugh and shook his head. "No. No, sir, you're not being sued."

I started walking toward the back door. "Then, come on in for a glass of sweet tea. It's a beautiful December day, and the heat has made me thirsty for some tea."

Whitley grabbed my arm. "Where did you go? Are you in any pain?"

I smiled as I leaned down and whispered in her ear, "The only pain I feel is the pain of not being inside you right at this moment."

Her face blushed as she pushed me gently away.

We got inside, and Mr. Mitchel sat down at the table in the kitchen as Whitley got out three glasses. I took out the sweet tea from the fridge and poured us each a glass. As I sat down, I gestured for him to start talking.

"Well, Mr. Morris, I'm afraid I'm here on some rather disheartening business. My law firm, um…we represent your father."

My heart dropped to my stomach, and Whitley reached for my hand.

"What has he done? Has he gotten into some kind of trouble?" I asked, trying to force the lump down my throat.

Mr. Mitchel looked away and then back at me as he shook his head. "Mr. Morris, your father passed away a few weeks ago. He'd left specific instructions for all of this information to be hand-delivered to you in person, here in Texas. I'm so very sorry to be the one to break this news to you. I understand that you and your father had a strained relationship."

I let out a gruff laugh. "Yeah, you could say that. He left my brother and me to fend for ourselves as teenagers with no parents and a huge ranch to take care of."

"Well, your father left everything to you with the exception of a small part of his estate to his granddaughter, Kate. He also—"

"Wait—he knew about Kate?" I asked as I took a quick peek over toward Whitley.

"Um, yes. He also knew about Miss Reynolds, and he asked for a handwritten letter to be personally delivered to her also. So, with you being here, it has helped me out, Miss Reynolds."

Whitley tried to give him a smile, but I saw her hands were shaking.

She looked over at me and asked, "How did he know?"

I shrugged my shoulders. "How did my father know about Whitley? I mean, I guess I could understand maybe someone telling him about Kate. But Whitley?"

Mr. Mitchel took a deep breath and slowly let it out. "Mr. Morris, your father was in constant contact with your foreman—a, um…Mr. Mitch Black. Mr. Morris would call him a few times a year to see how things were going on the ranch."

All the air in my lungs felt like it had been sucked out. I sat back in my chair and shook my head. "That motherfucker was in contact with my father and never once told me about it?"

"Well, I'm not sure what their relationship was or why Mr. Black didn't share this information with you, but yes, he had been in contact with your father over the last several years."

Why in the hell would Mitch keep this from me?

"So, what is my father's estate? I doubt he had any debt. He was always a fairly simple man," I said.

Mr. Mitchel let out a small laugh. "Mr. Morris, your father's estate is worth just over six million dollars. One million of that goes to Kate."

I dropped the glass of sweet tea that I was bringing up to my mouth as Whitley and I both said, "What?"

Whitley jumped up and started to clean up the spilled tea and broken glass. After she sat back down, I looked at Mr. Mitchel and shook my head.

"How? I mean, I knew my father was always well-off, but I just figured he made enough to do okay since he still sent the yearly taxes on the ranch even though he had signed it over to us long ago."

"Your father was a smart businessman. Most of his earnings were from stocks, investments, and racehorses. You're also now the owner of six racehorses. Two of which are highly talked about as Derby contenders for next year."

I sat up and just stared at him. "What are their names?"

Mr. Mitchel smiled. "Sunset Sky, Fast as a Bullet, Kate's Date, Lay it Low, Mike's Lucky Star, and Sweet Baby."

I felt tears building in my eyes. I'd heard of every single one of these horses, but I had never dreamed they were my father's. All were named after each of us. He must have used a different name as the owner.

"I can't believe it," I whispered.

Whitley took my hand in hers. "Layton? Are you okay?"

I shook my head. "He named them after us."

Whitley looked confused. "What do you mean?"

I looked down at her and smiled. "Sunset Sky was the name my mother wanted to call the ranch. When he saw a horse he thought was a winner, he'd say, 'That damn horse is fast as a bullet.' Kate's Date—well, that has to be for Kate. Lay It Low is what my father used to say when I got in trouble with my mother. He would tell me to lay it low until she cooled down."

Whitley smiled. "Mike's Lucky Star."

I smiled and nodded. "For Mike."

"What about Sweet Baby?" Mr. Mitchel asked.

I looked up at him and fought like hell to hold back the tears. "He called my mother Sweet Baby. I can see him now, walking up behind her as she cut up vegetables. He'd ask her, 'How was your day, sweet baby?' I can actually hear him saying it to her."

My heart was breaking all over again.

Why did he leave us? Dad…why did you leave us?

Mr. Mitchel stood and opened his briefcase. He pulled out a folder and three envelopes. One had my name on it, one was for Whitley, and one was for Kate.

"Mr. Morris, you'll want your lawyers to take a look at all of this. Your father was a major stockholder in an investment firm. All of that will be transferred to you. I'm guessing they will probably request for you to attend the next stockholder's meeting."

I rolled my eyes as Whitley let out a small laugh.

Motherfucker, not another investment firm. Why the fuck did my brother and father get involved with these companies?

"Where's the firm located?"

"New York City."

I saw Whitley suck in a breath of air. I was pretty damn sure we were praying to God it wasn't Roger's dad's company.

"Miller and Pike Investments," Mr. Mitchel said.

Whitley and I both let out the breath we had been holding. I glanced over to her, and she gave me a small smile.

"Do you have any other questions for me, Mr. Morris, before I head back to Chicago?"

I snapped my head over toward him. "Chicago?"

"Yes. That's where your father was living when he passed away."

"I see. Um…may I ask how he died?"

"Oh, yes, I'm so sorry. I don't normally take care of estates like this. Please forgive me. Your father had lung cancer. He battled it for a few years, but…" Mr. Mitchel looked down and away.

"Thank you so much for making the trip out here. Let me walk you out," I said. I leaned down and kissed Whitley on top of the head.

As I walked Mr. Mitchel out to his rental car and said good-bye, I noticed Mitch driving by, heading to the barn.

"Layton, don't go talk to him right now. You're upset, and now is not the time to do this." Whitley placed her hand on my arm.

Fuck! This was supposed to be the best day of my life, and it's turning out to be one of the worst.

"Will you go for a ride with me?" I smiled down at my beautiful girl.

She gave me that smile of hers that I loved so much as she winked and said, "I'd love to go for a ride with you."

➤➤➤➤➤➤➤➤➤➤➤➤➤➤❭❬❬❬❬❬❬❬❬❬❬❬❬❬❬❬◆

Whitley had been talking nonstop since we got into the truck. I knew she was trying to keep my mind off of just finding out that my father had

passed away—and the fact that he'd left me with five million dollars, six racehorses, and God knows what else was in all that paperwork.

And in the letter.

I wasn't sure I would ever read that letter.

As we got closer to the area I had set up earlier, my heart started pounding. I pulled up and parked. I looked over at Whitley and smiled. "You ready?"

"Ah…I guess so. Ready for what though?" she asked with a laugh.

"I have a surprise for you, baby." I jumped out of the truck as easily as I could. I was still in a lot of pain, but I was trying like hell to hide it from Whitley.

I walked over and opened her door. She jumped out of the truck and looked around.

As we started walking toward where I had everything set up, she grabbed my arm.

"Layton, are we going to the old house?"

I smiled as I pulled her closer to me and crushed my lips to hers. When I pulled back, she still had her eyes closed.

"I miss being with you, Layton. I miss feeling you inside me." She opened her eyes and smiled.

I grabbed her hand, and we made our way down the path that had been worn by the workers.

"Have you been coming here, Layton? I don't remember such a worn path."

As we came around the bend, Whitley dropped my hand and stopped as she let out a gasp. "Oh my God, where's the house?"

I stared straight ahead and smiled. "I had it torn down. It was time for me to leave the past in the past. All that house did was remind me of a time in my life when I was angry and hurt. I've moved on, thanks to you. I've forgiven my father, and I'm ready to start a whole new life."

I turned to see Whitley crying as she looked up at me.

"Layton…" was all she said.

I smiled as I leaned down and gently rubbed my nose against hers. "I want to show you something else."

She smiled as she took my hand, and we moved closer to where the house that my father had built for my mother once stood—the same house that had held too many memories of my mother for him to be able to stay with us, the house that had caused him so much pain he had to run and never look back.

As we got closer, the gazebo came into sight. The spot my father and mother had picked to build their house on was probably one of the best views on the whole ranch. It looked out over the hill country and just about

had a three-hundred-and-sixty-degree view. I had the gazebo built to face the west and east.

"Oh, Layton, it's absolutely stunning. I've never seen such an amazing gazebo."

I had overheard Whitley and Courtney talking about a book where the characters got married in a white gazebo overlooking the west. They got married right before sunset, and Whitley had mentioned how romantic it was.

I smiled at the gazebo I had built. It was a classic octagonal gazebo made from cedar.

"Good Lord, that thing is huge. Oh my, Layton! The flowers…they're all my favorite flowers. The roses…they smell heavenly."

I smiled as I looked at all the landscaping that had just been finished yesterday. Whitley turned and looked at me as we walked up toward the gazebo.

As she moved up the steps, she threw her hands up to her mouth. Both sides of the gazebo had seating areas. The front and back were open to the east and the west, and we could see perfectly out west.

"I had them clear out a few trees, so you can see the sunset even more now."

I had placed a blanket, a basket, and a cooler right in the middle of the gazebo. I had packed wine, fruit, and cheese.

"Layton, when did you do all of this?" Whitley asked as she looked back at me.

"This morning. Do you know how hard it was to pack up that basket? I practically killed myself, trying to pack it and put it into the truck before you got out of the shower."

Whitley laughed as she shook her head. She sat down and moved her hand along the blanket. "This blanket looks so old. Where in the world did you get it?"

I walked up and slowly sat down on the blanket.

"Are you hurting, babe?" she asked as she reached over for my hand.

Even though I was, I smiled. "Nah, I'm all right. Just still moving a bit slow is all."

She raised her eyebrow at me, like she knew I was lying.

"This was my grandmother's blanket. It's a very special blanket that my mother used to wrap Mike and me up in as we watched movies with her and my father on the sofa. She always used it when we went on picnics, which was all the time. She loved picnics." I smiled, thinking about how many times I'd watched her take the blanket out and lay it on the ground for all of us to sit on.

Whitley's face lit up, and she grinned bigger. "I wish I could have met her."

I put my hand on her cheek and moved my thumb up and down on her soft skin. "So do I, baby. So do I."

I cleared my throat and tried to stop the shaking in my hands. "Anyway, when my grandfather asked my grandmother to marry him, it was on this very blanket. My father took my mother on a picnic, and he also used this blanket when he asked her to marry him. It was on this ranch…in about this very same spot. That was why they built the house where they did." I looked out west and smiled. "I can almost understand why my father left. He loved my mother so much, and I can't imagine the pain he felt when she'd left him."

Whitley's eyes filled with tears. "Oh my God, that is the most romantic thing I've ever heard."

I reached into my pocket and pulled out the blue velvet box. Whitley started shaking her head as tears fell from her eyes.

"Whitley, you changed my whole life that day I saw you on the side of the road. You helped me put the past where it needed to be, and you showed me how to push my fears to the side, so I could learn to love again. I was so broken, but your love healed me and made me a better man. I don't want to live a single minute without you. When you're not with me, I ache to feel your touch and hear your sweet voice whisper in my ear how much you love me. I want to go to sleep every night and wake up every morning to you telling me you love me. I promise to always love you and take care of you. Forever. You are and will always be my forever. My everything."

I opened up the box, and Whitley let out a gasp as she started crying harder.

She barely whispered, "The ring," as she looked into my eyes.

"Whitley, would you do me the honor of becoming Mrs. Layton Morris?"

She started nodding. "Yes! Yes, a million times over!"

I took her hand and slipped the ring onto her finger as I silently thanked God that those were happy tears she was crying.

"Will you dance with me, baby?" I got up and reached for her hand.

She stood and tried to wipe away the steady stream of tears.

I walked over and opened up my laptop sitting on the seat. As I started up my laptop, I looked back at her.

"This song says everything that's in my heart."

I hit play, and "Changed by You" by Between the Trees started playing.

Whitley walked over and slammed herself into my body as she repeated over and over again, "I love you, Layton. I love you so much!"

As we danced to the song, I had an overwhelming feeling that we weren't alone. I looked up and saw light beams coming through the trees,

shining directly onto the blanket. I smiled, knowing that Mike and my parents were with me, with us. They would always be with Whit and me.

As the song finished, Whitley pulled back and looked into my eyes. I reached down and wiped away the wetness on her face.

"I've never in my life been so happy as I am in this very moment, Layton. I…I…" She closed her eyes and then opened them again. "I never thought I deserved this kind of love."

"Whitley—"

She held her finger up to my lips. "I never thought I deserved this kind of love because the love that I thought I knew…it wasn't love at all. You've taught me what love is, Layton—true, honest-to-God love. I'll love you forever."

I reached down and captured her lips with mine. I wanted nothing more than to pick her up and make love to her against this gazebo.

"God…I want to make love to you so damn bad, baby."

She smiled as she looked down toward the blanket and then back up at me. "As romantic as that would be, you would be in so much pain," she said with a giggle. "Let's go home, and I'm sure we can come up with another plan."

I looked down at the basket. "What about the wine? And the cheese?"

She threw her head back and laughed. "Did you bring a flashlight 'cause the sun is going to set soon?"

I just looked at her. "Really, Whit? You don't know me at all." I walked over and opened up the basket. I took out two flashlights, and then I sat down and motioned for her to sit in front of me.

She sat down, and I handed her the wine bottle and glasses. She poured us each a glass. After she handed me a glass, she gently laid back against me. I fed her a grape every now and then as we sat and talked while the sun slowly began setting.

"Layton, this is beautiful. Can I ask you something?"

"You can ask me anything, baby."

She turned her head and looked up at me. "Can we get married here?"

I smiled and nodded. "I was hoping that's what you would want."

"How did you know?" She pushed herself forward and turned around to look at me.

I smiled as I looked back out toward the sunset. "You and Courtney were talking about a book one day. You mentioned a gazebo and how the characters got married while looking out toward the sunset. In that moment, I knew that I was going to ask you to marry me in the exact spot where we would get married. This spot might have once held anger and hurt, but it started off with the love of my parents and their dreams of raising a family here." I smiled. "Now, it's our dream."

She smiled as a tear slowly moved down her cheek. "Is this where you were going to bring me on my birthday?"

I nodded. "Yes, but the gazebo wasn't here yet. I had made plans for it to be built, and it was going to be a Christmas present to you. Things changed, and I thought it would be better to ask you to marry me in the gazebo."

She shook her head and gave me a drop-me-to-my-knees smile. "Okay, next question."

"Go for it."

"The ring. Layton, how did you know about this ring? Did Anna tell you?"

I threw my head back and laughed. "I was there."

She looked at me with a confused expression on her face. "What? You were where?"

"The day you came into the jewelry store to get the picture of us put into Kate's locket, I saw you walking up when I was looking at rings. I hid behind the counter. I was there the whole time."

Her face dropped as she looked down at the ring. "You were there?"

"Yep. It was fate that you walked in when I was there. It was perfect really. You picked out your own ring and didn't even know it."

She threw herself into me, causing me to let out a curse.

"Shit! I'm so sorry, baby," she said as her eyes caught mine.

The look she was giving me started making my dick jump.

"Layton. Will you please take me home now?"

I jumped up and grabbed her hand. I started to make my way down the steps of the gazebo.

"Wait! Layton, what about all of this stuff? You can't leave it out here. The animals will get it."

I stopped and let out a sigh. I turned back, grabbed the grapes and cheese, and tossed it all back into the basket. I dumped out the wine as Whitley let out a gasp.

"That was perfectly good wine," she said.

I just looked at her. "There is no way in hell I'm letting an open bottle of red wine go anywhere near the inside of my truck. No fucking way."

She rolled her eyes as she bent down and grabbed the blanket, and she began to fold it up. We both turned to leave, and then we stopped dead in our tracks.

"Oh, wow!" Whitley said as we just stared at the beautiful red sky. "Oh yeah, totally getting married at sunset."

I smiled as I took her hand and led the way back to my truck. I didn't care how bad it hurt. I was making love to my fiancée tonight.

It's time to cowboy up for the sake of love.

TWENTY-EIGHT
-»»»»»»»»»»»«««««««««««-
Whitley

I sat on the back porch of Mr. and Mrs. Pierceson's house, watching the sunrise. I couldn't believe today was finally here.

My wedding day.

So much had happened in the last six months. Roger had gone to trial and had been found guilty of attempted aggravated assault and aggravated assault with a deadly weapon for shooting Layton.

Layton had settled everything with his father's estate. He had taken part of the money his father had left him, and he'd set up a college fund at Texas A&M. He'd also made a very large donation to the National Coalition Against Domestic Violence. Kate and Jen would never have to worry about anything with the way Layton had invested Kate's money. I would never forget the look on Jen's face when Layton had told her she'd never have to worry about Kate's future.

I glanced over to my left when I saw something moving out of the corner of my eye. Courtney came running up.

Jesus, what time did she get up to go for a run?

I thought back to the night before last when Court had been drunk and talked a little too much to Stacey and me. Stacey was our best friend from high school. She had flown in for the wedding a few days ago, and she had gone out with all of us. It was a good thing Anna had already left and gone home with Jen. Courtney had confessed to still being in love with Reed. My heart broke for her, and I had tried to talk to her a number of times yesterday about it. She'd said she was in love with Mitch, but Layton and I had both agreed that we thought Court loved Mitch, but she wasn't in love with Mitch.

Anna had been really pushing Reed to move in together, but he'd kept putting her off. Layton had said that at his bachelor party, Reed had gotten drunk, and Layton had to keep him away from Mitch because Reed had wanted to tell Mitch he had stolen the woman he loved.

Court and Reed needed to be locked up in a room for a few days to work their shit out.

Courtney came jogging up the steps with a damn smile on her face. She had on a light strapped to her damn head. I couldn't help but laugh at her when she stopped in front of me.

"What the hell, Court? Jogging at five a.m. Aren't you afraid of running up on some animal or something?" I shook my head.

"Ah hell, don't start with me. I already ran into Reed this morning."

I snapped my head up at her. "What? Where?"

She sat down in the chair and laughed. "Well, you'll never believe this, but he was out running on the road, and we ran right up on each other. He scared the piss out of me. I saw his light, but at first, I thought it was a car with only one headlight."

My mouth dropped open, and I just stared at her. "You're kidding me, right?"

She looked at me like I was the one who was crazy. "No, I really did run into him. He stood there for five minutes and lectured me. He said I had no business being out so early and in the dark even though it was the country. Then, I had to hear about how I should be wearing some sort of reflectors—because you know how much traffic comes down that road." She rolled her eyes. "We're out in the middle of Bumfuck, Egypt, for Christ's sake."

I let out a giggle. "I think it's kind of cute. He's worried about you, Court. You know, Courtney, we really should talk about the other night."

"Ugh, my God, Whit. Will you please just drop it? I was drunk and wasn't thinking clearly."

I let out a sigh and turned back to the sky getting lighter by the second. *Stubborn girl.*

"You know Reed loves you."

From the corner of my eye, I saw her head snap over and look at me. *Oh God. I'm so going to hell for this.*

"Did he tell you that?"

I slowly turned and looked at her. "Do you really want to know? I mean, you say you're in love with Mitch and all, so what should it matter how Reed feels?"

"Damn it, Whitley! Did he tell you that? Did he tell you he's in love with me?"

I let a small smile play across my face.

"Whitley, please just—"

Just then, the back door opened, and Anna came walking out. *Fuck me.*

"Hey, girls. What are you both doing up so early? Whitley, you should be getting your beauty sleep."

I tried smiling up at Anna, but over the last six months, I had really grown to dislike her—a lot. She was always trying to keep Reed and

Courtney apart. I didn't trust her, and I knew she was pushing Reed into moving faster than he was ready to.

"I wanted to watch the sunrise on my wedding day. Courtney here was out freaking jogging."

Anna glanced over toward Courtney, who was looking out at the sunrise. I knew she was pissed that Anna had interrupted our conversation, especially since I was just about to tell her that Reed had told Layton he still loved her.

"What were y'all talking about? The wedding?"

I just looked at her.

Rude-ass bitch.

I just smiled and nodded.

She smiled back and then let out a giggle. "Oh my God, I have to tell someone before I burst!"

I looked over and saw Courtney roll her eyes. I let out a small laugh as I watched Anna jump around like an idiot.

"Well…what is it?" I asked.

"Reed asked me to move in with him, and I'm pretty sure he's going to pop the big question soon!"

I sat up and both Courtney and I said, "What?" at the same time.

"He asked you to move in with him, Anna? Are you sure?"

Anna's smile faded as she gave me a dirty look. "Of course, I'm sure, Whitley. I don't think I would misread something like that."

She looked over at Courtney, and the smile that spread across her face told me she was only saying this because she must have overheard us talking just now.

She's totally lying.

Courtney got up and excused herself. "I need to go take a shower and start getting things ready. Duty calls for the maid of honor and all. I'll talk to you later, Whit."

Shit! Shit! Shit!

There was no way Courtney and I were going to have a chance to talk alone again. I looked back up at Anna, who was smiling as she watched Courtney walk back into the house.

"It was so nice of Mimi and Frank to let us all stay here. When are we going back to Layton's house?"

Anna wasn't even in my wedding party, so I had no idea why she'd stayed with us last night.

"I'm not sure." I got up and turned to walk inside.

"Whitley, are you okay? You seem…upset," she said with a fake-ass smile.

"Do you believe in Karma, Anna?" I asked.

She just stared at me as the smile disappeared from her face.

"He loves her, and you and I both know it. If they're meant to be together, there is nothing you can do. No amount of lying on your part is going to keep them away from that love. You and I both know that Reed did not ask you to move in nor did he ask you to marry him. I hope to God Karma comes back and bites you in the ass."

I turned and walked away from her. I had a wedding in a few hours, and the last thing I needed was this bitch's drama, but I made a mental note to let Reed know about Anna's little bit of *good news* that she'd shared with us.

➤➤➤➤➤➤➤➤➤➤❌◀◀◀◀◀◀◀◀◀◀◀➤

"Holy hell, Whitley. Girl, can you plan a wedding or what?" Courtney said as we walked around the reception area.

Two large white tents were set up in the backyard of Layton's house. I walked along the tables to make sure everything was just as I wanted. Each round table had a silver satin tablecloth on it with a centerpiece of white roses and silver candles. Every few feet, there were silver candlestick holders holding small bouquets of white roses and carnations.

They look perfect.

The plastic plates were all clear with a silver beaded accent around the rim. The fake silverware looked so real. If I hadn't known better, I would have thought it was all real and not plastic. I smiled as I looked up and saw all the clear bulbs hanging down from the top of the tent.

The food table was reclaimed wood doors being held up by old wine barrels. Huge glass vases with greenery were on each one.

It's perfect—beyond what I pictured it would look like.

I smiled as I looked around. "Once all these candles get lit, the light will reflect off of the clear bulbs and light it up even more in here." I glanced over toward the dance floor.

Between the two tents was a large dance floor. Small round tables were set up all around outside the tents and were also draped in the same silver satin cloth. Each one held a small votive candle placed in a small mason jar. Some of the trees had white and silver chandeliers hanging down from them. I couldn't wait to see what they looked like when all the lights hit them.

I walked up to the cake table. The cakes had already been delivered, but they were in the house. Layton had picked out a Texas A&M cake, of course. The bride's cake was a four-tier cake that a sweet girl in Llano had made. She was trying to start her business, and our wedding was her first wedding. The bottom tier was square followed by a round tier, then another square tier, and a round tier to finish it off. Layton and I had decided to go

with a silver letter M for the top of the cake. The small silver accents on the cake added just the right amount of elegance, but it wasn't over the top.

"How did the gazebo look, Whitley?" Jen asked as she walked up to me.

Jen had been helping me with my event-planning business since Courtney had been swamped with books to edit. I loved working with Jen, and I was shocked at how much we both envisioned the same thing.

I smiled as I winked at her. "It was perfect. I loved the silver carpet, and the candles lined up along each row of chairs were genius. Thank you for using LEDs. The last thing I want is for someone to knock a candle over!"

Jen smiled at me and nodded. "I'll have them lit ahead of time, so as the sun starts to set, they will light the area."

"I can't believe this is really happening!" I said as I looked at Courtney.

"Well, believe it, baby girl. I just happened to see your very nervous husband-to-be earlier, looking out the back window at you walking around out here," Courtney said with a laugh.

I spun around and searched every window.

"I already called Reed's cell phone and told him to stop fucking up his best-man duties by letting Layton get a peek of you."

I looked back at Courtney and laughed.

"Okay, Whitley, you need to go in and get ready," Jen said as she looked at her watch.

My heart started pounding as I made my way back to the house. Layton was upstairs in Mike's room with Reed, Mitch, Kevin, and a few other friends.

As I walked through the kitchen, Kevin came running down. He opened up the freezer and grabbed ice. He took one look at me and smiled. My hair was already pulled up and curled to tame my natural curls.

"Holy shit, Whitley. You look beautiful." He looked me up and down.

I looked at what I was wearing—sweatpants from Victoria's Secret and one of Layton's A&M shirts.

"Do I even want to know why you're getting ice?" I raised my eyebrow.

"Hmm...probably not. But I promise, there's not a lot of blood."

My heart dropped.

"What in the fuck are y'all doing up there?" Courtney asked as she started to follow Kevin upstairs.

She looked over her shoulder and smiled. "Honey, go in the bedroom. I'll be right there. Don't worry! It's all going to be okay. Go on."

I stood there with my mouth hanging open as I watched Kevin running up the stairs two at a time with Courtney following him.

"I'm going to kill him if he hurt himself," I said as Jen took me by the arm and led me to the master bedroom.

I heard a loud thump, and I just closed my eyes for a quick second and kept on walking.

Yep…his ass is grass if he hurts himself on our wedding day.

TWENTY-NINE

LAYTON

Kevin came bursting into the bedroom, and I let out a moan when I saw Courtney following behind him.

Shit!

She took one look around and slowly moved her hand up to her mouth.

"What. In. The. Fuck? What were y'all doing?" She looked around the room, and when her eyes caught sight of Reed, she let out a small gasp and went running over to him.

"Son of a bitch, Reed, hold up your head, so the blood doesn't get on the tux," Richard said as he tried to stop Reed's nose from bleeding.

"Oh my God, Reed!" Courtney pushed Richard out of the way. "What happened? Oh God…did you break your nose? Oh my God, you poor thing!"

Reed looked over at me.

"No, his nose isn't broken," I said in a pissed-off voice.

Courtney spun around and looked at me. "Layton! Why would you punch him? My God, it's your wedding day. What's gotten into you?"

"Um, Court, he didn't punch me," Reed said.

"Well, who in the hell did?" Courtney turned back to Reed.

"I did," Mitch said from across the room.

He was sitting in a chair with Scott, one of our friends from high school, still holding him down.

"What?" Courtney yelled. "My God, why would you hit him? And are you okay, baby?" She walked over to Mitch and looked at Scott. "Why are you holding him down, Scott? What's going on?"

Mitch stood and pushed Scott away. "Why don't you ask Reed? I'm sorry I punched you in the eye, Layton. I'm so tired of this fucking shit."

I gave him a weak smile as I watched him turn and walk away. Kevin had already given me the ice to put over my eye.

Whitley is going to kill me if I have a black eye in our wedding pictures.

Courtney stood there, stunned. She slowly turned and looked between Reed and me. "Is someone going to tell me what in the hell happened in here?"

"I think it's stopped bleeding, Reed," Richard said.

"Layton? Reed?" Courtney put her hands on her hips.

I glanced over toward Reed. "There was a disagreement of sorts. Reed and Mitch got pissed at each other, and Mitch started punching Reed. I jumped in to break it up, and Mitch accidently hit me."

Courtney's mouth dropped. "What were you fighting over?"

"Nothing. It was stupid, and it was my fault. I'll apologize to Mitch before the wedding," Reed said.

I quickly turned my head to look at Reed.

Why in the hell is he lying?

Courtney started shaking her head. "Are you ever going to grow the fuck up, Reed? *Oh my God.* If Layton gets a black eye, do you know how upset Whitley is going to be? It's his wedding day, Reed!"

"I know, Courtney. I know." Reed let out a long sigh.

"See…this is exactly why…" Courtney stopped talking.

Reed snapped his head up and looked at her. "This is exactly why…what?" he asked.

Courtney was staring at Reed. She walked up to him and looked at his nose. She went into the bathroom and came out with a wet washcloth.

"You have some, um…some dried blood still on your nose. You should probably go say sorry to Mitch. I have to go help Whit get ready."

They stood there for a good minute, just staring at each other.

For Christ's sake, why can't they just both admit that they love each other?

Mitch walked back into the room and cleared his throat. "Reed, I'm sorry. I didn't mean to provoke you and start this whole mess. Layton, I'll understand if you don't want me in the wedding."

Courtney looked around at each of us, confused as hell, before turning back to look at Reed.

Reed glanced at Courtney before he stood. "Don't worry about it. I better go check on things."

He started to walk away when Courtney grabbed his arm. "Wait, Reed, why did you say it was your fault…"

"It doesn't matter, Courtney. You better go help, Whit. It's getting close now." He moved past Courtney and walked around Mitch as he headed out of the bedroom and down the stairs.

Courtney looked at me and then slowly started walking out. She stopped in front of Mitch and asked, "Are you hurt anywhere?"

He shook his head, and she nodded before heading back down to Whitley.

Mitch turned to leave, and everyone else followed out of the room. I was alone now—sitting here on my wedding day, holding a fucking piece of ice up to my eye.

I swear if I get a black eye, I'm firing Mitch.

We'd already had it out the day after I asked Whitley to marry me. I'd confronted him about keeping in contact with my father. Things hadn't been the same between us since then. I really hated to lose him as a friend and as the foreman to the ranch because he really knew his shit, but it looked more and more like that might happen.

Kevin walked back into the room and smiled. "Dude, I saw Whitley."

I smiled at just the mention of her name. "Yeah? How did she look? I mean, I couldn't really tell, but it looks like her hair is all the way up with some curls hanging down."

Kevin laughed as he walked up and hit me on the back. "She looked beautiful. You're just gonna have to be patient."

I tried to smile, but all I wanted to do was hit someone. I was so frustrated. "Fuck! How much longer?"

Kevin looked at his watch. "Forty minutes. You'll have to head downstairs soon and make your way to the gazebo. You have to get there before Whit."

I nodded and picked up my mother's small cross necklace and put it into my pocket. She had given it to me when she was in the hospital. She'd told me that when I got married, I had to put it into my pocket, so she could be with me the whole time. I turned and picked up Mike's dog tags and put them into my other pocket.

"Let's go do this." I smiled and followed Kevin out and down the stairs.

The thought of Whitley getting ready in our bedroom was driving me insane. I just wanted to see her. I just wanted to talk to her for one quick second.

"Hold on." I walked up to the master bedroom door.

"Stop! Layton, you can't go in there," Kevin called out.

"I'm not. I just want to hear her voice." I knocked on the door. "Whit? It's me."

Courtney barely opened the door. "Layton! What are you doing?"

"I just want to hear her voice, that's all."

She rolled her eyes at me. "Gah! Fine. Hold on. Step back a bit, you overly romantic ass."

Courtney shut the door, and I heard her talking. The door slowly opened, and I smiled when I smelled Whit's familiar perfume—Coco Chanel.

"Hey, baby. I heard you and the boys had a little bit too much fun earlier," Whitley said.

I let out a small laugh. "Yeah." I reached my hand around the door. The moment she took my hand in hers, I felt my stomach drop.

God, I love this girl more than life itself.

"Whitley?"

"Yes, Layton?"

"I love you so damn much. I just want to hold you in my arms and never let go."

I felt her squeeze my hand.

"I swear to God, Layton…if she cries and messes up her makeup before she even gets down the aisle, you will have a black eye for sure!" Courtney called from inside the room.

"I love you, too, Layton, more than anything. I can't wait to see you."

I let out a laugh. "What are you wearing under your dress?"

She giggled. "Let's just say, you won't be disappointed."

Oh God. I want her. I need her.

"Let's just skip all this and leave for the honeymoon now."

"Okay, that's enough. You have to get ready, Whitley. And all this lovey-dovey shit is making me sick." Courtney pulled our hands apart. "You'll see her in a few minutes."

I took a step back as I watched the door close. I leaned up against the door and rested my forehead on it. "I love you," I whispered.

Reed slapped my back and pulled me away from the door. "Dude, let's go. We need to get down there."

I smiled as I looked at my best friend. I wanted him to be as happy as I was, and it sure as hell wasn't with Anna. Reed had just told me a few hours ago that Anna wouldn't stop bugging him about moving in with her. He was tempted to do it just to shut her up. Then, he'd talked to Whitley, and I'd never seen him so pissed in my life. When I'd tried to talk to him about it, we had kept getting interrupted.

As we made our way outside, I glanced over toward the master bedroom windows. In less than thirty minutes, I was going to be married to the girl of my dreams.

She is going to be mine forever.

THIRTY

Whitley

I stood in front of my wedding dress, just staring at it. My heart had been racing ever since Layton's little visit a few minutes ago.

"Okay. Hair, check! Makeup, check, check! Sexy-ass lingerie, check, check, check! The last thing is the wedding dress, my dear," Courtney said as she walked up next to me.

I looked around at Courtney, Stacey, and Jen. They were all dressed in silver column strapless knee-length dresses. There was just enough of a ruffle on them to make them look elegant, but they were super comfortable. The way the dress fit Courtney and her hourglass figure was sure to drive both Mitch and Reed crazy.

I turned back and watched as my mother walked up to me and smiled. "Can I help you put it on?"

I smiled and nodded.

I had flown back up to New York to go dress shopping with my mother. I closed my eyes and thought about the moment we found this dress.

New York

Four Months Earlier

When my mother held up the Sophia Tolli dress, I scrunched up my nose.

"Mom, the top is silver. I know I said white and silver, but I didn't mean my dress."

"Just try it on for me. Please. Humor your mother."

I put it on, and when I turned around and looked in the mirror, I instantly started crying. It was beautiful. The Paris satin and Italian silk were a perfect combination. The sweetheart neckline highlighted the stunning silver bodice, and the crystal and pearl brooches were stunning and added just the right touch. They would shimmer beautifully in all of the

candlelight. The draped Paris satin skirt had side pick-ups. The chapel-length train was breathtaking and would look perfect pinned up. I turned and looked at the detachable back silver bodice. It looked so old-fashioned.

It was so me that it was unreal. I glanced over toward my mother, who was crying.

I wiped my tears away and nodded. "Oh, Mom…" I began sobbing again. "It's breathtaking. Do you think Layton will like it?" I turned back and looked at myself in the mirror.

She let out a laugh and walked up to me. She put her chin on my shoulder. "You look like a princess. I just can't believe it."

"I know, Mom. It's the most beautiful dress ever."

My mother shook her head. "No, that's not it." The tears rolled down her face. "I can't wait to tell everyone I picked it out, and you loved it! Score one for mom."

My mouth dropped open, and I just looked at her in the mirror. We both busted out laughing, and then I told the saleslady I would take the dress.

➤➤➤➤➤➤➤➤➤➤➤❋◀◀◀◀◀◀◀◀◀◀◀◀◀

"Where are you, Whitley?" my mother asked as she held my dress up in front of me.

I smiled. "Thinking about the day we found this dress."

My mother raised her eyebrows and chuckled. "Come on, honey, we're running out of time."

By the time everyone got done fussing over my hair and makeup after the dress was on, I was ready to push all of them away from me.

"It's fine! Let's just go." I slipped on my Louboutin shoes.

I turned and looked at myself in the mirror one last time. I was wearing my grandmother's pin in my hair, my something old and borrowed. I had on diamond drop earrings that were a gift from my parents, and a simple silver diamond bracelet that Layton had given to me after the rehearsal dinner last night.

My mother tucked a blue hankie inside my corset and smiled. "Your father loved finding this little surprise," she said as she winked.

I felt my face blush as I quickly looked away.

I couldn't wait for Layton to see the lingerie I had on under the dress. Courtney had given it to me at the bridal shower, and I'd actually blushed when I opened it up in front of everyone. The fact that the lace was see-through was going to drive Layton mad.

I took one last deep breath and turned toward everyone. I smiled. "Let's do this shit!"

-》》》》》》》》》》》《《《《《《《《《《《《-

As we pulled up, my heart started pounding. Layton and Reed had gotten everything ready during the last few weeks. They had made the road smooth, so everyone could drive up to the wedding site in their cars. After the concrete had been poured last week, the path to the gazebo had been built. It was lined with LED candles and looked beautiful.

My mother and Court helped me out of the car and carried the train of my dress over to the walkway. I laughed at how wide Layton had made the sidewalk. He'd kept saying he didn't want my dress to drag on the ground.

"I still can't get over how big this sidewalk is. They sure as shit do everything big in Texas," Courtney said.

My mother and Jen both laughed.

"You said a bad word, Miss Courtney," Kate said as she looked at Courtney and shook her head.

"Oops, sorry, Katie Mac."

Courtney had gotten into the habit of calling Kate that ever since she had watched her one night when Kate had insisted she was allergic to mac and cheese and could only eat chocolate ice cream.

As the music began playing, I felt like I was going to throw up.

I frantically looked at my mother. "Mom."

She reached over and gave me a kiss on the cheek. She moved her mouth close to my ear. "Baby girl, you look breathtaking. Layton is going to shit his pants when he sees you," she whispered so that Kate couldn't hear her.

I let out a laugh and instantly felt calmer. My mother handed me my bouquet of white roses and smiled as she turned and made her way down the sidewalk.

My father walked up to me and smiled. "Whitley," he barely said. "My God…you are the most stunning creature I've ever seen. That bastard better know how lucky he is."

I smiled as my father held out his arm. I took it and turned to where the love of my life was waiting. I watched as Kate took off down the sidewalk, skipping and dropping white and red rose petals along the way. Jen went next, trying to quietly tell Kate to slow down.

Oh my God. I'm getting married. I think I'm going to puke.

My father placed his hand on top of mine. "Breathe, Whit. Just take deep breaths."

Courtney was up last, and she started to walk, but then she stopped and turned to look at me. "I love you, Whitley. Layton is one lucky son of a bitch."

"That's what I said!" my father said with a laugh.

When Courtney went up and over the hill, they changed the music to the wedding march.

I looked at my father. "Dad...I can't move."

"Do you love him, Whitley?"

I closed my eyes and pictured Layton's face with his beautiful blue eyes and smile that melted my heart every time. I could hear him whispering in my ear how much he loved me as we made love. I snapped my eyes open and looked at my father.

"More than anything. I love him so much, Daddy. It scares me."

"Then, are you ready to marry him?"

I smiled and nodded. I started down the path that would lead me to Layton. As we turned the corner, I saw all of the chairs filled with people.

Oh shit. Who in the hell are all of these people? I don't remember inviting all of them.

I started to slow down.

My father whispered, "Whit, look at him. Look at Layton."

I snapped my eyes up, and immediately, I was looking at Layton. I sucked in a breath of air. "Oh...God..." I whispered.

He had the biggest smile on his face. He looked so handsome, and I instantly felt that familiar ping between my legs. He was dressed in a black tux with a silver vest and light silver–blue tie.

As we drew closer, I felt my stomach twisting and turning. Layton walked up, and my father leaned over and whispered something in his ear. Layton pulled back and just stared at my father in horror as everyone started laughing. I turned and tilted my head as my father kissed me on the cheek.

"Take care of my little girl. She's my whole world," my father said.

"She's my whole world, too, sir." Layton looked into my eyes.

As soon as his hands touched mine, I was suddenly calm.

We turned and walked up to the preacher.

Layton just stared at me. "My God, you're the most stunning, breathtakingly beautiful thing I've ever laid eyes on."

I was just about to say something when Kate piped up and said, "Thank you, Uncle Layton!"

We all looked down toward Kate and laughed.

Layton squatted down and used his finger to call Kate over to him. "I was talking to Whit, baby girl, but you...my goodness. You look like a princess. You take my breath away, too."

Kate wrapped her arms around Layton's neck as I fought to hold back tears from watching the display. As Layton stood, I was hit with the notion that I wanted to have a baby. I wanted to start a family right away. Layton turned back toward the preacher.

I held up my hand. "Um, Layton…can I ask you something?" I whispered.

Layton looked between the preacher and me. "Uh, of course, sweetheart."

I leaned in and whispered in his ear, "I want to have a baby—right away."

He stepped back and looked at me as a smile spread across his face. He pulled me to him and kissed me with so much passion that I wanted to let out a moan.

"Um…we haven't gotten to that part yet, y'all," Reed said as he tapped us both on the shoulders.

Layton smiled against my lips. "I love you so damn much, Whitley."

"I love you, too, so very much."

THIRTY-ONE
LAYTON

I sat and watched Whitley making her way around to everyone, thanking them for coming. Her smile would always be my undoing. I was still flying high from her telling me she wanted to start trying for a baby right away.

Reed walked up and slapped me on the back as he sat down. "How's it feel?"

"Amazing, like I'm flying high, and I don't want to ever come down."

Reed smiled. "What did Whitley's dad say to you?"

I shook my head and laughed. "He told me his best friend was part of the mafia in New York, and all it took was one phone call, so I'd better never hurt his baby girl."

Reed threw his head back and laughed his ass off. "And Whit? What did she say to you?"

I looked at Reed and smiled. "She wants to try for a baby right away."

Reed reached his hand out for mine. "That's awesome, dude. I'm so happy for both of you." He took a sip of Shiner Bock.

I watched him as he looked out toward the dance floor. Christina Aguilera's "Candyman" was playing, and Courtney was dancing with Kate all over the dance floor.

"She looks stunning in that dress." I looked at Court and then back at Reed.

"Yeah, she does. Too bad that fucker boyfriend of hers is ignoring her while he's over there talking to Karen Rhodes. Who talks to his ex-fiancée at a wedding where his current girlfriend is the maid of honor?" Reed asked.

I took a sip of beer and nodded. I'd already noticed how Mitch had been talking to Karen practically the whole night.

Courtney was now standing alone in the middle of the dance floor as Brad Paisley's "I Can't Change the World" began playing. Reed jumped up and made his way over toward her. She had started walking off the dance floor when he reached for her arm.

I sat there and watched the two of them dancing. I glanced over toward Mitch. He was so caught up in his conversation that he hadn't even noticed them dancing.

Whitley walked up and grabbed my beer as she sat down. "Wow. This is exhausting." Then, she noticed Reed and Courtney dancing. She sat up and dropped her mouth open. "Oh. My. God. They're dancing together. Where's Mitch?"

I gestured toward him and Karen.

Whitley turned, looked at them, and then back at me. "Who is she? He's been ignoring Court and talking to her almost all night."

"Old fiancée."

"Prick." Whitley turned back toward Reed and Courtney.

I noticed when Courtney quickly wiped a tear away.

I shook my head as Whitley took my hand in hers.

"What happened today?" she asked.

I glanced over at her and tilted my head. "What do you mean?"

She smiled and shook her head. "Don't think I didn't notice the black eye that someone had tried to cover up with makeup."

I laughed as I took my beer back from her. I took a deep breath and slowly let it out. "Mitch started egging Reed on for some reason. Started saying all this shit about Courtney. Reed asked him to stop, and Mitch wouldn't. I have no idea what's gotten into Mitch lately. But Reed got pissed and pushed Mitch. He told him to stop talking. The next thing I knew, Mitch was on top of Reed, punching him. I jumped up and tried to pull Mitch off of him, and he punched me by mistake."

"What? Holy shit, Layton! Are you okay?" She put her hand on the side of my face.

I guided her hand up to my lips and kissed it. "Yeah, baby, I'm fine, but Reed's nose wouldn't stop bleeding for the longest time. I was sure it was broken."

"What was Mitch saying that pissed Reed off?"

"He just kept talking to Kevin about how good Courtney was in bed. Mitch has never talked about anyone like that. He was clearly trying to get Reed worked up, almost like he wanted Reed to go after him. Then, he mentioned something about being sick of this shit. I'm assuming he meant Court and Reed."

Whitley sat back in the chair. "Huh, how weird. Courtney mentioned that Mitch has been working really late a lot and going into town all the time. She said she feels like they're drifting apart."

I didn't want to say anything to Whitley until I had proof, but I was pretty sure Mitch was cheating on Courtney. Richard had mentioned how he'd thought he saw Mitch coming out of Karen's house one night, but he wasn't one hundred percent sure it had been Mitch.

I'll kill that fucker if I find out he's cheating on Courtney.

The DJ got on the speaker and announced it was time for the bride's and groom's songs. Whitley and I had decided we would each pick a song. We had drawn straws to see whose would get played first. I'd won.

As we walked out to the dance floor, I glanced over toward her father, who smiled at me.

Huh, that's a change, considering he has been giving me the evil eye all night.

We stopped in the middle of the floor, and I used my finger to pull Whitley's chin up. I looked into her beautiful green eyes.

"I love you so much, baby. I feel like this song was written just for you. If I could write you a song, this would be it."

As Keith Urban's "All For You" began playing, I pulled her against my body.

The words began, and she grabbed my shirt as she buried her head into my chest. I could feel her sobbing, so I held her closer to me. As she looked up into my eyes, my heart slammed into my chest, and I felt tears building.

"Please don't cry."

She smiled. "They're happy tears. I've never been so happy in my life, Layton. Thank you."

We danced in silence as I held her close to me.

The song ended, and the DJ announced that we had decided to do things differently with the last song being mine to Whitley, and now, it was time for her song to me.

"My turn," she said with a wink. "Without your love, Layton, I don't know how I could live. You're not only the love of my life, but you're also my best friend."

Tim McGraw's "My Best Friend" began playing as I looked into her eyes. This time, it was her turn to reach up and wipe away my tears.

"God, I love you so much. I just can't even begin to tell you how much I love you." I leaned down and gently kissed her lips.

She pulled back slightly and smiled. "How about if you show me later?"

I laughed as I pulled her closer to me.

➤➤➤➤➤➤➤➤➤➤➤➤❳❲❰❰❰❰❰❰❰❰❰❰❰❰❰➤

As the night wore on, I was getting more and more pissed at Mitch. He'd only danced with Courtney once. The rest of the time she'd been dancing with Kate.

My heart was breaking, and I was just about to make my way over to talk to him. He was talking and laughing with Richard. Whitley stepped in front of me with that drop-me-to-my-knees smile of hers.

"You ready to leave?" She wiggled her eyebrows up and down.

All thoughts of Mitch quickly disappeared. "Fuck yeah, I am!" I said with a smile and a wink.

We had already done all the traditional stuff, like throwing the bouquet and garter belt. Now, it was time to leave.

We made our way to my truck, getting pelted with birdseed while bubbles surrounded us along the way, as everyone cheered us on. I was so glad Whitley hadn't changed out of her wedding dress. I wanted to slowly peel it off of her. It was so damn beautiful that I almost wanted to make love to her while she was wearing it.

As we made our way down the driveway, she turned and looked at me. "I don't think I can wait until Austin."

I looked at her, stunned. "What? What do you want me to do, Whit? Pull over on the side of the road? It's only an hour and a half to the hotel, baby."

She leaned back in her seat and let out a sigh. "I need you, Layton. God, I just need to feel you. I've wanted to just sneak away all night. I can't take it any longer. Do you know how hot you look in that tux?"

I felt my dick getting harder, and I tried to adjust myself. I glanced over and looked at her.

"Can't we just go back to the house?"

"What? No! Oh my God, Whitley. Your parents are there. Do you want your dad to kill me?"

"Layton, we're married. I'm pretty sure my father and mother know what we're going to be doing tonight."

I shook my head.

No. Not a chance in hell. I value my life way too much.

⤙⋗⋗⋗⋗⋗⋗⋗⋗⋗⋗⋗⋗⋖⋖⋖⋖⋖⋖⋖⋖⋖⋖⋖⋖⤚

As I drove, I noticed Whitley trying to stay awake. Before I knew it, my princess was out cold and snoring away. I pulled up to the W Hotel in Austin and smiled. I was finally going to bury myself deep inside her after wanting her all day.

Our flight wouldn't be leaving until two the next afternoon. We were going to Europe for three weeks for our honeymoon because Whitley couldn't make up her mind on where she wanted to go, so I told her we were going to see it all. I'd never seen her so excited.

I'd asked Reed to stay at the ranch and take care of things while we were gone, knowing Whitley had made arrangements for Courtney to stay at the house also to watch the dogs. I smiled, thinking about the two of them living together under the same roof for three weeks.

As I pulled up to the valet parking, I jumped out and ran around to get my sleeping beauty out of the car. She snuggled her face into my neck as I carried her through the lobby. I was completely intoxicated by her smell.

"I fell asleep," she mumbled.

I let out a small laugh as I kissed her on the top of her head.

She looked up at me. "I feel like Cinderella." She scrunched up her nose and smiled that sweet smile of hers.

"You're more beautiful than Cinderella." I walked up to the reception desk.

I slowly slid her down, and she smoothed out her wedding dress.

"Oh my! Your wedding dress is stunning!" the girl behind the counter said.

Whitley tried to wake herself up, and she smiled. "Thank you so much. I feel like a princess in it!"

"Well, you certainly look like one," the girl said.

After we checked in, we made our way over to the bar to grab a quick drink. Before we knew it, other people had bought us rounds, and we had four drinks sitting in front of us. Whitley finished her first drink and looked at me with passion-filled eyes. I jumped up and thanked everyone for the drinks and tipped the bartender. I took her by the hand and led the way to the elevator.

By the time we made it to our room, I was hurting from how hard my dick was.

I will never get tired of being with Whitley. Every time with her feels like our first time.

I opened the door, picked her up, and carried her into the room. I started to kiss her as I brought her over to the bed. She ran her fingers through my hair as she let out a soft, small moan.

"Shit, Whitley, I want you so much." I set her down.

She slowly turned around and looked over her shoulder. I reached my shaking hands up to her corset and started to untie it. She reached up and held her dress to keep it from falling down.

As she turned around, she looked up at me, biting on her lower lip.

Motherfucker. I want to be inside her more than I ever have.

She smiled as she let the dress fall and pool at her feet. I sucked in a breath of air as I took in what she still had on. She was wearing a white lace bustier with silver accents on it, and it was practically see-through. Her breasts were pushed up and looked amazing. My eyes traveled down to the garters holding on to her stockings. Her white matching thong also had silver accents on it. I was pretty sure my mouth was hanging open as I looked her body up and down. I was feeling greedy to be inside her.

I reached out my hand, and she placed her hand in mine. I stepped backward and helped her out from the dress. I walked her away from the

dress and turned her some. I walked over, picked up her wedding dress, and brought it to the sofa where I gently laid the dress across it.

As I turned back to look at her, I almost fell to my knees. The sight of her standing there—dressed in a bustier, thigh stockings, and high-heel shoes—was almost too much for me to take in.

I've never seen her look so beautiful.

I was completely breathless. I couldn't pull my eyes away from her. I couldn't even move. I stood there and watched as she slowly moved her finger up her stomach to between her breasts and then up to her mouth where she gently bit down on her finger.

"Mother of God."

She let out a giggle as she slowly kicked off her shoes. She moved her hands down and unclipped her stockings. She lifted her leg up and set it on the coffee table where she slowly rolled her stocking down and tossed it to the side. Then, she repeated the motion with her other leg.

My heart was beating so fast and hard. If she were to touch me with her hand, I would come on the spot.

She walked over and said, "There is a surprise in there." She peeked down between her breasts.

I smiled as I reached in and pulled out a blue hankie. I snapped my eyes down to hers as she giggled.

"My something blue."

She turned her back toward me. "Will you take the bustier off, please?"

Jesus, I thought my hands had been shaking from taking off her wedding dress. I couldn't even grab the buttons on the bustier to undo them.

After I finally unbuttoned the bustier, she turned around and took a few steps back until she hit the end of the bed. She was still holding the bustier up. She smiled as she took it in her hand and set it to the side of the bed. The only thing she had on was her panties.

"What do you want me to do, Layton?"

I couldn't stop looking at her hourglass body. She was absolutely fucking perfect.

"Um…"

She smiled and sat down on the bed. She slowly lay back and began moving up the bed until her head was on the pillow.

I quickly started taking off my clothes. I'd never removed a tux so fucking fast in my life. I deserved some kind of reward for fastest undressed groom. I walked up to her and stood next to the bed as I watched her look my body up and down while she licked her lips, and her eyes filled with passion. The way we were taking each other in was like we were seeing each for the first time.

"Layton, I've never wanted you as badly as I do right now. I can't take it any longer."

I swallowed hard. "Touch yourself, baby."

Her mouth dropped slightly open as she took her hand and slowly put it in her panties. She used her other hand and began playing with her nipple.

Oh my God...I'm not going to last thirty seconds.

She started moaning as she moved her hand faster. "Oh God...Layton."

I moved onto the bed and took her hand out of her panties as I began to pull them off. As she lifted her hips, I couldn't take it any longer. I buried my face in between her legs, and she started to call out my name as she ran her hands through my hair. The more she called out in pleasure, the harder my dick got until I couldn't take it any longer. I made my way up her body and slowly pushed myself into her.

"Jesus, you're so warm and wet, Whitley."

"Yes. Oh God...Layton, it feels so good. Kiss me, Layton. Please kiss me."

"Whitley, I just—"

She shook her head. "I don't care right now. Please just kiss me!"

I slammed my lips to hers, and our tongues began moving frantically with each other.

"Oh, you feel so good. I'm...oh God...I'm going to come, Layton," Whitley whispered against my neck as she grabbed on to my arms.

I began moving faster and harder until I couldn't hold off any longer. I moved my lips down her neck and up to ear as I started to come. "I'm coming...baby. I love you so much, Whitley."

Whitley moved her head and looked into my eyes as she smiled that beautiful smile of hers. I held my body up by my elbows as we both tried to catch our breaths.

"Layton, that felt so incredible. I've wanted you all day. I could hardly stand being near you because I wanted you inside me so much."

I pushed her hair back and smiled. "It's just the beginning. I kind of wanted our first time as husband and wife to last just a little bit longer though," I said with a wink as she smiled bigger. "We have a lot of baby-making practice to do over the next three weeks."

She nodded and giggled. "I guess it's a good thing I didn't pack my birth control pills."

I sat up and looked at her. "Didn't you pack before the wedding?"

She nodded and looked at me with so much love in her eyes. "I was going to ask you before we left. If you had said no, I would have just grabbed them before we left, but...I was kind of hoping..."

I reached my hand around her neck and pulled her in for a kiss. "I love you, Mrs. Morris."

She grinned. "Say that again."

"I. Love. You. Mrs. Morris." I kissed her in between each word.

She lay back down as I kept repeating the words and kissing her all over her body.

"I don't think I want to leave. I want to stay in this hotel for the next three weeks," she said.

I laughed as I got up. I walked over and grabbed the champagne that they had stocked in our room and poured us each a glass.

"Then, how could I make love to you under Italy's stars? Or on a secluded beach in France?"

She wiggled her eyebrows up and down. "Well, with those kinds of promises, how can I refuse? Until tomorrow, I want to be with you as much as possible. With my parents being at the house for almost a week and no sex with you, I thought I was going to die."

I looked down at my dick and back up to her. "Looks like he's up for the challenge." I set my glass down and made my way over to my wife.

"Layton," she whispered, "make love to me."

I gently entered her body as she grabbed on to my ass and began moving along with me. The sounds she was making only made me want to go slower to make this last longer.

"Whitley, I love you."

"I love you, Layton. I love you so much."

As we slowly and sweetly made love again, I couldn't help but think of us possibly making a baby during our honeymoon. I was overcome with love and happiness as Whitley softly called out my name while I poured myself into her body.

While I held Whitley in my arms, I couldn't help but think of Reed and Courtney. I only wished they would both open their eyes and see that the two of them were meant to be together. They could be sharing the same love and passion as Whitley and I did.

I rolled over and pulled her body up against mine. "I'll love you forever, Whitley, and I can't wait to see your belly grow with our child."

"I'll love you forever, too, Layton. I can't wait either. I want that more than anything." She smiled as she gently kissed me.

➤➤➤➤➤➤➤➤➤➤➤❮❮❮❮❮❮❮❮❮❮❮❮

I wasn't sure how long I lay there, watching her sleep. No longer did I feel lost and alone. I didn't feel angry or hurt. I was no longer broken. I had been healed by the love of this girl in my arms.

As I started to drift off to sleep, I dreamed of Whitley walking toward me, holding our child in her arms. I tried so hard to see if it was a boy or

girl, but something caught my eye. I looked beyond Whitley and saw Mike and my parents walking behind her.

As they all drew closer to me, Mike smiled.

Well done, my brother. Well done.

EPILOGUE

It wasn't lost on me how Mitch had been talking to Karen during almost the whole reception. When I'd questioned him about why he was paying more attention to his ex-fiancée than me, he had gotten angry and said they were old friends just catching up. I wasn't even sure why she was at the wedding. I didn't remember seeing her name on the guest list.

I'd felt Reed's eyes on me all night, and every time I looked at him, a shiver had run up and down my body. Walking down the aisle, I couldn't help but look at him. The look in his eyes when he saw me had caused my whole body to start trembling. I closed my eyes and thought about the dance we'd shared.

Did I make a mistake by choosing Mitch over Reed? I love Mitch, but I don't love him like I love Reed. If I were honest with myself, I'd say I love Mitch, but I'm not in love with him like I am with Reed.

But Reed will just end up hurting me.

I was beginning to think that Whitley had been right. I was looking for that fairy-tale love I'd read about in all my books. I truly believed Mitch was going to make my dreams come true. The first time we'd made love, he had even told me, *I'm going to make it my life's mission to bring all your dreams to life.*

I closed my eyes and tried to remember that night. Reed's smile kept invading my thoughts. I opened my eyes and shook my head.

Stop this, Courtney! Stop this now.

I looked around to see how many people were still here. Almost everyone had already left, including Mitch. He'd said he had a headache, and when I'd begged him to stay with me, he'd said there was no way he could sleep with me in one of Layton's beds or even in Layton's house. I had rolled my eyes and told him he was being ridiculous, but he'd said he was heading home and would be getting up early to take care of some cows he thought would be calving soon. He'd told me he wouldn't be by the house until around noon. I'd also noticed that things had not been the same between him and Layton at all.

I let out a deep breath as I watched Anna arguing with Reed. All they ever did was fight. Reed glanced over my way, and I quickly turned away.

I walked up to Stacey, who was sitting down on top of one of the tables. She was half-drunk out of her mind.

I bumped my shoulder against hers. "Hey, you doing okay?"

She nodded. "Do you know how close I came to going home with Richard? God, I just want to be fucked by a Texas cowboy. That pretty much makes me a slut, doesn't it?"

I threw my head back and laughed. "Richard? I thought you had your eye on Kevin."

"Oh, I did until I saw him sucking face with some girl on the dance floor. I think I'm really drunk and ready to go to sleep."

I helped her off the table. "Do you need help, sweetie, making it up to your room?"

She shook her head and started off toward the house. I watched her stumble around until Whitley's dad took her by the arm and helped her into the house. Stacey, Jen, Kate, and Whitley's parents were all staying at the house tonight, and then Stacey and Whit's parents were heading home tomorrow.

When Layton had told me to take the master bedroom, I didn't argue. They were going to be gone for three weeks, and they had asked me to house-sit and watch the dogs.

I heard shouting and turned to see what was going on.

Anna pushed Reed. She started shouting, "I gave you all these months for nothing! I hate you, Reed Moore. Don't. Ever. Call. Me. Again."

As she turned and started walking off, she made her way over toward me with nothing but pure hate on her face.

Ah hell. This isn't going to be good.

She walked up to me and stopped as she looked me up and down. "I can't believe this."

I just stared at her. "Is everything okay, Anna?" I asked.

She threw her head back and laughed. "No, Courtney, everything is not okay. I hope you're happy now." She shook her head. "What a waste." She turned and walked away.

I glanced back over to where Reed had been standing, but he was gone. For one brief second, my heart dropped. I wanted so badly to talk to him to find out what had just happened between him and Anna.

Once everyone was gone, I slowly started making my way into the house.

Everything can be cleaned up later because I certainly don't have the energy to do another thing.

I walked into the master bedroom and saw my notification light blinking on my phone. I picked up my phone to see I had a voice mail from Mitch. I was guessing it was probably him telling me he had made it home okay.

Ugh, I need out of this dress like right now.

I peeled off the dress and stood there, looking at myself in the mirror. I was wearing a white bustier that really pushed my breasts up and had made the dress look even better. I smiled at how I looked, but then I frowned.

Too bad Mitch isn't here to appreciate it. I bet Reed would have.

I slipped off my shoes and made my way back over to my phone. I opened it up and hit play to start the voice mail. I was just about to sit down and take off my stockings when I heard Mitch talking.

"Karen, she's not going to be coming here tonight. She is staying at Layton and Whitley's house, baby. We have all night and all morning. I told her I had things to do in the morning. Besides, that fucker Reed has been pining after her all night. Let him go take care of her tonight since they both want each other so much. She's done nothing but want him from the beginning. Baby, it's just us now. She was just a rebound fuck."

I threw my hands up to mouth as I sat down on the bed and heard Karen moaning.

Oh God. No. He was supposed to love me forever. He promised to make all my dreams come true. He was different...he was...safe.

The message kept playing, and I foolishly kept listening until I heard her calling out Mitch's name. I reached over and stopped it.

I feel sick.

Just then, the door to the bedroom started opening. I jumped up, and Reed came walking in. He stopped dead in his tracks when he saw me. His eyes traveled up and down my body before he looked into my eyes.

"Holy shit, Court. I didn't know you were staying in this room!"

I couldn't say a word. I couldn't even move. All I wanted to do was run into his arms while I begged him for his forgiveness. I needed to ask him to just hold me and make the pain and hurt go away.

"I just came in to grab some of Layton's sweatpants for in the morning when I go for a..." He stopped talking.

He must have just noticed I'd been crying. As he walked toward me, I began backing up until I hit the wall.

"Courtney, what's wrong?"

I shook my head. "Nothing."

He walked up to me and lifted my chin and looked into my eyes. "You've been crying. Baby, tell me what's wrong."

Oh God.

The sound of him calling me baby about had me drop to my knees.

How stupid am I.

Here, I had pushed the only man I ever truly loved away because I thought he was going to hurt me. And the man I thought would make all my dreams come true had totally destroyed my whole world tonight.

"What happened before the wedding?" I asked.

"What? What do you mean?"

I put my hand on his chest to keep him from coming any closer to me. If he stood any closer, I was afraid I'd walk right into his arms.

"When I went upstairs and saw you. Why did Mitch hit you?"

Reed took a step back. "It doesn't matter, Court. It's over and done with."

"It matters to me. Please don't lie to me. Please not tonight, Reed. I *need* the truth."

He shook his head and turned away before looking back into my eyes. "Mitch started talking all this shit about you to Kevin. I'd never heard him talk about you at all, let alone the shit he was saying. He was only doing it to rile me up. I really tried to just ignore him since it was Layton's wedding day, but Mitch had already been drinking. Then, he said…he said—"

"He said, what?"

"He said you were the best fuck he's ever had, and he looked right into my eyes as he said it. I lost it, Courtney. I'm so sorry. I went up, pushed him, and told him to shut the fuck up. That was when he jumped on me and started punching the shit out of me. Layton jumped in and tried to pull Mitch off of me, and Mitch hit Layton. He says it was a mistake, but I'm pretty damn sure it was done on purpose. Things haven't been the same between them since Layton found out Mitch had been in contact with Layton's dad all those years."

I stood there, stunned. Everything was slowly starting to make sense.

Was Mitch trying to get Reed to tell me what he'd said? Was he hoping I'd leave him, so he could be with Karen?

I looked back at Reed. His green eyes caught mine, and they were filled with so much hurt that it actually made my heart ache. Then, it hit me.

Why did Reed get so upset? I need to hear it from him, not Whitley or Layton.

"Why would he want to rile you up? And how did he know talking about me would upset you, Reed?"

He stood there, staring at me. A part of me wanted him to touch me so badly. His eyes traveled up and down my body, and I instantly felt the wetness between my legs.

I'm so confused. I'm so upset and so hurt about Mitch, but I want Reed so badly. But…I can't be hurt again. All men ever do is hurt me.

"You looked beautiful tonight, Courtney." Reed looked back into my eyes.

I felt my whole body shaking.

If I hadn't heard that message and Reed walked in, would I be standing here like this with him? Or would I have made him leave?

He took a step closer to me, and I sucked in a breath of air. I willed him to move closer, and when he did, I closed my eyes. I could feel the heat coming from his body.

When he started to talk again, I jumped and opened my eyes, startled by the gentleness in his voice.

"Do you really want to know why he was egging me on, Court?"

I slowly nodded and whispered, "Yes."

I could see my chest heaving up and down as he looked deeper into my eyes.

"Because he knows I love you and that I've loved you since the moment I first saw you."

I sucked in a breath of air as he leaned in closer and put his lips up to my neck.

I closed my eyes and whispered, "Yes,"

"As much as I want to make love to you right now...I'd never let you be unfaithful to Mitch. I love you too much, Courtney, to let you do something you'd ever regret. Besides, you made your choice long ago."

With that, he took a step back before turning and walking into Layton's closet. I stood there, leaning up against the wall. I could barely stand.

As he walked by, I tried to call out for him. I wanted to tell him what Mitch had done to me, how he had been the one who was unfaithful. I wanted to tell Reed I loved him, too, and how I'd made the biggest mistake of my life by being with Mitch.

But I couldn't move or talk.

As he slowly turned around and looked at me, I felt tears running down my face. He gave me a weak smile before walking out the door. After he quietly shut it behind him, I fell to the floor and began crying hysterically.

I just let the only man I ever truly loved walk out the door, and I didn't even tell him that I love him, too.

As I lay on the floor crying, I thought of all the dreams I'd had...

Forever gone.

Forever broken...again.

THE End

➤➤➤➤➤➤➤➤➤➤➤➤❯❮❮❮❮❮❮❮❮❮❮❮❮❮❮

But a true love story never truly ends...

LOOK FOR **REED** AND *Courtney's* STORY...

BROKEN
Dreams

SPRING 2014

If you or someone you know is a victim of abuse,

please contact the National Coalition Against Domestic Violence.

www.ncadv.org

1-800-799-SAFE (7233)

Thank You

I'm so blessed, blessed beyond words, and there is only one I can thank for that. So, I drop to my knees each day, and thank God for this amazing journey he allows me to travel each and every day.

Heather Davenport—You truly are a blessing in my life. Thank you SO much for all of your input and for always being honest with me when you read these little stories of mine. Thank you for everything you do for me with nothing expected in return. I hope you know how much I appreciate it all. I love ya, girl!

Gary Taylor—Thank you so much for being such an amazing friend. Thank you for being on the cover of this book for me. It means more to me than you will ever know. Hard to think it was all those months ago we talked about it and then to have Tiffany on the cover as well makes it all the more special. Thank you for going on that walk and finding the road. It's perfect. Love ya, cowboy!

Molly McAdams—Oh, Molly, how I adore you. I'm absolutely gutted when we can't meet for our weekly lunches. I think they keep me sane, and your smile brightens my whole week. You truly are a blessing in my life, and I love you, girl! I'm still slightly upset I missed the pancake release party for *Forgiving Lies*. I might or might not get over the devastation by the end of the year. #PeasAndCarrots

Jovana Shirley—Can't do all this without you! You're an amazing editor, and more importantly, an amazing friend. Thank you for all that you do for me. You are my rock star, and I hope you know that!

Kathy Bankard—Thank you for everything you do for me. I appreciate it more than you will ever know! Thank you for providing the quote used at the beginning of this book. My sweet quote fairy, you start my days off with a smile every time. Love ya, girl!

Gigi Aceves—LOL! What can I say? You make me laugh—all the damn time. Your videos bring me to tears, and I'll never be able to thank you for all that you do for me. I'm blessed to have you in my world! Love ya, girl!

The Most Wanted Girls—My admins: Maegan, Liz, Gigi, Pamela, Kathy, Kerri, Shelly, Angeline, Trish, Jennelyn, Carmen, Nina, Heather, and Amanda. Thank you girls for being the best admins and friends ever. I don't think I could do it without y'all. I wish I could hug each of you every day and tell you how much I love y'all.

To the rest of the Wanted girls—I SO wish I could name each of you, but a few of y'all are popping into my head: Jamie Bourgeois, Lori Perreira Peixoto, Carron Scott, Laura Hansen, Amanda Brown, Jennifer Aldridge, Maya Dujak, Kim Motzer Reisdorf, Amanda Thompson, Lisa Waugh, Angie Davis, Jacinta Brown, Nancy Minot, Alexandra Louk, Heather McNeal, Shelly Barton-Lazar. Oh man, I could go on and on. And y'all know I suck at names, so I'm pretty damn impressed I got the ones down that I did! THANK YOU! THANK YOU! THANK YOU! The fact that you spend so much of your time and energy to pimp out my books blows my mind. I'm in awe of each of y'all every day. I know for a fact that you do it for other authors as well, and I'm just in awe by your generous hearts. Thank you girls from the bottom of my heart!

Kristin Mayer—Thank you for my editing kit and for the magic of the eight ball! Love you, girl!

Liz Aguilar—My own personal bubble gum pimp and the lover of TTFN. Love you, Liz!

My Beta Readers: Jemma Scarry, JoJo Belle, and Heather Davenport—I love you, girls! Thank you for taking the time out of your lives to read my books.

To my readers/friends—None of this would be possible without y'all. Every day I wake up, I smile, knowing that at least a few of y'all are going to make my day with a note, a funny post, a comment to tell me that you recommended the book to someone, or just a simple, *Hey*. Thank you for

your support and for your love of these characters. They are so very dear to my heart, and it is a privilege that I'm able to share them with y'all. I hope you get lost in their world just as much as I do.

Darrin—I just don't even know what to say. You are my rock—my true love who has always been by my side since the very beginning. I love you so much, and I can't thank you enough for your support in all of this. Even when it takes me away from you so much, you still support it, and that makes me love you even more.

Now, on to bigger things—yes, yes, I know when you read the books that some things seem *very familiar*. Get over it, babe. I'm always going to use what you do and say and put them into my books. Think of it as memories forever frozen in time! Besides, you give me SO much material that I feel like it's my duty to share it with the world. I love you, and I'll love you forever, Darrin.

Lauren—You are growing up before my eyes. Please stop. It makes me so sad, and not to mention, it makes me feel old. You make me laugh, and sometimes you make me want to scream when you roll your eyes at me. I don't know where you got that from (rolling my eyes as I type that).

You are becoming such an amazing young woman, Lauren. Always stay true to yourself and know that there is nothing in this world you can't do if you want it bad enough. Believe in yourself and your dreams always. I love doo!

Mom—I miss you so much. I hope that I've made you proud of the person I strive to be each and every day. Love you, Mom.

SONG PLAYLIST
-»»»»»»»»»«‹‹‹‹‹‹‹‹‹‹‹‹-

"Army of Me" by Christina Aguilera—Whitley packs up her New York apartment and leaves.

"Undo It" by Carrie Underwood—Whitley and Courtney leave New York.

"Cold As Stone" by Lady Antebellum—Layton finds out Olivia is getting married.

"Simple Life" by Drake White—Layton drives Whitley home for the first time.

"Clarity" by Zedd—Layton and Whitley are driving in his truck.

"Something to Do with My Hands—Layton walks into Joe's bar.

"Dancin' Away with My Heart" by Lady Antebellum—Layton dances with Misty at Joe's bar.

"What About Love" by Austin Mahone—Layton and Misty dance while Whitley gets jealous.

"Right Round" by Flo Rida—Whitley dances with Richard as Layton gets jealous.

"Best of Me" by Christina Aguilera—Whitley tells Courtney she is afraid all men will be like Roger.

"Keep It to Yourself" by Kacey Musgraves—Layton reads the text messages from Olivia.

"Let There Be Cowgirls" by Chris Cagle—Whitley and Layton are horse racing.

"Whatever She's Got" by David Nail—Whitley and Layton dance at the hot dog stand.

"5-1-5-0" by Dierks Bentley—Whitley and Layton dance at the hot dog stand.

"Goodbye" By Kristinia DeBarge—Whitley dances with Richard when she is drunk.

"Whatever You Do, Don't" by Shania Twain—Whitley thinks about Layton at the coffee shop.

"Safe and Sound" by Taylor Swift—Layton tells Whitley about his past.

"I Don't Want This Night to End" by Luke Bryan—Layton and Whitley drive around the ranch in the rain.

"I Want Crazy" by Hunter Hayes—Layton and Whitley play in the rain and mud.

"New Favorite Memory" by Brad Paisley—Whitley and Layton make love for the first time.

"You Look Good in My Shirt" by Keith Urban—After Layton tells Olivia to leave, he turns to see Whitley standing in his T-shirt.

"Feelin' Love" by Paula Cole—Whitley touches herself after seeing Layton wearing flip-flops.

"Pontoon" by Little Big Town—Layton tells Reed they are going to have a pontoon party.

"Big Promises" by Keith Urban—Whitley and Layton dance at the pontoon party.

"Why Wait" by Rascal Flatts—Whitley and Layton dance at the pontoon party.

"Buttons" by Pussycat Dolls— Whitley and Layton dance provocatively at the pontoon party.

"Never Let Her Go" by Florida Georgia Line—Layton and Olivia dance at the pontoon party.

"Done" by The Band Perry—Whitley sees Layton dancing with Olivia.

"Brave" by Sara Bareilles—Whitley tells Layton about Roger abusing her.

"Honey Bee" By Blake Shelton—Layton tells Richard that Whitley is officially off the market.

"Circles" by Christina Aguilera—Courtney hears Reed talking about her and tells him to never talk to her again.

"I Hate Boys" by Christina Aguilera—Courtney is upset about Reed.

"Heart Attack" by Demi Lovato—Courtney talks to Whitley after Reed tells her that he only slept with Anna to forget Courtney.

"On My Way" by Boyce Avenue—Layton tries to get to Whitley when he finds out Roger is in town.

"Better Than I Used to Be" by Tim McGraw—Reed talks to Whitley in the hotel room. He tells her he loves Courtney, but he is not good enough for her.

"Changed By You" by Between The Trees—Layton asks Whitley to marry him.

"Waiting on a Woman" by Brad Paisley—Layton waits to get married.

"Candyman" by Christina Aguilera—Courtney and Kate dance at the wedding reception.

"I Can't Change the World" by Brad Paisley—Reed dances with Courtney at the wedding reception.

"All for You" by Keith Urban—Layton's wedding song to Whitley.

"My Best Friend" by Tim McGraw—Whitley's wedding song to Layton.

"Told You Sold" by Cassadee Pope—Courtney finds out Mitch has been cheating on her.

CPSIA information can be obtained at www.ICGtesting.com
Printed in the USA
LVOW01s1802080114

368612LV00018B/1171/P

Why Coconut Oil?

You've probably heard at least some of the excitement about the benefits of coconut oil, and hopefully the introduction confirmed some of that hype and introduced you to benefits you weren't already aware of. However, those of you who still aren't convinced might be wondering, "What makes coconut oil so special?"

That's an excellent question. The difference between coconut oil and the other "cures" on the market is that this one has a long-standing history. A quick search on the internet will provide all the evidence you need. You'll find works like this book, as well as testimonies by people who have used coconut oil and loved it. There are hundreds of stories and personal accounts of how coconut oil has improved the health of individuals just like you. This is a multi-purpose oil that can change your life in a few days – and *that,* my friend, is a completely hype-free statement.

What is It?

In technical terms, coconut oil is extracted from the *cocos nucifera,* or the coconut palm tree. Basically, the oil is taken from the meat, which is the solid part of a ripe coconut.

There are different types of coconut oil you should be familiar with. The knowledge will help you decide which type (or types) is best for you to use. In some cases, you may want to purchase more than one type for different purposes.

Refined Coconut Oil

Refined coconut oil has been processed. You may prefer refined coconut oil for cooking, as the flavor is more subtle and the oil can withstand higher cooking temperatures. Note that the refining process can involve the use of harsh chemicals, and frequently refined coconut oils are actually RBD oils – refined, bleached and deodorized. I definitely recommend grabbing unrefined coconut oil as well, to ingest raw. If you are planning on cooking and need an oil with a mild flavor and a high smoke point, refined coconut oil may

be a good option for you. Additionally, it is the most widely available coconut oil.

Some refining processes are better than others, so pay close attention to where you buy your refined coconut oil. Make sure you're not getting something that's been refined through a process you don't agree with. While chemically refined coconut oil is NOT what you want, there are healthier refined alternatives. Some coconut oil is refined using diatomaceous earth or steam. Read the label carefully before making a purchase.

Unrefined Coconut Oil

Unrefined coconut oil is as close to nature as it gets - short of cracking open your own coconuts. This is pressed raw coconut. Look for "virgin," "extra-virgin" or "unrefined" on the label.

Note that unrefined oils are sometimes strong and can overpower foods when you cook with them. I recommend taking unrefined oils in raw form, and saving the refined coconut oil for cooking.

I prefer to research the brand before I buy. This is to determine whether or not
I agree with their method of extracting coconut oil. The majority of unrefined coconut oil manufacturers avoid the use of chemicals, but there are exceptions.

How is it Extracted?

The extraction of coconut oil for consumption as a food product dates back to as early as 2000 BC in India. According to research conducted by Dr. K. T. Achaya, a world-renowned expert in food and nutrition history, records from the Harappan civilization mention the cultivation and extraction of coconut oil, but there is no description of the techniques used to extract the oil. By 1500 BC, a

giant mortar and pestle known as a ghani was in use.

Today there are two dominant extraction processes used in the manufacture of coconut oil. One is a dry method, which equates to the meat being scraped from the shell and then dried using kilns, an open flame, or even sunlight. This separates the oils from the fibrous mush, but can also introduce contaminants. The mushy substance is normally fed to animals that do not have sensitive stomachs, as it is susceptible to bacteria and disease.

The other process, called the wet version, involves many more steps and results in less coconut oil from the same number of coconuts. The meat of the coconut creates an emulsified product that is a combination of oil and water. The trick is separating the two. Currently, many variations of the wet method exist and may include a combination of extreme temperature changes, or even the use of shock waves. Wet method technology is not cost effective, and provides no advantages over the dry method, despite the percentage of product which can be lost due to the occasional contamination problem using the dry technique.

There are other methods of expressing coconut oil which are becoming more common. These include cold-pressing, centrifugation, and expeller-pressing. If you are looking for a strong coconut flavor, use the cold-pressed or expeller-pressed varieties. They are frequently exposed to higher temperatures, and thus have a nuttier flavor. For a milder flavor, use the centrifuged coconut oil (www.foodrenegade.com, 2011).

Why should you care how coconut oil is made? One method isn't necessarily better than the other, but knowing how the coconut oil on the shelf is processed will definitely explain the difference in price. Rest assured that the cost is well worth it. Understanding production

methods can also help you determine which brand you want to buy as some use chemicals and others do not. Some have an intense coconut flavor, while others are virtually tasteless. It's up to you to buy coconut oil according to your preference.

Centuries Old Benefits We're Rediscovering

The benefits and properties of coconut oil are not new discoveries. For centuries, coconuts and coconut oil have been the key source of fats for tropical and subtropical cultures. With more research being done, we've found that the benefits stretch far beyond the fats coconut oil provides. Eating coconut oil or using it as part of your grooming routine can help with things such as:

- ✓ Having soft, silky hair

- ✓ Getting rid of bad skin so that you have the smooth and even skin tone of your teens

- ✓ Reducing stress levels- This can help to make your busy, chaotic day go more smoothly.

- ✓ Creating cholesterol levels that are manageable.

- ✓ Improving your ability to lose weight.

- ✓ Having a better immune system to help you fight off all those colds your kids or coworkers show up with.

- ✓ Aiding your digestive process so that your body gets the proper nutrients and reduces bloating.

- ✓ Creating the right atmosphere for your body to speed up metabolism.

- ✓ Helping to relieve kidney problems.

- ✓ Preventing heart problems.

- ✓ Preventing diabetes, and relieving its symptoms if already present.

- ✓ Killing viruses, including AIDS, mononucleosis, herpes, and many others.

- ✓ Maintaining strong bones.

- ✓ Relieving digestive disorders, including Crohn's disease.

- ✓ Helping protect against cancer.

- ✓ Helping relieve symptoms associated with chronic fatigue.

- ✓ Killing bacteria.

- ✓ Killing and preventing yeast overgrowth.

- ✓ Killing parasites, such as tapeworms and lice.

✓ Providing protection against the sun.

Coconut oil also has numerous domestic applications. It can be used as a cleaning agent, to help care for your family pet, and even to make candles and deodorant!

What's Behind the Miracle?

We are all skeptical of purported 'miracle cures,' and with good reason. Once in a while, however, there are products that are worth investigating further. This report has made a lot of claims about the virtues of coconut oil. I bet you are wondering how coconut oil accomplishes everything I've said it can do. This section should help to clarify any questions you have.

There are numerous fatty acids in coconut oil. These acids act as cleansers. They are soothing to the body while fighting off bacteria and fungi. Coconut oil contains powerful amounts of medium chain triglycerides (MCTs), which are behind many of the health benefits. We'll cover what these MCTs mean for our health later on. Additionally, coconut oil is an antioxidant and is antimicrobial!

Lauric Acid

Lauric acid is a fatty acid found in coconut oil, and is the primary antiviral and antimicrobial agent found in human breast milk. While the mechanism is unclear, it is known that lauric acid can be converted by the body into something called monolaurin. Monolaurin helps the body to combat disease and illness by destroying the protective casing around viruses, fungi, and bacteria – leading to the death and destruction of these microorganisms. Recent changes to the human diet have largely eliminated lauric acid, as misunderstandings of the function of saturated fats led to diets devoid of healthy sources of medium-chain fatty acids. Coconut oil is comprised of roughly 50% lauric acid, from which an estimated 3% can be metabolized by the body directly into monolaurin. The remaining lauric acid, while a less potent antimicrobial agent than monolaurin, is still an effective germ killer, and coconut oil is one of the best natural sources for this vital fatty acid (Lieberman et al,

2006).

Medium-chain Fatty Acids

Unlike many other oils, such as vegetable oil and various seed oils, coconut oil is predominantly comprised of medium-chain fatty acids, also referred to as medium-chain triglycerides. These types of acids are easier for the body to digest, and are not likely to be stored as fat. Medium-chain triglycerides work very much like carbohydrates, but lack the glucose contained in them. By increasing the bioavailability of energy while reducing glucose, the body is able to function more efficiently – in turn encouraging weight loss and better overall health. Additionally, nearly all of the medium-chain fatty acids found in coconut oil contain antimicrobial properties which are still being investigated, but are known to be beneficial to human health. These healthy fatty acids include lauric acid, capric acid, caprylic acid and myristic acid (Lieberman et al 2006). Some individuals take supplements of the healthy fatty acids found in coconut oil, but this is often prohibitively expensive. Coconut oil is considered an excellent, cost-effective alternative to direct dietary supplementation with monolaurin and other healthy fatty acids. Additionally, coconut oil does not require chemical extraction processes, which may make it easier for the body to utilize.

Myths about Coconut Oil

There is plenty of good information available regarding the benefits of coconut oil, but much of it is eclipsed by rumors and false information. While you are able to identify which statements are downright untrue, some myths can be convincing. Getting the facts is vital to making your own choices about whether or not coconut oil is right for you. Ignoring the hype about what is hot and what is not is the best way to get the results you want from any product, especially coconut oil.

Saturated Fat

A common belief regarding coconut oil is that it can increase your risk of heart attack. This is based on the misconception that *all* cholesterol is bad cholesterol, and that *all* saturated fats are bad fats. In truth, your body requires a ratio of LDL and HDL cholesterol in order to function properly. There is also *no* proof that the saturated fats in coconut oil raise your bad cholesterol. Recent articles in the BBC and NY Times have discussed the positive benefits of including coconut oil in your diet. Saturated fats are not all alike, and the virtue of coconut oil lies in its composition – the medium-chain triglycerides we discussed earlier are exactly what makes coconut oil different from the majority of saturated fats. Coconut oil can actually increase the good cholesterol in your body while decreasing the bad cholesterol. The good cholesterol produced by your body with the help of coconut oil can clear arterial blockages, prevent the build-up of arterial plaque and work to protect the cardiovascular system.

Weight Gain

Another common myth states that the saturated fats in coconut oil cause weight gain, making it more likely that people who use it will become obese. This is the opposite of the truth. An experiment in the 1940s attempted to make cows fat by feeding them coconut oil. The result was the contrary to what researchers had intended – the cows were leaner, more active, and hungrier! The saturated fats - also known as medium chain fatty acids - that are contained in coconut oil help to increase the body's metabolism. This makes your thyroid function better and actually causes your body to use ingested food more efficiently (Peat, 2006). Coconut oil is occasionally used in weight loss plans for this reason. Regular use can dramatically increase your chances of weight loss success.

Effects on Diabetics

There are rumors that coconut oil is sweet to the taste and therefore must have a bad effect on the blood sugar levels of a diabetic. First of all, coconut oil is *not* overly sweet. Second, research on mice has shown that coconut oil can be effective in reversing Type 2 diabetes and protect against insulin resistance, a condition responsible for diabetes in many individuals (Medical News Today, 2009). Coconut oil actually stimulates the pancreas to promote greater insulin production. This means that when used regularly, coconut oil can actually reduce the onset of diabetes.

A Skin Irritant

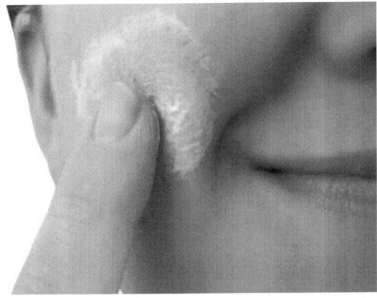

These days, it's all about looking great, and word is getting around that coconut oil will bother the skin. I can confidently refute that from personal experience.

The beauty industry has known about coconut oil for quite some time. The compound cocamide-DEA is frequently found in soaps, shampoos, and other beauty products. This compound, contrary to providing the positive benefits of coconut oil, is a suspected carcinogen and a frequent irritant for individuals with allergies. While derived from coconut oil, it is NOT coconut oil. Confusion over this has led to some of the bad press surrounding coconut oil itself. It is important to note that cocamide-DEA is a chemically derived, highly processed product that bears little resemblance to actual coconut oil. The dangerous part of this compound is not what is derived from coconut oil, but what is added to it. The diethanolamine compound (DEA) is the suspected cause of health problems associated with cocamide-DEA (David Suzuki Foundation, 2012).

The response of the cosmetic industry to the bad news about cocamide-DEA has been beneficial for coconut oil lovers. Many products now contain less processed forms of coconut oil. Additionally, the global economic crisis has spurred many women to creating their own beauty products at home. There are numerous blogs on the internet that provide recipes for homemade cosmetics, skin care products, and soaps. The ingredient of choice for these thrifty women: coconut oil!

Coconut oil can be a great soothing treatment for skin, especially if it is already irritated by sunburn, bug bites, or allergic reactions. In fact, coconut oil has antimicrobial components in it that can heal the skin if it is damaged. There are, however, some forms of coconut oil that are not refined and could contain dust or other irritants. Dermatologists and nutritionists recommend that a high quality refined coconut oil be used on the skin. Additionally, for topical treatments a coconut oil extracted using the wet method may be your best bet, as the risk of contamination with skin irritants is significantly lower.

Sticky and Not Absorbed by Skin

There is a widely held belief that coconut oil is thick and sticky, making it tough to absorb into the skin. Again, this is a myth. Coconut oil is a favorite for massage and tanning oils because of its easy absorption. Virgin coconut oils are of higher quality, but in general coconut oil is thin and smooth. Using the product on a daily basis can leave the skin feeling soft and silky - not oily and slick.

Oilsandplants.com, a website devoted to the use of natural cosmetics, provides a recipe for body butter which is 50% coconut

oil. Other sites devoted to homemade skin care products provide similar formulas, and many organic skin care companies sell coconut oil based cosmetics and creams. For example, Burt's Bees, a company known for its skin care products, sells many products made from coconut oil. Check for yourself – you'll be amazed at how many items in the skin care aisle are made from coconut oil. And just think, with raw coconut oil, you can save yourself money on skin care products by either applying coconut oil directly, or making coconut oil based lotions, creams and cosmetics at home!

Goes Bad Easily

The other day I met a woman who refused to spend money on "something that goes bad so quickly." This is a common misconception, but in reality, coconut oil has a longer lifespan than many other marketed oils. According to shelflifeadvice.com, olive oil's maximum shelf life is approximately 3 months. You can keep unrefined, purified coconut oil indefinitely. Even refined coconut oil lasts for 18 months without going rancid!

Terrible Taste

Everyone has different tastes, and you can't make someone like or dislike the taste of something. However, both Melissa Clark and Tara Parker-Pope of the NY Times have written articles attesting to coconut oil's delicious flavor. Parker-Pope went so far as to include several recipes for cooking with coconut oil in her piece (Clark, 2011; Parker-Pope, 2011). It can be used in the same way as other oils such as vegetable and olive oil, and really adds to the flavor of the food. Coconut oil has a higher smoke point than many cooking oils, as well – a fact which makes it a healthier cooking oil than most widely available oils. Personally, I also think it tastes and smells

good!

Why All the Bad Press?

With so many great benefits to coconut oil, it is hard to see where all the myths came from.

Much of the misinformation about coconut oil resulted outdated reports focused on saturated fats in general. The reports that actually discussed coconut oil dealt with hydrogenated coconut oil, a product which is high in unsaturated trans-isomer fats (trans fats), and can wipe out the positive fatty acids and antioxidants in the body. It is best to avoid hydrogenated oils — coconut or not! Those reports got one thing right – anything hydrogenated is detrimental to your health. When possible, use raw, virgin coconut oil. If you need to use refined oil, stay away from the hydrogenated forms.

Remember, you can always confirm what I'm telling you simply by trying it for yourself. Maybe take a few tablespoons a day, or rub a little onto your skin. That way, you'll be able to prove to yourself that coconut oil works and bust all these myths in just a few days. Have fun!

Good vs. "Bad" Fats

Deciding what you are supposed to add to your diet to improve your health is a difficult task – and all the advertising out there doesn't help a bit. Even advice from the healthcare community can be confusing; filled with information that is good today and bad tomorrow. How are you going to stay on track if the "experts" can't figure it out? A good example of this kind of scenario is the saturated fats argument.

For years the professionals have been saying that saturated fats are to be avoided, because they damage your health and can lead to things like heart disease. The fact is, not all saturated fats are the same, and not all should be shunned. This "one size fits all" kind of labeling can steer you away from substances that can actually help you.

Coconut oil has saturated fat in it. The interesting thing is that in

countries where coconut oil is a major part of the diet, heart disease is rare. Coconut oil is, as discussed earlier, different from the majority of saturated fats due to its medium-chain fatty acid content. Nutritionists are beginning to recognize the vital difference between coconut oil and other saturated fats. Many now recommend that their clients use coconut oil in place of the unsaturated oils that were once considered the healthiest options on the market. Those 'heart-healthy unsaturated fats' are now being blamed for increased levels of cancer and fat retention in the liver (Peat, 2006)! Given this evidence, it seems that saturated fat is not the enemy after all – at least, not when it's good fat. Some saturated fats should be avoided, particularly those that have been tampered with by manufacturers who add hydrogen atoms during the heating process. The purpose of hydrogenation is to make food last longer on the shelf, but I'd rather buy clean, healthy food that spoils faster than longer-lasting food that can give me a heart attack. Additionally, many saturated fats possess natural anti-oxidant qualities – meaning they don't necessarily need to be hydrogenated to have a long shelf life.

Coconut oil is one of the few oils that provide you with medium-chain fatty acids. These are more easily digested than long-chain fatty acids. They are broken down into free fatty acids, and are directed straight to the liver. Uniquely, medium-chain fatty acids are also absorbed directly into cell mitochondria, where they are used as energy — not stored as fats in the body like long-chain fatty acids. *Energy* is produced, *not* body fat. This is a very important distinction that is often overlooked. The fat contained in coconut oil also promotes better thyroid function, which provides you with a body that burns energy more efficiently. Remember the study done on the cows? Their more efficient bodies were responsible for their leaner, healthier physiques.

Low Fat – Good or Bad?

Many people are shocked to learn that those "low fat" foods on the shelf at the grocery store are better left untouched. They can actually cause more harm to your health than good! How is it that our beloved coconut oil is maligned by many while the praises of these low fat abominations are sung?

Dr, Mark Hyman, author of UltraMetabolism, states that:

"Dietary fat is not a major determinant of body fat. The Women's Health Initiative, which is the largest clinical trial of diet and body weight, found that 50,000 women on low-fat diets had no significant weight loss. Yet another study looked at people who followed four different diets for 12 months -- and found no dramatic differences between those who followed low-fat, low-carb and very low-carb diets (Hyman, 2010)."

Call me dramatic, but if you took the time to consider the circumstances I think you'd see why this is true. In some cases, people are overweight because they are partaking in a low-fat diet. Think about how your grandmother's generation used to eat - full fat everything. Yet, here we are, a fat society on low-fat diets.

If you're eating enough fat, you will feel full and satisfied. The opposite is true for those poor souls on low-fat diets – they never feel as if they've eaten a complete meal.

After a while, the idea of being stuck on a diet becomes a terrible thing. Dieters revert back to old habits, consuming foods that are unhealthy. This can lead to feeling guilty about not sticking to the low-fat foods. But sticking to that diet and never feeling full takes its

toll once more... and so the cycle continues.

If you are eating healthier, fattier foods like coconut oil consistently, you'll feel full longer. You'll tend to consume less in the long run. Your body also won't be fooled by those awful chemicals in the "fake" foods on the shelf.

Understanding the difference between good saturated fats and bad fats is an important step when choosing the right supplements to add to your diet. Foods that have been hydrogenated or tampered with to extend their lifespan will contain the fats that can cause problems for your body. The only benefit to those products is that they help extend the shelf life of the foods — avoid them!

Coconut oil is made up of medium-chain triglycerides. It, along with palm kernel oil, is your best bet for getting these medium-chain fatty acids. Individuals who consume this type of fat tend to have more energy, lower body fat, and a lower body weight. Coconut oil also contains fewer calories than other fats. You can easily digest the fat in coconut oil, making it a win-win all the way around.

Cooking with Coconut Oil

The fat contained in coconut oil can be used in baking, as well as in savory dishes. It tastes great and can be used as a substitute for vegetable or olive oil.

The majority of coconut oil consumers prefer to use refined coconut oil in their cooking, since it tends to taste less like coconut. I find that many raw virgin coconut oils do just fine, because they've not been exposed to a "cooking" heat.

General Health Benefits of Coconut Oil

Heart Health

Coconut oil can provide significant protection against heart disease.. You've probably heard that you should not eat saturated fats because they clog arteries. Actually, this is true of only some saturated fats. The fat in coconut oil can help clear arterial plaque and safeguard the heart. In part, this is true because it increases your body's metabolism, and the types of fat it contains are capable of directly entering cell mitochondria to be used as fuel. You can use coconut oil to prevent heart disease by adding it to your food, taking it orally by spoon every day or even taking it within a drink such as coconut water or coconut milk – while both coconut water and coconut milk provide health benefits, they are not the same. Coconut water is lower in fat and contains less sugar than coconut milk.

Weight Loss

Coconut oil affects the way your body uses and stores the foods that you take in, which can help with weight loss when used as part of a healthy diet and exercise regime. It can even boost your metabolism! This means your body can burn calories much faster than it did before. Using coconut oil regularly is a safe, reliable way to lose weight. It isn't going to make you lose beyond what you need. It will, however, bring your body up to speed and allow your thyroid to function properly. When you combine the use of coconut oil, a proper diet, and good exercise, you get a winning formula for weight loss and the ability to build a powerful body.

Healing Power

The healing power of coconut oil is unlike any other product on the market. The oil can be converted into monolaurin in the body, which is an anti-fungal, anti-viral, anti-bacterial component that increases the immune system and protects against potential illness and disease. It is also believed to have healing components that allow the body to recover much faster when used topically. Monolaurin is only found in one other natural source: breast milk. Lauric acid, the component which the body converts to monolaurin, is one of the most powerful ways that mother's milk protects breastfed infants.

Perhaps one of the most impressive values that coconut oil brings to the table is its ability to fight disease. The antimicrobial properties held in coconut oil can, according to numerous studies, help to fight many viruses and yeast overgrowths, such as influenza, candida and HIV (Lieberman et al, 2006).

Coconut oil is resistant to the formation of free-radicals and can improve the body's immune system. This makes it a valuable

resource which can be used to cure many conditions and protect the body against others. The oil is being studied by many scientists, nutritionists and doctors for its ability to:

- ✓ Destroy the viruses that are responsible for herpes, hepatitis C, AIDS, measles, influenza and SARS.
- ✓ Destroy the bacteria that are the main cause of infections of the throat, gum disease, urinary tract infections, pneumonia, cavities and other diseases.
- ✓ Kill yeasts and fungi that are responsible for athlete's foot, diaper rash, thrush, ringworm and candidiasis.
- ✓ Kill parasites such as tapeworms, giardia and lice.
- ✓ Provide energy to the body quickly, giving it a better chance to fight off illness.
- ✓ Increase the production of insulin and improves the use of blood glucose.
- ✓ Protect from cancers such as breast and colon cancer.
- ✓ Improve digestion and how the body absorbs nutrients such as amino acids, vitamins and minerals.
- ✓ Relieve the symptoms of diabetes and helps prevent against the disease.
- ✓ Assist in decreasing the symptoms of pancreatitis.
- ✓ Relieve symptoms from Crohn's disease and improves bowel function.
- ✓ Protect the body against bladder infections and kidney disease.
- ✓ Help to relieve symptoms of chronic fatigue syndrome.
- ✓ Improve the condition of skin afflicted with psoriasis,

dermatitis, eczema and other chronic irritations.

- ✓ Help relieve kidney stone symptoms.
- ✓ Provide relief from gallbladder issues.
- ✓ Reduce the symptoms of cystic fibrosis.
- ✓ Protect against osteoporosis.
- ✓ Prevent premature aging through protection from harmful free radicals.
- ✓ Reduce the onset of epileptic seizures.
- ✓ Provide a protective layer on the skin from infection.

Building up your immune system by taking coconut oil daily can really help you to fight off even basic illnesses like colds.

Skin and Hair Conditioning

Using coconut oil as a way to treat skin irritation, including sunburn,

rash, and superficial cuts and bruises will help to heal the skin faster and provide relief from irritation. It is important that you use refined coconut oil for these purposes, as unrefined coconut oil can contain sediment, dust, and other particles that irritate your skin further.

Coconut oil is great for massage because it is easily absorbed by the skin - making it feel lighter and less dense.

Coconut oil, when combined with a mixture of zinc oxide, can be used in place of sunscreen to help protect your skin from UV rays, while maintaining softness and keeping your skin from drying out. This is a good way to get younger-looking skin, because it promotes elasticity along with rejuvenation.

Coconut oil can be used for occasional hot oil deep-conditioning hair treatments. You can also use it fairly regularly to promote stronger hair follicles. This will give your hair a shiny healthy look.

Going Deeper Into How It Works

We've already briefly touched on some things in this chapter. Now, I'm going to take the opportunity to go even more in depth into the "how" and "why." Hopefully the knowledge you gain here will help and encourage you to get started with coconut oil as soon as you can.

Heart Disease

As we've discussed, there is a common misconception that you should avoid anything made up of saturated fat if you want to protect yourself from a heart attack. That's one reason for the myth that individuals with concerns about heart disease should stay away from coconut oil, which is made up primarily of saturated fat. That is the *wrong* school of thought. There is a lot of information that implies that coconut oil can actually protect the body from heart related disease and illness.

Coconut oil is comprised of medium-chain fatty acids (MCFAs), which actually increase the presence of HDL cholesterol in the body. HDL is known as the "good cholesterol" that helps clear the arteries and protect the heart against disease and stroke. Most studies of cholesterol levels include a combination of the good and bad cholesterol also referred to as HDL/LDL. Grouping them together gives the wrong impression that cholesterol and saturated fat are dangerous for the heart. It is much more effective to examine the two separately. The twofold job of coconut oil is to reduce bad cholesterol and increase good cholesterol.

There are studies that show that virgin coconut oil that has not been hydrogenated has the ability to lower LDL and increase HDL in the body. This translates into higher levels of the "good" cholesterol and a decrease in the "bad" cholesterol. A decrease in bad cholesterol

results in fewer clogged arteries, and lowers the risk of heart disease and stroke.

The FDA recommends that in order to live a heart healthy lifestyle, people should live a life free from excess LDL - the "bad" cholesterol - and that saturated fatty acids can increase the levels of the LDL in the body, thus making it more likely that a person will suffer from heart disease. While this is true, there is a great deal of evidence that shows that people should not cut out saturated fats completely, but instead need to have a balance of fats such as monounsaturated fats, saturated fats, and polyunsaturated fats in order to keep their LDL and HDL levels in check.

In order to accomplish this goal, the use of non-hydrogenated coconut oil is suggested. Staying clear of hydrogenated oil is best because the process of hydrogenation adds hydrogen atoms to the fat molecule. This changes the makeup of the oil by creating trans-fat, the consumption of which poses a significant risk of heart disease.

Coconut oil contains another extremely helpful natural resource, polyphenols. Polyphenols are plant compounds that can contribute a high level of antioxidants to the body. Antioxidants significantly reduce the likelihood of heart disease, especially when ingested regularly. You can easily add a dose of coconut to your food or just take it straight each day.

There is no consistent recommendation for how much coconut oil you should take daily in order to benefit from its use. The type of oil you buy and its purity will significantly impact how effective it will be, and how quickly. Discuss taking coconut oil with your doctor or nutritionist in order to determine how much is right for you. You could also begin by substituting butters and oils in your diet with coconut oil.

The increase in the metabolism provided by the medium-chain fatty acids contained in coconut oil makes it possible for the body to use energy more effectively. This means that your body will work better, will be less likely to be overweight and will create less strain on the heart. These factors also contribute to positive cardiovascular health. The more control the body has over the use of the nutrients it consumes, the less taxed the body will be.

In addition, coconut oil naturally contains the compound lauric acid, which your body can convert to monolaurin – you know this part is exciting to me! This is a disease fighting agent that can do everything from increase the human immune system to stopping viruses and diseases in their tracks. It can also help the body to recover quickly from internal and external injury.

The combination of fatty acids found in coconut oil works as an antibiotic, antibacterial and antiviral agent that can protect the body from some of the illnesses that regular antibiotics are no longer able

to defeat. Some of the toughest bacteria such as *Staphylococcus aureus* have been killed using coconut oil. This means that the coconut oil is able to help the body fight against immuno-compromising illnesses.

In fact, coconut oil is actually believed to be a potential antidote for aluminum phosphide poisoning. Aluminum phosphide is a mitochondrial poison used to control rodent populations in grain storage facilities. According to a report by a team of Iranian doctors in the journal *Human and Experimental Toxicology* in 2005, coconut oil in combination with other therapies was effective in treating an individual suffering from aluminum phosphide poisoning.

Coconut oil is now being viewed more often as beneficial for those who are concerned about heart health. With all of the new facts coming to light, it is easy to see why many people are changing the way they think about saturated fats, and are choosing to add coconut oil to their diets.

Factors that can help make sure that your reap the positive benefits of coconut oil in your diet include making sure to purchase extra virgin coconut oil, and oil that is not hydrogenated. This will ensure that you are helping the body to increase the metabolic function, process foods more appropriately, avoid weight gain, induce weight loss as appropriate and keep the heart healthy. Along with increasing the body's immune system and providing the body with an ability to fight disease, illness and injury, coconut oil is generally advantageous for the body.

Individuals who currently are suffering from heart disease should consult with their physician before any dietary changes, including the addition of coconut oil. While there are no side effects reported from using coconut oil, some individuals may experience allergic reactions. If you are unsure if you have a coconut allergy, or have any questions as to whether or not coconut oil could be beneficial for you, contact your doctor or nutritionist before you get started.

Germs/bacteria

I'll bet when you think of coconuts you never think about using them for protection against germs and bacteria. Scientists have known about coconut oil's ability to help protect the body from bacteria, fungus and viruses since the 1960s. The same medium-chain triglycerides whose benefits we have been discussing throughout this book can also inactivate bacteria, viruses and fungi. As a result, topical use of coconut oil may be beneficial when applied to an infected area of the skin. In essence, it reverses the damage and helps to heal the area. In addition to its use against common skin infections, coconut oil has been found to be effective on some types of antibiotic resistant germs. That's great news for those who suffer from illnesses each year but find that antibiotics are no longer effective.

Coconut oil's germ fighting and immune boosting capabilities have been noticed by doctors battling the most dangerous bacterial infections, including MRSA. One of the dietary changes recommended for individuals suffering from MRSA or Staph is the replacement of their standard dietary oils and fats with coconut oil (Moore, 2011b).

The effect of coconut oil as a topical agent is also experienced by those suffering from an imbalance of *Candida albicans* yeast. You might not realize it, but this yeast is present in the human body naturally and is typically kept from doing any harm or making you feel sick by the other healthy organisms and bacteria in the body. If you have taken heavy doses of antibiotics or antimicrobial agents, you may lack necessary healthy bacteria and organisms to fight off excess fungi such as yeast.

Once an individual develops an imbalance of Candida, it can be very hard to restore the normal balance of bacteria and fungi. The use of coconut oil, along with major changes in diet, can be very effective.

When using coconut oil you might go through what is called a "die-off" if the coconut oil kills off the unhealthy organisms too quickly. A "die-off" occurs when the body ends up filled with toxins resulting from the rapid death of numerous micro-organisms. As a result, many cocnut oil users have stated that they get sicker before they get better.

Doctors are now trying more natural ways to boost immune systems and fight against viruses. That's one of the reasons many doctors are less likely to hand over a prescription for antibiotics before trying other remedies. The overuse of antibiotics to treat or fend off illness is the cause of antibiotic resistant disease and illness. Coconut oil may be used to fight against antibiotic resistant diseases and viruses, providing a viable alternative to antibiotics and other medicines for

individuals with compromised immune systems that need help fighting infections.

Weight loss

Coconut oil and weight loss - you already know I recommend it. Here's more on *why* I suggest it. The short and medium chain fatty acids in coconut oil help encourage weight loss. It also boosts your metabolism, thus helping to improve thyroid function and keeping the excess weight off. Using it as cooking oil each day is a good way to receive these benefits without drastically altering your regular diet. It is easy for the body to break down and also helps improve digestion. The fatty acids contained in coconut oil are effortlessly digested, making it easy for the body to convert into energy. This means that the energy is used almost immediately by the body,

resulting in less weight gain. The best part is how easy it is to integrate coconut oil into your everyday life. You can use it in cooking or add it as a salad dressing. You can simply take it as is each day, or even drink it in coconut water. The body reacts quickly to coconut oil, making it a workable solution for weight loss.

The detoxification effects of coconut oil can also benefit your weight loss efforts. Cleansing the body of toxins can lead to a real change in how your body deals with the food you digest. Making sure foods are processed properly is essential to the effective use of the calories. Your body will burn calories faster if it is working properly.

For some people with weight issues it is all about obtaining the proper metabolism. Getting some natural help from coconut oil can turn your metabolism around, thus making it easier for your body to burn calories and use nutrients properly. You will find that you can manage the glucose in your food better if your thyroid function is normal. In fact, many people say that with coconut oil as a regular part of their dietary habits they have fewer snack cravings. You can imagine what a change this can have on your weight gain.

If you are new to coconut oil you will want to start out slowly. Although it digests easily it can be a big change for you. Starting with a teaspoon a day is a good way to get used to the idea. You can move up to 5 or 6 tablespoons as you feel ready. Make sure you pick a good quality coconut oil, as this makes a big difference in how well it will work. Organic is the best way to go if you want to avoid exposure to nasty chemicals and pesticides, and stick with unrefined extra virgin oil to get all the benefits coconut oil has to offer you. You can find lots of coconut oils on the market - find a good one and stick with it to obtain good results quickly.

It's important that you stick to a healthy diet as well. Make sure that

the foods you are taking in will be easily digested and work in favor of your goals. Coconut oil will help you keep your body functioning well, but you have to supply it with the right fuel if you want great results. Stay clear of junk food and make smart choices.

Hair and Skin

Getting great skin doesn't have to mean buying every cosmetic product on the market or spending a fortune on all kinds of treatments. You can get great hair and skin with coconut oil. The product's versatility allows it to be used as a topical agent and as a food, both of which produce excellent results. Typically, coconut oil is used to treat damaged hair by warming the oil up until it is easy to use and applying it directly to the hair. This treatment can be left overnight for severely damaged hair, or can be removed after thirty minutes for less drastic repairs. Coconut oil can also be used as an effective treatment for dandruff, and has been shown in studies to kill head lice.

You can use the coconut oil as a part of a regular hair treatment each week as well as add it to your dietary regimen as cooking oil. It is easy on the digestive system, thus making it simple to add to your diet. Even if you don't damage your hair with chemicals and blow drying, your hair can have a lack luster look after some time. The oil can completely renew the youthful look of your hair and skin.

You are probably thinking that the typical course of action when it comes to fatty and oily things is to stay clear to promote healthy skin and reduce acne. So why would you want to try coconut oil as a treatment for your skin? The answer is actually very sensible. Acne is typically caused by infection or bacteria on the skin. Coconut oil's antibacterial properties might help your acne to disappear!

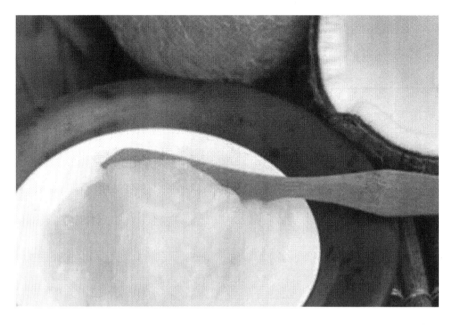

Using coconut oil topically is a good first step to getting healthier hair and skin and fighting acne. When using coconut oil topically you want to get the best you can find and not skimp on price. The oil also contains a great deal of Vitamin E and the more natural the product you purchase the more vitamins the oil will likely have retained. Adding it to your diet is another great way to promote good health. Make sure to eat properly and drink plenty of water in order to keep your skin looking healthy from the inside out. Although the coconut oil will help you to heal your acne, it will not cure it. You will need to continue with treatments and make sure you keep your skin as clean as possible.

Coconut oil is also beneficial in the treatment of chronic skin conditions like psoriasis and eczema. While it isn't a cure for these conditions, applying coconut oil topically can reduce the itching and help improve the appearance of your skin. Individuals with allergic dermatitis will be happy to learn that coconut oil, unless a coconut allergy is suspected, is also an effective treatment for allergic

dermatitis. It can help skin stay moist and heal quickly, and costs significantly less than creams and lotions that are commonly recommended for the same purpose. Topical application of coconut oil can also be used to treat ring worm and other fungal skin infections.

In the section below, I'll share even more tips on how to use coconut oil to improve your skin and hair, to solve common household problems, and to improve your overall health!

Ways to Use Coconut Oil

After reading this book, you should realize that it's clear that coconut oil is the way to go. Now let's get into some practical uses. There are an incredible number of possible uses for the oil, some of which seem logical and others that seem totally unusual!

We've touched on the health benefits of coconut oil already, so I want you to use this list as a jumping off point to get inspired about using it in your own life.

Skin

✓ The oil can be used to help with reduction of acne. Topically apply to any spots you see. Can be used (lightly) as a face lotion to prevent acne and moisturize the skin.

- ✓ Can be applied to reduce the appearance of skin tags and warts. Rub oil onto skin tag each night. The skin tag may eventually fall off.

- ✓ Treat skin ailments like psoriasis or eczema. The oil is wonderfully healing! Apply liberally over affected areas for healing.

- ✓ Use as a lip balm for the hot and cold weather. Dab on to cover lips.

- ✓ Use to treat a cold sore that is on its way. Dab on the spot to prevent and heal.

- ✓ Prevention for stretch marks. Apply liberally to skin, as you would a lotion. This can aid in stretch marks fading over time.

- ✓ Create a skin moisturizer by whipping in a mixer.

- ✓ Combine the oil with oatmeal and cinnamon for a great scrub for the face. Not only will it feel great, but it will make you look great as well.

- ✓ The oil is an effective makeup remover that also moisturizes as you use it. Dab onto eyes, and wipe with a cotton ball.

- ✓ The oil works very well in moisturizing nails and cuticles naturally. Apply small amounts to cuticles, allowing it to absorb before pushing cuticles back.

- ✓ Apply coconut oil to your damaged, dry and cracking heals for softer skin in no time.

- ✓ Coconut oil works very well in reducing signs of aging when

applied to wrinkles and fine lines as you would a fine eye cream.

✓ You can even create your own deodorant using the coconut oil. One excellent recipe for deodorant is as follows:

Coconut Oil Deodorant Recipe

Ingredients:

15 drops of essential oils
½ cup of beeswax that has been grated
2 Tbs. of baking soda that is free from aluminum
15 drops of tea tree oil
2 Tbsp. cornstarch or arrowroot
1 Tbsp. Shea butter
2 Tbsp. coconut oil

Directions:

- Start by melting the coconut oil with the beeswax at low heat with the occasional stir.
- Once the coconut oil and beeswax mixture starts to melt, add the Shea butter until everything is melted together and completely liquid.
- Take the mixture from the heat and start to stir in the arrowroot or cornstarch, baking soda and the essential oils until well mixed.
- Quickly pour the mixture into the container (an old deodorant stick works great) you have set aside before it starts to solidify.
- A few hours later you will have your deodorant.

Hair

✓ Coconut oil can be used in the treatment of lice. Just follow

these simple steps: Remove as many lice as you can with a comb. Then, apply and massage coconut oil into the scalp. Use a louse comb and pull from the scalp to the hair ends. Shampoo. Apply coconut oil and leave on for the day, reapplying as needed. Repeat combing step. Repeat as needed until lice are gone.

- ✓ Excellent for treating the damage done to hair from coloring. Apply liberally to hair ends, allowing it to sit. Wash out, and repeat as often as necessary to restore moisture.

- ✓ Treats cases of dandruff. Apply to scalp and allow it to sit for an hour. Be sure to only use only enough to coat the area, as it can be difficult to wash out of your hair.

Pets

- ✓ Healing and soothing for hot spots – acute moist dermatitis - on dogs. Apply liberally as needed.

- ✓ For the treatment of fleas in animals. Apply liberally to skin to suffocate fleas and soothe the animal.

✓ Add to a bowl of dog food to improve symptoms of arthritis and joint pain.

✓ The oil can easily be used as a natural way to clean your pet's ears with the help of a cotton swab.

Household

✓ Can be used to clean the shower and the tub. Apply to wet rag, and rub tub in a circular motion. Spray with vinegar and rinse to clean.

✓ Coconut oil can be used to remove gum from a number of locations such as carpets and shoes.

✓ It works well in place of regular lubricants like WD-40. Use as you would any lubricant.

✓ It works very well to condition wood, especially cutting

boards. Apply as you would a wax.

- ✓ It can be used to treat (season) cast iron cookware. Apply as you would a seasoning.

Health

- ✓ Apply the oil on the inside of the nose to stop a runny nose or heal a sore dry nose.

- ✓ Treat fungal infections like athletes foot by combining with a few drops of tea tree oil.

- ✓ Use the coconut oil as an option for treating ringworm. Dab it on the area with a Q-tip.

- ✓ Use as a source of relief from sore throats. You can mix it with honey to gargle and soothe.

- ✓ The oil can be used as a treatment for yeast infection. Place it in an applicator, or use a finger to insert the oil.

- ✓ For relief of bladder infections symptoms and treatment of the infection, ingesting coconut oil can be the key.

- ✓ Can be used as a massage oil for muscle aches. Warm the oil in your hands, rubbing it over the sore muscles. It's even better if you can convince your partner to do it for you!

- ✓ Apply to burns to help soothe and ease the irritation.

- ✓ It can be used as a great bath soak along with other essential oils. Add a dab of lavender oil mixed with bath salts.

- ✓ For bug bites and other wounds, apply coconut oil for fast

healing and soothing of discomfort. Dab on with a Q-tip.

- ✓ The oil works well to soothe hemorrhoids. Apply as you would a hemorrhoid cream.

- ✓ It can be used to help in soothing the symptoms of rashes and skin irritations. Apply to the affected area.

- ✓ Coconut oil increases a mother's milk production when taken daily. This is because it helps to balance the body.

- ✓ It improves the immune system when ingested on a regular basis, fighting against virus and disease.

- ✓ The oil will help you to regulate your body functions if used daily.

Cooking

- ✓ The oil is a great addition to foods that you normally use butter on, such as popcorn.

- ✓ Coconut oil is a great additive to frozen desserts like homemade ice cream and smoothies, not only providing healthy components, but a great flavor as well.

Weight

- ✓ Ingesting coconut oil before you eat may help keep your appetite at bay.

- ✓ Add to a drink for a boost of energy. A small amount (a teaspoon up to a tablespoon) can be just what the doctor ordered!

Scientific Evidence

I've touched some on the science behind the benefits of coconut oil, but I definitely felt it important to really highlight this evidence. I am including studies you can turn to, to investigate scientific findings related to coconut oil. Note that these studies are just the tip of the iceberg! There are literally thousands out there. I've included a few as starting points, to show you that the evidence behind coconut oil is not just anecdotal, as many would have you believe. You can use Google Scholar as a search engine to investigate more. Use key terms such as "coconut oil, lauric acid, MCTs, medium chain triglycerides" and so on.

First, it's important to realize that there is no harm that can come from trying coconut oil as a remedy. As always, I must advise you to speak to a trusted health professional before using coconut oil for any major health issue in your life. With that said, it's always okay

to use it in conjunction with other things you're doing.

Works Cited

I have cited numerous articles and reports throughout this book. This section lists those sources. Numerous other sources are available online and in the library. I hope you take the time to read them and learn even more about coconut oil and its benefits!

Achaya, K. T. (1994). Ghani: A traditional method of pressing oil in India. Food, Nutrition and Agriculture.
http://www.fao.org/docrep/T4660T/t4660t0b.htm
Clark, M. (2011) Once a villain, coconut oil charms the health food world. New York Times.
http://www.nytimes.com/2011/03/02/dining/02Appe.html?pagewanted=all&_r=0

David Suzuki Foundation. (2012) Chemicals in your cosmetics: DEA.
http://www.davidsuzuki.org/issues/health/science/toxics/chemicals-in-your-cosmetics---dea/

FoodRenegade.com (2012) How to choose a good coconut oil.
http://www.foodrenegade.com/how-to-choose-a-good-coconut-oil/

Hyman, M. (2010) Why eating a low-fat diet doesn't lead to weight loss. Huffington Post. http://www.huffingtonpost.com/dr-mark-hyman/why-eating-a-low-fat-diet_b_634011.html

Lieberman, N., Ening, M. G. and Preuss, H. G. (2006) A review of monolaurin and lauric acid: natural virucidal and bactericidal agents. Alternative and Complimentary Therapies.

Medical News Today (2009) How coconut oil could help reduce the symptoms of type 2 diabetes.
http://www.medicalnewstoday.com/releases/163249.php

Moore, M. (2011) Can coconut oil help with Staph and MRSA?
http://www.staph-infection-resources.com/staph-mrsa-treatment/coconut-oil-benefits/

Parker-Pope, T. (2011) Cooking with coconut oil. New York Times.
http://well.blogs.nytimes.com/2011/03/02/cooking-with-coconut-oil/

Peat, R. (2006) Coconut oil.

http://raypeat.com/articles/articles/coconut-oil.shtml

Shadnia, S., Rahimi, M., Pajoumand, A., Rasouli, M. H., and M. Abdollahi. (2005) Successful treatment of acute aluminum phosphide poisoning: possible benefit of coconut oil. Human and Experimental Toxicology.
http://www.ncbi.nlm.nih.gov/pubmed/15957538

Medium Chain Triglycerides are Key

We've already discussed that coconut oil coconut oil contains MCTs, or medium chain triglycerides. This is fairly unique because MCTs are more easily digested and converted into energy.

The fact that MCTs are broken down so easily has led to their use in problems such as jaundice and cystic fibrosis. There are an incredible number of benefits to MCTs, and the scientific literature is clear on that!

Resources:

Kaunitz, H., Slanetz, C.A., Johnson, R.E., Babayan, V.K., & Garsky, G.(1958). Nutritional properties of the triglycerides of medium chain

length. Journal of the American Oil Chemists Society, 35(10), 10-13.

Energy

MCTs are easily converted to energy in the body! The fact that MCTs are so prevalent in coconut oil bodes well for those who consume it.

Resources:

Fushiki, T and Matsumoto, K "Swimming endurance capacity of mice is increased by consumption of medium-chain triglycerides," Journal of Nutrition, 1995;125:531.

Vitamin Absorption

Coconut oil has been found to improve the absorption of beneficial nutrients. This helps make up for a diet that may be lacking in certain nutrients. Coconut oil improves the absorption of vitamins A, B, D, E, K, beta-carotene, CoQ10, and more. This includes various minerals. Coconut oil improves the health of malnourished children and babies.

Resources:

Salmon, W.D., and Goodman, J.G., (1936). Alleviation of vitamin B deficiency in the rat by certain natural fats and synthetic eaters. Journal of Nutrition, 13, 477-500.

Greenberger, N.J. et al. (1967). Use of medium chain triglycerides in malabsorption. Annual of Internal Medicine, 66, 727-734.

Antimicrobial, Antifungal, and Antiviral Properties

MCTs have antimicrobial properties. Coconut oil has the power to kill bacteria, fungi, viruses, and parasites. Even HIV and bacteria that are resistant to common antibiotics can be eliminated by coconut oil.

Resources:

Isaaces, C.E., Litov, R.E., Marie, P., & Thormar, H. (1992). Addition of lipases to infant formulas produces antiviral and antibacterial activity. Journal of Nutritional Biochemistry, 3, 304-308.

Isaacs, C.E., and Scheneidman, K. (1991). Enveloped viruses in human and bovine milk are inactivated by added fatty acids (FAs) and monoglycerides (MGs). FASEB Journal, 5, p. A1288.

Matsumoto, M., Kobayashi, T., Takenaka, A., & Itabashi, H. (1991). Defaunation effects of medium chain fatty acids and their derivatives on goat rumen protozoa. The Journal of General Applies Microbiology, 37(5), 439-445.

Preuss, H.G., Enig, M., Brook, I., & Elliott, T.B. (2005). Minimum inhibitory concentrations of herbal essential oils and monolaurin for gram-positive and gram-negative bacteria. Molecular Cell Biochemistry, 272, 29-34.

Hierholzer, J.C., and Kabara, J.J. (1982). In vitro effects of monolaurin in compounds on enveloped RNA and DNA viruses. Journal of Food Safety, 4, 1-12.

Kabara, J.A. (1978) Fatty acids and derivatives as antimicrobial

agents – A review. The Pharmacological Effects of Lipids: American Oil Chemists' Society, Champaign IL.

Kitahara, T., et al. (2004). Antimicrobial activity of saturated fatty acids and fatty amines against methicilin-resistant staphylococcous aureus. Biological &Pharmaceutical Bulletin, 27, 1321-1326.

Ogbolu, D.O., et al. (2007). In vitro antimicrobial properties of coconut oil on Candida species in Ibadan, Nigeria. Journal of Medical Food, 10, 384-387.

Ketones

Some MCTs are converted into ketones in the body. Ketones provide energy for the brain, including cell repair and growth. This is the reason coconut oil is cited as helping to treat things like Alzheimer's, Parkinson's, and Huntington's. In fact, coconut oil treatment is thought to work better than prescription medication, in many cases.

Resources:

Neal, E.G. et al. (2009). A randomized trial of classical and medium-chain triglyceride ketogenic diets in the treatment of childhood epilepsy. Epilepsia, 50, 1109-1117.

Alzheimer's, Diabetes, Cancer and Other Ailments

The components in coconut oil help to fight and prevent a host of diseases and ailments. Here is a just a sampling of the scientific findings related to its use a medical aid.

Resources:

Awad, A.B. (1981). Effect of dietary lipids on composition and

glucose utilization, by rat adipose tissue. Journal of Nutrition, 111, 34-39.

Lim-Sylianco, C.Y. (1984). Anticarcinogenic effect of coconut oil. The Philippine Journal of Coconut Studies, 12, 89-102.

Reddy, B.S., & Maura, Y. (198$). Tumor promotion of dietary fat in azoxymethane-induced colon carcinogenesis in female F 344 rats. Journal of the National Cancer Institute, 72, 745-750.

Burke, V., and Danks, D.M. (1966). Medium-chain triglyceride diet: Its use in treatment of liver disease. British Medical Journal, 2, 1050-1051.

Kuo, P.T., and Huang, N.N. (1965). The effect of medium chain triglyeride upon fat absorption and plasma lipid and depot fat of children with cystic fibrosis of the pancreas. Journal of Clinical Invest., 44, 1924-1933.

Hilmarsson, H., et al. (2006). Virucidal effect of lipids on visna virus, a lentivirus related to HIV. Arch Virol, 151, 1217-1224.

Echel, R.H., et al. (1992), Dietary substitution of medium-chain triglycerides improves insulin-mediated glucose metabolism in NIDDM subjects. Diabetes, 41, 641-647.

Hostmark, A.T., Spydevold, O., & Eilertsen, E. (1980). Plasma lipid concentration and liver output of lipoproteins in rats fed coconut fat or sunflower oil. Artery, 7, 367-383.

Heart Health

MCTs are used by the heart and can improve oxygen cycling and heart health. Coconut oil can be very helpful for those who suffer

from heart ailments.

Resources:

Kaunitz, H., & Dayrit, C.S. (1981). Coconut oil consumption and coronary heart disease. Philippine Journal of Internal Medicine, 30, 165-171.

Prior, I.A., Davidson, F., Salmond, C.E., & Czochoanska, Z. (1981). Cholesterol, coconuts, and diet on Polynesian atolls: a natural experiment: the Pukapuka and Tokelau Island studies. American Journal of Clinical Nutrition, 34, 1552-1561.

Felton, C.V., Crook, D., Davies, M.J., & Oliver, M.F. (1994). Dietary polyunsaturated fatty acids and composition of human aortic plaques. Lancet, 344, 1195-1196.

Eraly, M.G. (1995). Coconut oil and heart attack. Coconut and coconut oil in human nutrition, proceedings. Symposium on Coconut and Coconut Oil in Human Nutrition, Coconut Development Board, Kochi, India, 63-64.

Cholesterol

Contrary to popular belief, consumption of coconut oil does not lead to high cholesterol.

Resources:

Nevin, K.G., & Rajamohan, T. (2004). Beneficial effects of virgin coconut oil on lipid parameters and in vitro LDL oxidation. Clinical Biochemistry, 37(9), 830-835.

Blackburn, G.L., Kater, G., Mascioli, E.A., Kowalchuk, M.,

Babayan, V.K., & Bistrian, B.R. (1989). A reevaluation of coconut oil's effect on serum cholesterol and atherogenesis. The Journal of the Philippine Medical Association, 65, 144-152.

Halden, V.W., Lieb, H. (1961). Influence of biologically improved coconut oil products on the blood cholesterol levels of human volunteers. Nutr Diets, 3, 75-88.

Weight Loss

Coconut oil is an inexpensive weight loss aid! There are numerous studies that show this is the case, but here is a sampling.

Resources:

Assuncao, M.L., Ferreira, H.S., dos Santos, A.F., Cabral, C.R., & Florencio, T.M. (2009). Effects of dietary coconut oil on the biochemical and anthropometric profiles of women presenting abdominal obesity. Lipids, 44(7), 593-601.

Baba, N. (1982). Enhanced thermogenesis and diminished deposition of fat in response to overfeeding with diet containing medium-chain triglycerides. American Journal of Clinical Nutrition, 35, 379.

St-Onge, M.P., & Jones, P.J. (2003). Greater rise in fat oxidation with medium-chain triglyceride consumption relative to long-chain triglyceride is associated with lower initial body weight and greater loss of subcutaneous adipose tissue. International Journal of Obesity & Related Metabolic Disorders, 27(12), 1565-1571.

Beliebter, A. (1980). Overfeeding with a diet of medium-chain triglycerides impedes accumulation of body fat. Clinical Nutrition, 28, 595.

Make Coconut Oil Your Answer!

The number of ways coconut oil can be used in and implemented into your life is endless. More excellent results are being discovered every day. Whether you are using it to soak in a baking soda and coconut oil bath to cleanse your body or you are using it to replace your current cooking oil, you will enjoy the results. Coconut oil adds something more to whatever you are using it for, and the fact that it is all-natural is a big bonus. Using coconut oil that is not hydrogenated, thereby not tampered with at the core, is vital to getting the results that you are looking for with the oil. I recommend organic, virgin, unrefined coconut oil for your health and happiness.

Made in the USA
Lexington, KY
08 September 2014